JUSTICE DENIED

BERMUDA'S BLACK MILITANTS, THE "THIRD MAN,"
AND THE ASSASSINATIONS OF A POLICE CHIEF AND GOVERNOR

MEL AYTON

STRATEGIC MEDIA BOOKS, LLC

13-digit ISBN 978-0-9852440-4-0
10-digit ISBM 0-9852440-4-6

This book is dedicated to my granddaughter Isabella.

Justice Denied would not have been possible without the assistance of many people, including former police officers who had first-hand knowledge of the murder investigations and who knew many of the participants in the conspiracy to murder the Governor. Some of them wish to remain anonymous — and for good reason. They are either still living on the island or they live in Britain or the United States and continue to visit Bermudian relatives and friends. There are four former police officers to whom I owe a special debt of gratitude: Territt Cabral, Alan Armstrong (pseudonym) Peter Clemmet, and Nick Bolton, and two former high-ranking police officers involved in the murder enquiries who still live on the island and wish to remain anonymous. Another former police officer, Philip Swift, was instrumental in facilitating important contacts who knew a great deal about the incidents I write about. I also wish to express my gratitude to Baroness Sharples who agreed to be interviewed for this book.

CONTENTS

As Mel Ayton will tell you in his book *Justice Denied*, coaxing truth out of hiding in the British territory of Bermuda is no small task. There its isolated inhabitants keep their codes of silence, while racial and political agitation seethes just below the surface on this only 20-square mile chunk of presumably dead volcanic rock some 600 miles off the coast of North Carolina.

Readers will find that very little has changed in Bermuda from the 1970s, when Ayton reminds that the struggle for equal rights was the high point of Bermuda's history—and murder its lowest—until now.

The political murders bear out Bermuda's self-fulfilling prophecy of racial rage, at one time barely noticeable as tourists flocked to the Queen's Jewel in the Atlantic, when quiet afternoon tea parties blinded visitors to the swirling emotions of those who were oppressed and often to the arrogance of those oppressors.

Perhaps the best way to introduce you to *Justice Denied*, which on my fourth reading intrigues me even more than my first, is to tell you how Mel Ayton and I met—corresponding on a now defunct blog Bermuda Free Speech Forum. (Locals and foreigners both tread lightly on an island where loose lips have gotten more than a few locals their mortgages pulled or foreign workers their sudden returns home.) The blog's anonymous few, many who had left Bermuda, but who remained in touch with key players, exposed truths that local media either did not know or dared not to print.

Our conversations began early in my own review of a young Canadian tourist's 1996 murder in Bermuda, more than eight years after it, with gossip and injustice continuing to surround the rape, torture and murder of 17-year-old Rebecca Middleton. I found that Mel Ayton's queries and conversations with forum members early in the Twenty First Century seemed to draw strange parallels between tales of the 1970s and secrets I was finding.

I discovered an eerie similarity between attitudes of the Twenty First

Century and Ayton's dialogues about those violent political murders of the early 1970s, the gory hangings of the two men held responsible, the secrets of that "third man" (and perhaps others), and the main characters, many of whom now hold thrones of power in Bermuda. For me, it became obvious that more than a few in Bermuda and in the United Kingdom, tasked with good governance of its territory, but which some islanders consider its colonial master, continued to advocate amnesia.

Meanwhile, perhaps the most forbidden public topic—until Mel Ayton's research unleashed a mass of media attention--were those shocking political murders that more than a few attempted to sweep under the rug.

Ayton has written a superb portrait of an enraged island on the verge of collapse, a situation so explosive that Bermuda had to bring in British soldiers, Scotland Yard, and a tuxedo-clad hangman from Canada, making his approach with his assistant by sea to foreboding Casemates Prison, land approach deemed too dangerous during island-wide violence.

Despite rare access to public information in Bermuda, Ayton's decade of research exposed what he demonstrates clearly is the real story behind the murders, the hangings, and the riots that ensued. His sources aren't the usual Rolodex of experts, but eyewitnesses, including himself, to the violence and rage that surface all too often on this tiny island.

It's fortunate that Mel Ayton took on the job of telling the story behind the murders and riots because the media could not. It's not surprising that when the Mid Ocean News, perhaps the strongest investigative arm of Bermuda's media, died suddenly in 2009, its mourners were few.

But, in fact, Ayton charges that even this newspaper, which perceived itself as purveyor of truth "pay(ing) no mind to any sort of political pressure or otherwise," had their "hand…forced." (It would not be the first time—in the late 1990s the newspaper published an issue with a blank page, ripping out a major story as presses rolled, owing to political pressure).

Ayton reports that--despite his having provided to this newspaper by 2005 "all the important 'conspiracy' information…that decidedly pointed the finger of guilt at a number of Black Beret members and associates who planned and initiated the assassination of the Governor using Burrows and Tacklyn as 'hit men'"--the Mid Ocean News "at no time mentions an important witness to the conspiracy who later became a police officer… whose testimony proved without a shadow of a doubt that he and others had 'reconnoitred' Government House and the homes of public officials as part of their assassination plans."

In his in-depth project, Ayton's exclusive personal and professional testimonies combine with Scotland Yard documents, and British Foreign and Commonwealth Office (FCO) communications, sent during the horrific period of the murders, to disclose the sociology and psychology of those days, as well as the legal and ethical questions that continue to trouble the island, where the same arguments and rage seem hidden not far beneath paradoxical smiles: "Welcome to Bermuda…another world."

Ayton's choices on how to develop the story are confident. The reader first learns of the international shock of the murders. Ayton makes a stellar turn, introducing us to the opulent island, which to this day continues to hold the dubious distinction of being alone among Britain's territories in recent times to have had its royally-appointed leaders assassinated, a secret many still prefer not to share.

Ayton's character detail—both victims and accused—deliver outstanding examples of professional journalistic follow-up for which he is well known, having investigated and published investigations of the controversies surrounding the John F. Kennedy assassination and the murders of Senator Robert F. Kennedy and the Rev. Martin Luther King.

His reporting of details that only those directly involved would know, along with official secret communications, and trusted correspondence with the murdered governor's widow, all were the products of hard digging and commitment. Moreover, having served as a prison guard in Bermuda (later an educator and Fulbright scholar), Mel Ayton personally experienced the seething emotions that lie beneath the once broiling volcanic rock that millions of years ago bore this tiny island with international influence greater than its size. Guarding felons at stony Casemates Prison, Ayton knew personally--not only the two men who swung to their deaths in gallows hastily constructed just for this occasion—but, also, the alleged "third man" who might have escaped the same fate.

Ayton exposes a little known militant organization, the Black Beret Cadre (BBC), born in the late 1960s, and modelling itself on America's Black Panthers.

Ayton guides readers to the graves of Governor Richard Sharples and his aide Capt. Hugh Sayers at historic St. Peter's church in St. George, to historic Casemates Prison, better forgotten, some say, with racial anger, by both blacks and whites, disguised by claims of equality, economics, and workers' rights, threatening to surface, irrevocably.

Ayton's image of Bermuda, corroborated by government statistics, is one of economic woes caused by tourism competition, off-shore industries flocking to friendlier environments because of high import duties, shipping problems, union shut downs, increased debt, cool intolerance to foreign workers and employment time limits, violence against tourists and locals, prosecutions compromised, and gang warfare—no longer a matter of "Saturday night specials" (bats to the back of biking gang warriors heads). Sadly bullets have been known to fly, even where children play.

Ayton has compiled a portrait of an island in denial when it comes to crime and politics that threatens to cast a dark shadow on Bermuda, neither sugar coating, nor shaping his work into morbid excess.

Mel Ayton doesn't take the simple road. Authors hope to believe that if we fling ourselves into projects, establish our credentials for accuracy, which Ayton has long ago accomplished, truths will be accepted graciously. So we write our hearts out, come up with copious quantities of previously unpublished information, and we expect publishers to seize it. But this is not the "real world" of the author.

The proprietorship of *Justice Denied* frightened more than a few publishers, despite Ayton's judgment and clarity. Fortunately, Ayton and his agent didn't despair. Readers will find that in this new publication, Ayton tells the story wisely and clearly, deciphering the obvious tale and leading us through a maze that some in Bermuda continue to deny exists.

Because secrets ultimately are never well kept, Ayton's labour makes it possible for the reader to understand the realities of an isolated tribe, consumed by its own sense of self importance and an often alternate reality.

Ayton has compiled a portrait of an island in denial when it comes to crime and politics that threatens to cast a dark shadow on Bermuda, neither sugar coating, nor shaping his work into morbid excess. Although charades recounted here likely will make your blood boil, as does mine, Ayton's tenor is not anger, but objectivity.

Thus, while questions may remain as to how Bermuda will deal with its oncoming global challenges, Ayton's *Justice Denied*, in my view, dispels those myths of the 1970s political murders and quells the efforts of those who wish to avoid serious grappling with the politics and crimes of Bermuda.

Dr. Carol Shuman,
a psychologist, former newspaper reporter, editor and author

"The past is the present, isn't it? It's the future too. We all tried to lie out of that but life won't let us."
Eugene O'Neill

During 1972 and 1973 the North Atlantic British Colony of Bermuda, which had become a 'playground' for vacationing Americans, was suddenly thrust into a climate of fear when a spate of murders, including political assassinations, occurred. Bermuda became the only British territory ever to have the Queen's representative murdered in cold blood and the first nation to suffer the violent effects of the importation of 1960s American black power militancy.

The first murder was committed on 9th September 1972 and the victim was Bermuda Police Commissioner (Police Chief) George Duckett, an expatriate officer who had previously served in a number of British colonies around the world. Duckett had been lured to the back porch of his home, Bleak House, North Shore in Devonshire, where he was ambushed by his killer, or killers.

The Bermuda Police, ill equipped to deal with a major murder enquiry, sought the assistance of Scotland Yard who had been involved in previous murder investigations on the island in the past decade. Scotland Yard flew a team of detectives out to the colony. A substantial reward was offered by the Bermudian Government, but neither money nor murder squad detectives could raise any clues to the killer's identity. The new Governor of Bermuda, Sir Richard Sharples, a sailing friend of UK Prime Minister Edward Heath, suspected the involvement of a Black Power organisation, the Black Beret Cadre. The Black Berets were a group of Bermudians who modelled themselves on the American Black Panthers. Although a number of Black Beret members were interviewed none were charged with the murder.

Following the British detectives' return to London, and exactly six months to the day since the Police Chief was killed, Governor Sharples and his aide Captain Hugh Sayers were shot dead in the grounds of the Governor's mansion in the capital city of Hamilton. Sir Richard's Great Dane, Horsa, was also shot dead. Once again a team of detectives were requested to investigate the crime. Scotland Yard's Chief Superintendent Wright and Detective Inspector Basil Haddrell led the team. With no more evidence than that three black men were seen or heard running from the scene of the latest shootings and a conviction that the two murders were linked with that of the Police Chief, the detectives conceded defeat for a second time and left what investigating could still be carried out to the local police. Their task was extremely difficult as Deputy Governor Ian Kinnear found. "I would be less than frank", Kinnear said, "if I said (the police) had received (help) in the investigation of the (murders). In a small, tight-knit community, there is a natural tendency to avoid getting involved or implicating others".

The British newspaper, *The Sunday Times*, described the murder of Sir Richard Sharples as "a deep and personal tragedy" and editorialized : "It had been widely assumed that, after the outbursts of protests that led to some violence in 1968 and 1970 Bermuda had settled down to working out its destiny by parliamentary means…many reforms, a new and democratic constitution and the opening of more posts to black Bermudians have been made since the troubles of 1968. Yet these considerations can leave many bitter and disgruntled people at the bottom of the heap who blame their lack of success or status on race and the British connection." (1)

The funeral of Sir Richard provoked intense feelings of shame except for a number of black Bermudians who lined the funeral route. They had come to 'mock' according to a Foreign Office official. If evil is the absence of empathy, it was certainly abroad in Bermuda that tragic week. The official continued to describe the atmosphere on the island as, "…a mixture of shame, embarrassment, a desire to shed responsibility". The Chief Justice said it was, "a sick society with marked racial tensions".

The assassins of the police chief and Governor were so confident of their ability to elude police they struck again in the capital city Hamilton on April 6th 1973. Two white shopkeepers, Mark Doe and Victor Rego, were found dead on the floor of their store. They had been shot with a .32 pistol although some .22 bullets were left at the scene of the crime. The .22 bullets indicated a link with the murder of George Duckett. With what now appeared to be a further embarrassment to the Bermuda Government, Scotland Yard detectives were once more called to investigate. A new and enlarged police team arrived in Bermuda and in desperation the Bermuda Government offered a reward of three million dollars for information leading to the apprehension of the killers.

In September 1973, the Bank of Bermuda was robbed of $28,000 by an armed man, Buck Burrows, and on the 18th October detectives, acting on a tip off, arrested him. After a second man, Larry Tacklyn, was arrested and charged, and with a large reward still outstanding, information began to trickle in confirming their involvement in the five murders.

In November 1975 the Governor's assassination Inquest Report concluded that both men had been responsible for the Governor's assassination, "with other persons unknown".

In 1976, Burrows and Tacklyn were charged with the murders of Sir Richard Sharples, Captain Hugh Sayers, Victor Rego and Mark Doe. Burrows faced an additional charge of murdering the Police Chief. Burrows was found guilty of murdering Police Chief George Duckett, Governor Sharples, Captain Sayers, Mark Doe and Victor Rego. Tacklyn was found not guilty of murdering the Governor but guilty of murdering the two store owners. Both men were sentenced to death and hanged. It emerged that though the two men were simply professional criminals they entertained some sympathy with the Black Power movement and the Black Beret Cadre in particular, and this had established the political motive for the crimes. During his trial Burrows sent a written confession to the prosecutor in which he admitted killing the Governor "along with others I shall never name".

After the two assassins were executed in Casemates Prison on December 2nd 1977 revenge racial riots occurred throughout the island. They were incited by the Black Berets and the intemperate remarks of leading radical Progressive Labour Party politicians. Rioters attacked police stations and business premises, especially in the capital city of Hamilton. A state of emergency was issued that included a call-up of the Bermuda Regiment and the despatch of troops from the United Kingdom.

***

For the past 30 years the people of Bermuda had been given a whitewashed version of what exactly occurred when the murders were investigated and the two killers were brought to trial. However, as many Bermudians had suspected all along, not all of those involved in the murders of the Police Chief and the island's governor had been brought to justice. As Tim Hodgson, one of Bermuda's leading reporters commented in an email to me, "Not all of those involved in the Sharples conspiracy were brought before the courts. Although they were never charged, a chain of circumstantial evidence recorded in the (UK Foreign Office) files strongly suggests the complicity of several other individuals in the 1972/73 killings." (2)

However, even though the British Foreign Office files added to the sum of knowledge of the true circumstances surrounding the murders it was the release of the Scotland Yard Murder files that put the true story of the murders in the proper perspective. Additionally, further research by this author and interviews with former police officers who were involved in the murder investigations have provided a context that had been missing when two of Bermuda's leading newspapers ran a series of stories during the past decade which had been based on the newly released files.

The Scotland Yard Murder files, released to me in 2004 and to the general public in 2005, reveal how a group of Bermudians, an 'unholy alliance' of underworld criminals and a remaining hard-core of Black Beret activists, conspired to commit murder, assassination and robbery. Self-styled 'Godfather' Bobby Greene, who owned a restaurant in the Court Street area of Hamilton, led the 'underworld element'. He was the mastermind behind the spate of robberies in the early 1970s and was a known drug importer/dealer. The Governor's assassins, which included members of the Black Berets, a Black Panther-type organization, spent most of their free time at the restaurant. In fact, it was known as a meeting place for the Black Berets. A former police officer stated, "Bobby Greene was the mind behind the weapons and cash. Not knowing for a fact but I would say the Black Beret Cadre used him (in recruiting the assassins)." Greene died in 2005.

The Scotland Yard Murder files also reveal that the Black Berets had "reconnoitred Government House" on at least four occasions and watched the homes of leading politicians in the years before the actual shootings. And the planned attack on Police Chief George Duckett was taken straight from an urban guerrilla manual that was amongst literature read by Black Beret members. Additionally, Black Beret leader John Hilton 'Dionne' Bassett had been seen firing a .38 revolver, the same type of weapon used to kill the Governor. This information was never revealed during the trials of the Governor's assassins.

My research has also uncovered a number of suspicious links in the case. Dionne Bassett, founding member and original leader of the Black Berets, left the island on the 30th September 1972 shortly after George Duckett's murder and was known to harbor a deep hatred of the Police Chief. He eventually returned to the island but was never charged with any offence. Bassett died in the 1990s. In 1971 senior Beret member Phil Perinchief, who was characterized by UK and Bermuda authorities as the leading 'intellectual' and 'ideologist' of the movement, had shared a cell in Casemates Prison with Bassett. The files reveal that, whilst in prison, they were given "special privileges" for some unknown reason. Allegedly, Perinchief flew to Canada hours before George Duckett's murder. However, Scotland Yard detectives discovered no evidence that could link him to the assassinations of the Police Chief, Governor, the Governor's aide Captain Hugh Sayers or the murders of the Hamilton shopkeepers.

A 'third man' was also involved, according to Scotland Yard detectives, and he fled the island after the Governor's assassination with one of the two named assassins. (*Author's Note: Until the Bermuda Government establishes a royal commission to look into the real facts of the murders he must remain anonymous for legal reasons. Throughout this book he will be referred to as 'the third man')*

The third man was connected to the assassination by a shotgun shell found in his home. A warrant for his arrest was issued but was never acted upon. A government report stated that US police had been contacted and asked to "keep an eye" on him but he was never extradited. He returned to the island a few years later but the arrest warrant had mysteriously gone missing. As a former police officer source stated, "With regard to arresting (the third man) I don't believe there was much choice - the whole file including warrants, information etc had gone, I believe from the court registry. … I have a vague memory of an arrest on arrival prior to them discovering everything missing. I do not know why it was not reinvestigated with fresh information etc, maybe too much was missing. Maybe a deal was struck?"

The missing arrest warrant, according to the ex-police officer source, indicates there were people in high places who conspired to prevent the arrest of the third man. "My opinion is and was," he said, " that if they brought (him) back this would create such a political mess with the Bermuda Industrial Union (Allied with the opposition black party)…. The government had enough on its plate. The island was divided 50-50 on the race issue. They had enough trouble dealing with all the black participants (in the murders)….. I guess the feeling was if anything comes to light that can directly involve and get a confession from someone or point to (the third man) that they could put before the courts, it's better to have him at arms length and being watched."

The motive for stealing or destroying the arrest warrant, the source alleges, was a fear that riots would ensue. This suspicion was supported by a Foreign Office memo from a British official stationed in Bermuda in 1973 which stated, "Our case against (the third man) and the real ring leaders hang only on one shotgun cartridge and inadmissible evidence. At most (he) might be sent down for six months or a year if he returned to Bermuda. I am strongly of the opinion that would do more harm than good to the whole situation. Therefore, it seems to me infinitely more preferable that he should stay up in (North America) and the more we can harry him the better. The more we can drop stories into the press the better – our only means of communication with him – that might make him say 'God, they know that do they? I wonder how much more they know' The more we can make him and his friends still here in Bermuda, against whom we have no case at all, feel nervous and jittery, the better."

In September 2004 I received a letter from Sir Richard's widow, Baroness Sharples. She knew about the 'third man' and wrote, "(He) was the third involved, he went to the USA at that time where he was under observance, returned to Bermuda many years later, where I was informed he would not be arrested if he did not step out of line…". (3)

According to a former police officer, Neville Darrell, who wrote about the assassination of the Governor in his scant 90 page book "*Acel d'Ama*", he asked one of the two men named as the governor's assassins if anyone else had assisted in the murders. The assassin replied, "Neville, you'll be surprised, man, who was involved. Yes sir, man, you'll be surprised."

In the period 2004/2005 information I discovered in the Scotland Yard Files was given to a former senior police officer involved in the murder investigations. He wished to remain anonymous as he still lived on the island. The senior officer reached the rank of Superintendent which put him in the top half dozen officers on the island. According to one of his former colleagues in the force, "… he was an honest man and took his job seriously and professionally…he was one of those people who if he told you to do something you did it not only because it would be an order but because you knew it was right and that he would back you up if there was subsequently any problems; you could trust him…..He was privy to a great deal of information and procedures…..He was someone with 'status'". (4)

The senior officer said the information I supplied to him went beyond anything published in the *Mid Ocean News'* series on the assassinations. He also said I was correct in my conclusions about who was to blame for the assassination of the Governor and the police chief and that I was "… accurately centred in the middle of the nest." (5)

ONE

FLAWED PARADISE

"Each riot I as a young man could identify with, I too had frustration building up – 1965, 1968, 1970, 1977; and I can almost say that there will be another…because we are the majority, because we have not had our equitable share in the community, not just in terms of finance, but in terms of upward social mobility."

Pitt Riot Commission witness, 1978

MANY PEOPLE GET muddled about the British colony of Bermuda's exact location. It is easy to assume it lies in the Caribbean. However, while the Caribbean lies south of Florida, Bermuda sits in the Atlantic Ocean, some 600 miles east of North Carolina, surrounded by the Gulf Stream which accounts for the island's wonderful all year round climate.

Geography is not the only difference. Many islands in the Caribbean were once British colonies and this was once reflected in their culture. Today, however, they are increasingly Americanized – young people in Barbados, for example, seem keener on Basketball than cricket. Bermuda, on the other hand, has always retained its 'Britishness'.

Bermuda is sometimes known as the Bermudas or Bermuda Islands and is allegedly named after the Spaniard Juan de Bermudez who is credited with discovering the islands in 1515. (1) Prior to its settlement by the British in 1609 Bermuda was unoccupied. The island has the distinction of being the oldest and most populous remaining British Overseas Territory. Its first capital, St George's, was established in 1612 and is the oldest continuously inhabited English town in the Americas. The origins of the settlement were the shipwreck of a flotilla of ships that had been sailing to Virginia to relieve a colony of pioneer settlers. The wreck is believed to be the inspiration for William Shakespeare's final play, *The Tempest*.

On a map Bermuda looks somewhat like a fishhook with a curve at the south-west and the shaft extending north-east. There are some 150 islands in Bermuda but a total area of only about 21 square miles. Only about 20 of the islands are inhabited and are linked by a chain of bridges. The islands' wonderful climate and beauty attract thousands of visitors each month. It has been a second home over the years to prominent figures like Mark Twain, the Vanderbilt family, Mayor of New York Michael Bloomberg, Ross Perot (who has his own 'Perot Island') and Hollywood actor Michael Douglas. 31 years ago, just months before his murder, John Lennon arrived in Bermuda on a private yacht. On a visit to the island's botanical gardens with his son Sean he spotted a freesia called 'Double Fantasy' providing him with the title of his final album which was largely composed during his stay.

***

Since 1684 Bermuda has been a self-governing British Colony. It is divided into nine parishes, with Hamilton and St. George considered autonomous corporations. The capital and chief port is Hamilton on Great Bermuda. It is a small city with an area of only 180 acres. On St George's Island at the east end of the group is the picturesque old port of St George's. Nearby is the United States Naval Air Station. The population in 1970 was about 60,000, excluding tourists. About 60% of the population is black and there is also a large Portuguese population. A writer for the Bermuda Trade Development Board described the island as, "...a gleaming group of coral isles, riotous with tropical colour, set in an azure sea, warmed by a golden sun that will flood your veins with youth. It is a soft road, paved with cushions of green, spume-flecked velvet, bordered with white flowers of healthy salt-spray." (2)

Bermuda is the oldest self-governing overseas territory in the British Commonwealth. Its 1968 constitution provides the island with formal responsibility for internal self-government, while the British Government retains responsibility for external affairs, defence, and security. The

Bermudian Government is consulted on any international negotiations affecting the territory and participates, through British delegations, in the UN and some of its specialized and related agencies. Queen Elizabeth II is head of state and is represented in Bermuda by a governor, whom she appoints. Internally, Bermuda has a parliamentary system of government which includes the premier as head of government and leader of the majority party in the House of Assembly. Britain thought of Bermuda as a crucially important naval station ever since the UK lost its American bases in the wake of the War of Independence. Bermuda provided a link in the chain between its interests in Nova Scotia and those in British Guiana and the Caribbean. A Naval squadron was based on Ireland Island, site of Casemates Prison, and a Naval Station, HMS Malabar was situated there. Also SNOWI (Senior Naval Officer West Indies) had its headquarters there and Britain's rule of the Western Atlantic was assured. The station was responsible for fuelling passing warships.

In times of international crises, especially during the Cold War, Bermuda became ever more important to the United States in its efforts to track Soviet submarines in the Atlantic. The island was crucial to the security of the United States during the 1962 Cuban Missile Crisis. For that purpose a squadron of Lockheed P-3 Orion jet-prop surveillance aircraft flew missions at all hours picking Russian submarines out of 200 feet of water as they stalked around the American coast. The island also became vital to NATO's communications interests as a 'listening station' as evidenced by the Canadian-run radio station at Daniel's Head. During the 1980s the US Kindley Field Air Base, which was leased to the Americans by the British in 1941, was the scene of VQ-4 flights, unmarked Hercules that flew in and out on missions to unstated destinations, the radio listening and tracking.

As naturally beautiful as the place is below the surface of this paradise are all the familiar problems of any western society - degrading educational standards, high prices for even the basics of existence, burgeoning and increasingly violent crimes and a growing sense of fear for the future. Bermuda also has the 5th highest prison population in the world – 445 people in prison per 100,000 population putting Bermuda behind Russia and the USA, likely due to the high drug importation rate.

Movements for independence have also provided challenges to the United Kingdom and Bermudian governments over the years.

The history of Africans in Bermuda is unique amongst British colonies. The very first blacks in Bermuda were brought for their skills in pearl diving and agriculture. The small size of the colony ultimately forced Bermudians to turn to the sea rather than agriculture (shipping, piracy and the salt trade) as the climate and lack of land made slave plantations unfeasible. As a result black slaves served in a wide variety of occupations. While whites exhibited some racial bias by passing laws restricting black slaves' freedoms there was a lack of violent and hateful prejudice exhibited in other Caribbean colonies, the United States or elsewhere in the British Empire.

When the slaves were freed Bermuda provided blacks the opportunity to develop. For the previous one hundred years the island saw the growth of black participation in the business community and political life. However, the vast majority of Bermudians were denied equal educational opportunities and consigned to life as labourers, hotel workers and other work in the tourist industry. The bitterness this engendered remained with many blacks despite the progress toward complete equality which began in the late 1950s and especially the early to mid 1960s.

However, as Bermudian journalist Larry Burchall wrote, "Black Bermudian slaves and white Bermudian slave owners contrived mutually acceptable arrangements. These arrangements worked to the advantage of both sides. White slave-owners could feel generally safe; black slaves got treated with less routine cruelty. Our Bermudian racial history is the history of these 'arrangements'. This 384 year old arrangement history is devoid of significant bloodshed, without frequent violent rebellion and minus major or minor bloody conflict. Most countries have histories redolent of bloody conflict and rebellion. Histories littered with thousands of corpses, years of slaughter and tales of widespread atrocities. The history of the black man in the Caribbean and the Americas is a history of bloody conflict and frequent rebellion against widespread inhuman treatment.... The history of the black man in Bermuda is a history without bloody conflict and – relatively - minor rebellion. The history of black Bermudians is primarily a history of accommodations and adjustments - history of petitions, committees, representations, victimizations, mutilations, boycotts, segregation, discrimination and assassinations. But Bermuda's 384 year racial history shows few deaths which can be attributed to any kind of direct racial confrontation within Bermuda."(3)

The attitude of whites has been characterized a 'paternal' and 'condescending' in much the same way some moderate Southerners in the United States treat African Americans during the segregationist period of the 20th century. (4) Bermuda's system of segregation in the 20th century did not emulate the American 'white South' where hardly a black family had a member or friend who had not been beaten, framed or wrongfully imprisoned. The white South had been a place where untold victims had been imprisoned for crimes they did not commit. It had been a place where black men had been convicted on false charges of rape and murder. White cops were notorious for raping black women with impunity like their slave-owning forebears. The Southern court system was designed to eliminate all forms of human rights when it came to the treatment of the black man.

The difference in attitude was notable in the way white Bermudians displayed none of the overt racist vocabulary and approach white Southerners adopted. This 'British' attitude to change was reflected in the 1953 elections when black Bermudians saw Britain as the 'mother country' not at all 'oppressive or colonial' (5) In fact, many Black Bermudians during this post-war period looked to Britain to settle many of their grievances. In 1966 a Bermuda Constitutional Conference attended by representatives from both of Bermuda's main political parties the UBP and the PLP was held in London. At the beginning of 1967, a new Parliamentary Election Act became law, granting 'one man, one vote' to every British subject older than 21 and resident in Bermuda for three or more years. That summer a new Bermuda Boundaries Commission approved the division of the nine parishes into 40 voting constituencies.

Black Bermudian leaders also developed a relationship with the British Labour Party whose policies were built on equalitarian and non-discriminatory principles of government. Instead of blaming the British colonial power, black Bermudians turned their resentments towards the white islanders who they believed had long used their economic power to suppress blacks.

As the movement for equality for blacks in the United States reached its apogee after the *Brown v Board of Education* US Supreme Court ruling in the mid-1950s Bermudian blacks began to emulate their American cousins by taking firm direct action against an unequal structure of power. A peaceful boycott against segregated seating in cinemas was organised in 1959. Mass picketing and a boycott had closed the cinemas and it lasted two weeks until the owners agreed to an open seating policy. The hotels quickly followed the cinemas agreeing to accept reservations for dining and dancing from black Bermudians. Within a decade all commercial government and eventually private facilities were desegregated.

Black Bermudians also became more active in challenging racial barriers in the workplace. In 1963 the Progressive Labour Party (PLP) was established led by a group of men and women who had courageously fought against racial discrimination during the 40s and 50s. The party's main goal was to fight for the causes of the black working class – hotel workers, dockyard workers, transport and municipal workers and workers in the tourist industry. It formed strong links with the powerful Bermuda Industrial Union.

In 1964 the predominantly white United Bermuda Party (UBP), headed by Henry Tucker, was formed and Bermudian politics entered a new era, as a semi-autonomous colony which governed itself with a domestic agenda and left security and foreign affairs to the Governor of Bermuda and the British Government.

Racial segregation was made unlawful in Bermuda in 1969 when the Race Relations Act of that year expressly equated it, for the purposes of the Act, with racial discrimination. However, Bermuda was ruled by an aristocracy, generally called 'Front Street' or 'The Forty Thieves' a term used to describe expatriate and white Bermudian businessmen who controlled the economy and the political power. Their power came from the instruments of economic patronage – jobs, loans, credit and recallable mortgages.

It was not until the 1960s that Bermudian whites realized the winds of change had to accommodate new realities – realities that were beginning to change the social and political world of black citizens in Bermuda's neighbour, the United States. From the 1960s onwards Bermudian blacks were fortunate in being led to equality with whites by black leaders like future premier, Sir Edward Richards, Sir John Swan, Mayors Cecil Dismont and Lawson Mapp, Stanley Ratteray, Jim Woolridge, Russell Levi Pearman, Sir George Ratteray, Jerome Dill, Clarence James, Gerald Simons and Gloria McPhee.

The 1960s and the Black Power Movement

In 1959 and 1965 black union members demonstrated in support of their civil rights and a desire to benefit from the growing prosperity tourism had brought to the island. During both periods of union activity violence erupted. As Barbara Hunter wrote in describing the 1965 Bermuda Electric Light Company riots, "...how very strong the feelings of black Bermudian workers were against the barriers that had been put in their way for so long, and at the same time how little understanding most white people still had in regard to the situation." (6) According to Hunter, "The police, apparently acting within the law, forced a way through the picket line so that non-striking employees could get to work, and the strikers viewed this as 'aggression' by the police, and replied with weapons." (7) The riots of February 2nd 1965 were a turning point in the history of the BIU because membership skyrocketed and the disturbances brought many problems of inequality among the black and white populations out into the open.

Rightly or wrongly, it was during this period of unrest that young black Bermudians began to voice their hatred for the Police Force, which was dominated by British expatriate police officers. There is little doubt some officers who had arrived in Bermuda from other colonial police forces like Cyprus, Palestine and Rhodesia had adopted a superior attitude to the 'locals'. However, those officers who had stepped out of line in their treatment of islanders were swiftly dealt with by the courts. One example of ill-treatment of Bermudian blacks occurred in 1965 when a group of three young police officers injured a man on a moped who had failed to stop at their road block on Cedar Avenue, Hamilton. The officers used their truncheons on the young man and were subsequently prosecuted for 'unlawful wounding'. One of the officers was even sentenced to a term of two months imprisonment. (8) Another officer involved in the 1965 BELCO riots was fined £40 for 'unlawful assault'. (9)

Nevertheless, antipathy developed between the police and the many black Bermudians who saw the police force as an 'agent of oppression' Furthermore, feelings were exacerbated when the white population began to voice their concerns that if a black government came to power their rights would be trampled on.

This antipathy towards the police was described by a former expatriate police officer as having its origins in the, "problem (of) investigating crime in Bermuda". According to Philip Swift, "Bermuda has always suffered from a lack of information coming from the public. I suspect a small amount of it was fear driven, I doubt sympathy was a factor. The biggest barrier I found was that you have what is essentially a law-abiding, friendly, decent population in which everyone knew everyone else. People grew up together, they mixed well and they were neighbours on the 21 square miles. They like to gossip but claim to pay little attention to one another's business. I believe that most were prepared to let what goes on go on...it did not affect their lives and the only way it would was if they put their head above the parapet and said something. Bermudians are laid back (some would say slow or lazy), I prefer (the term) 'relaxed'. Take the attitude further and you have people who could say, 'Well, it's happened, what good does it do if I say something...all they do is potentially bring trouble on themselves'."(10)

This antipathy may also have developed from the experiences of young black Bermudians during visits to the United States in this period. Confrontations with local police forces were a constant during the height of the Civil Rights movement.

Like their neighbour, Bermuda began to experience black militancy in the 1960s through the auspices of the American 'Black Power' movement – a movement which rejected non-violent methods of protest and appealed to the impatience of blacks who wanted full economic and political rights immediately. Black Power advocates in Bermuda began to emulate their American counterparts by voicing their opinions at every opportunity and proclaiming that if those rights were not immediately implemented they would be taken by force.

In the mid to late 1960s young black Bermudians were inspired by a number of individuals and organizations within the US 'Black Power' movement. Stokely Carmichael, a former SNCC (Student Non-Violent Co-ordinating Committee), who has been credited as the first person to use the term 'Black Power', caught the imagination of many when he advocated strong left-wing answers to the problems of blacks in America and in the Third World. H. Rap Brown, a SNCC leader in 1967, began to develop extremist rhetoric in his appeal to blacks to rise up and destroy the 'corrupt and evil white power structure', encouraging rioters in cities across America to burn and loot.

Young Black Bermudians were also influenced by the Black Muslims, an American organization that encouraged dreams of a separate black community within the United States. They were especially taken with the example of Malcolm X who had been assassinated in 1965 by fellow Muslims. Malcolm X's autobiography, which contained extremist anti-white statements, became a best seller in Bermuda as well as the United States.

In 1966 the PLP issued a statement which set out their philosophy, "The workers can no longer sit back and do nothing since we now have the right to vote the agents of social injustice out of office. The party will no longer hesitate to fight for the rights of black people even if we are accused of being racists…The party is not convinced that any constitutional changes – short of independence – will solve the present problems of the workers…. The Party is convinced that the power structure and the UBP are indivisible. At the same time the party is not convinced that the power structure has departed from their policy of priority to whites." (11) In July 1967 several members of the PLP attended a 'Black Power' conference in Newark, New Jersey the scene of one of the worst ghetto riots in American history.

The 1968 Riots

This background of growing militancy by young black Bermudians, supported and condoned by the PLP, led to further unrest as the 1960s continued. When Dr Martin Luther King Jr was assassinated on April 4th 1968 feelings of anger and resentment towards whites were felt amongst many Bermudians, young and old. The 1968 Bermuda riot occurred only three weeks after King was assassinated – the evening of April 25th, Bermuda Floral Pageant Day. On Thursday afternoon April 25th a large crowd had gathered in Hamilton for three events – the annual Floral Pageant Parade, the 'Fair For All' held in Hamilton Hall and a political meeting organised by the PLP.

The Floral Pageant Parade and the PLP meeting ended without any disturbances. However, large crowds had gathered at the entrance to the *'Fair for All'*. The crowd grew increasingly impatient waiting to enter the event. The spark came when a group of white teenagers, claiming to be helpers, were admitted ahead of the crowd which was made up of mostly black Bermudians. Some individuals spread the word that whites were being unfairly admitted ahead of blacks who had been waiting for a considerable amount of time to gain entrance. The catalyst was the arrest of a black Bermudian by a white off-duty police officer. In the ensuing struggle the crowd erupted resulting in many arrests. Word spread about alleged strong-arm tactics by the police and the purported unfair treatment of blacks. Crowds assembled at the police station in Hamilton and riot police were called in to deal with a potential major disturbance. The crowd was forced back to Court Street and the police showed restraint in dealing with the crowd even though a number of black militants were inciting the crowd to violence. (12)

On the following Friday and Saturday an outbreak of disorder occurred when shop windows were smashed and a building was set on fire in the north section of Hamilton. Most of the fires were in the white business area of Hamilton. At 1.30am on Saturday 27th April the Governor, Lord Martonmere, declared a State Of Emergency and a curfew was imposed from 7pm to 6am. The Bermuda Regiment was called up and the Reserve Constabulary called out to assist regular police forces.

Lord Martonmere also requested that a Royal Navy ship, HMS Leopard, be diverted to Bermuda where it anchored alongside Front Street, Hamilton. On Sunday, 28th April, a company of the Royal Inniskilling Fusiliers arrived from the UK. However, they were not used in riot control as the police had by this time managed to gain control of the disturbances. In his efforts to quell the disturbances Martonmere broadcast an appeal to islanders saying he had a "…heavy heart tonight. I love Bermuda, and it was with a real sense of horror and distress that I saw parts of Hamilton in flames last night and heard of the serious physical injuries inflicted on some of our citizens. This is not the Bermuda I know, which is a country where people are happy and are learning to live together regardless of race…we should ask ourselves what has happened, what has gone wrong?" (13)

Ten citizens were injured during the riots and six police officers suffered minor injuries. Damage to property was estimated to be $1,000,000. A three man commission chaired by Sir Hugh Wooding was appointed to inquire into the causes and they concluded that the riots had been sparked by purported 'racial favouritism', a deep-seated hatred of the predominantly white police force by young blacks, and stop and search methods used by the police which suggested 'harassment'. The Commission also blamed 'juvenile delinquency', a shortage of low-cost housing, the high proportion of single-parent families, alcohol and drug abuse and the slow implementation of anti-discrimination laws. (14) The Commission added, "Full employment…. was experienced during the 1960s so that everyone was assured of a job. However, job opportunities remained restricted for many black Bermudians thus continuing an historical trend which had seen a large proportion of blacks working in menial positions for black Bermudians to pursue further education and the circle became complete when senior positions proved to be closed to these same black Bermudians because of lack of education. At the same time, policemen, teachers, accountants and executives in hotels and business places continued to be recruited from abroad." (15)

The Commission also placed blame on the PLP and its political platform which was based on, "…racial solidarity and denunciation of the UBP for alleged insincerity, assumed a positive racial character. The Commission considered that the campaign could not have failed to have a major influence on those who participated in the disorders, even though nothing was further from the PLP's intentions than the incitement to civil disorder." These claims would be repeated nearly ten years later when the Governor of Bermuda concluded that the PLP had incited the 1977 riots. (16)

In the 1968 election which followed the riots the United Bermuda Party made great strides in persuading black Bermudians that new constitutional changes would bring them into full citizenship. The party put forward 39 candidates, 13 of them black. As a result the UBP won 30 out of 40 seats and the PLP won 10, up from 6 in 1963 – 91.4% of the registered electorate voted. The UBP elected E.T. Richards, a black Bermudian, as its Deputy Government leader. The PLP chose black lawyer Lois Browne Evans as Parliamentary leader and Walter Roberts as Deputy.

Since the early 1960s Lois Browne Evans had been the central and dominant force within the PLP. Lois Brown Evans had a dream to rid the island of all vestiges of colonialism and began when she was on hand to witness Nigeria's independence. She was so admiring of the country she considered settling there. Her socialist philosophy (sometimes characterized as 'Marxist') and authoritarian tendencies distorted the purported democratic nature of the party and led to its first two great purges – the first of which occurred in the 1960s when moderates and progressives were expelled from the party for disagreeing with her. (17)

Evans's brand of socialism scared most black Bermudians, at least those mature enough to make up the majority of black voters. Her support really came from the black Bermudian 'intelligentsia', Bermudians who had gone to college in the United States and become radicalized with left-wing ideals. She also received support from black youth. It has been said that the PLP would have won power long before 1998 had the party embraced a more moderate socialist ideology. The reason given was that white middle class and black working class Bermudians have a lot more in common with each other than they had with white rich Bermudians. This never occurred because the party refused to abandon its Marxist and Third World brand of Socialism. In fact, by their embrace of revolutionary heroes like Franz Fanon and Herbert Marcuse the PLP had more in common with Bermuda's growing army of black militants than the average black Bermudian voter. By default the UBP became the party of multi-racial and moderate policies and appealed to a majority of white voters and middle class blacks.

The Government riot enquiry began the following August. The Commission appointed to investigate correctly pointed to the disaffection of Bermudian black youth as one of the main causes of the riots. It also pointed to the growing alienation many youths felt towards Bermudian society and especially the antagonistic feelings they had for the Bermuda Police Force.

The Commission also highlighted another issue which caused disaffection – the economic 'apartheid' which existed on the island and which was related to its history. A white member of the Race Relations Board testified to the Commission that,

"It is a fact that the economy of the island is practically entirely white-owned. This factor is historical, and now the picture in Bermuda has changed. If a coloured person wishes to attain his own form of economic independence, this is extremely difficult to do because most of the products, agencies and good things are already taken up." (18)

The Commission's report was released in March 1969 and described the riots as 'racial' because of the "tensions which have been simmering for more than three centuries". The Commission recognised that white-owned businesses should do more for the disaffected black youth.

In May 1969, five years after America's historic Civil Rights Bill, Bermuda passed its own version of this landmark legislation, "to prohibit discrimination on racial grounds and to penalize incitement to racial hatred and related acts", although most of the Bill's provisions were already in effect under different legislation.(19) The Act, however, did not satisfy the PLP who saw the 'inciting racial hatred' parts of the act as aimed mainly at black Bermudians. According to Barbara Harries Hunter, "The controversial clause in the Racial Relations Act relating to incitement of racial hatred may well have been included in direct anticipation of the Black Power Conference of July 1969 in Bermuda." (20) The leading organizer of the conference was a PLP leader, Roosevelt Browne, who later became a committed supporter of the Black Beret Cadre.

The Government was so concerned about the July 1969 conference two Royal Navy ships, HMS Mohawk and HMS Arethusa, were alerted and extra Royal Marine Commandos were added to their compliment. The conference also caused alarm amongst many white Bermudians. Although the conference speakers ranged from moderate to militant, many of the participants used radical anti-white invective which whites found disturbing. Additionally, to coincide with the conference, the Bermuda

Recorder published an article, '*Who Are The Black Leaders?*' in which the new militancy amongst many black Americans was praised. The article stated, "All blacks, no matter how disapproving of some Black Panther deeds and methods, feel better just because there is an organization of bold and daring young men of their own who have proven physical courage…Through all the ghettos we were constantly hearing of the black man's need to regain his 'masculinity'. Organizations like the Black Panthers do precisely that. In black eyes, gangs of that type are the elite corps of fighters which gives the whole community a new sense of pride. They do for the great mass of the black community what the guard's brigade does for any Britisher, what military victory in Palestine did for the entire community of Jews the world around. Someone of their breed has proven his manhood."(21)

Following the conference, the PLP alienated many of their liberal white supporters by adopting an attitude that was too militant in nature. The PLP emphasis was now on '*Black is Beautiful*' and the notion that, as blacks were the majority race on the island, they should be in control. The PLP also began to promote black history which was often Marxist-based. Black pride and black economic power were also put on the agenda. They were meant to raise the esteem of black Bermudians but effectively placed barriers between the two races.

Out of this new atmosphere of black militancy arose the Black Beret Cadre, a 'Black Panther' copy-cat organization. The Black Berets were created by black Bermudians who had been inspired by the rhetoric of Eldridge Cleaver, H. Rap Brown, Malcolm X, the Black Muslims and African-American 'black nationalist' groups who believed that violence was the only solution to the problem of equal rights.

At first the Black Berets were given some respect from the black establishment because they were supported by two ministers of the African Methodist Episcopal Church. The Black Berets also initially espoused moderate language in their publications, fearful they might fall foul of the new race laws. However, as time passed, that changed. Gradually, the Black Berets became comfortable enough to issue statements which effectively called for the overthrow of the Bermudian government by '*any means necessary*'.

Prince Charles' 1970 Visit To Bermuda

A visit by the heir to the British throne, Prince Charles', was organized for October 20th to the 22nd, 1970 to coincide with the 350th anniversary of the island's parliament. Events earlier in the year gave rise to concerns for his safety. In March 1970 arsonists torched the Old Devonshire Church; an historic landmark built in 1716. It was the second oldest church on the island. The device used was a crude bomb made from gas cylinders. Lord Martonmere was convinced the incident was "deliberate sabotage" by the Black Berets. He cabled London, "…this latest occurrence, if proven against Cadre, indicates new phase of bolder, more determined attacks against authority and confirms belief that Cadre is a serious danger to security. Further sabotage attempts and confrontation with authority are therefore considered possible." (22) Within a day or two Lord Martonmere's suspicions were confirmed when police found evidence that the Black Berets were indeed behind the fire bombing of the church. (23)

Shortly before Prince Charles' visit to the island the British Foreign Secretary, Sir Alec Douglas Home, voiced his opinion that Black Power militants might make an attempt on the prince's life. However, Home said he was against the cancellation of the visit as it would be "…a great blow to Bermuda and to the Governor (Lord Martonmere) personally…We should also have to weigh how much impact cancellation might have both on the security situation itself and on race relations in Bermuda against any conceivable risks which (in the light of the pending reports from the Governor, the Scotland Yard man and the Security Liaison Officer) might conceivably be thought to exist…Clearly Black Power and such militant manifestations of it as the Black Beret Cadre will not simply go away – especially in a racially divided society like Bermuda – however moderate and sensible the Government's policies may be and however good a public relations machine it may have. And so long as there are militant Black Power organizations in the colony, then so long can we expect at least occasional outbreaks of violence. The immediate question touches not so much on these broad issues but on the more immediate issue as to whether, at the present time, there is any significant risk in relation to the Prince of Wales' visit which ought to be borne in mind in deciding whether or not it should go ahead as planned." (24)

In response to the fears for the prince's safety a bodyguard of Royal Marines was sent from the UK to bolster his security. They were supported by an officer from Scotland Yard's anti-terrorist branch and they worked in tandem with Bermuda's Police Chief George Duckett who had overall responsibility for the security arrangements

However, three weeks before the prince's visit the political situation was deemed to be 'unstable'. Two workers' strikes were having their effect on the island's tourist trade – one strike took place at the airport and the other at a car dealership. Although the pickets were peaceful the Black Berets saw an opportunity to use the strikes to create new unrest. On October 2nd 1970 a demonstration was organised outside Hamilton's City Hall and later at Central Police Station. Two or three hundred people joined the march. Soon events took a turn for the worse. Police and private cars were stoned and damaged by thrown bottles and three police officers were slightly injured. The incident began when police arrested three men fighting among themselves. The crowd which included many young people, some aged no more than ten, attacked the police. Crowds eventually disbursed in the early morning hours of October 3. However, the authorities found nothing to indicate any overall plot by any organisation. (25)

Former Police Officer Territt Cabral remembered those events more than thirty years later. Cabral, a Portuguese Bermudian, was born and raised on the island and knew a number of Black Berets well. Cabral was on duty with the duty station officer, police officer Neville Darrell, at Hamilton Police Station the evening of the attack on City Hall when the crowd attacked the Police Station with petrol bombs. The station's officers had all been out on patrol when the attack began leaving Cabral and Darrell alone inside the building.

Darrell walked outside the police station and asked the crowd to disburse. Many were carrying weapons as well as petrol bombs. Cabral and Darrell decided to radio for backup. Cabral, who had been standing outside the police station when Darrell called for assistance, saw the crowd begin to close in. He ran inside and locked the doors and they were soon joined by

Police Officer Ernie Moniz who instructed Cabral to close and lock the back gates to the Police Station. "As I was closing the steel accordion-type gate, this guy threw a (petrol bomb) at me", Cabral said, "Thank God the flame went out as he threw it. It hit the gate, the (bottle's) glass shattered and all that gasoline went over me. I had to go to the hospital to get my eyes cleaned out and the shards of glass removed from my eyes. I was back in about an hour and then the chase began. It was a long night. Some members of the Black Berets were there during this time." (26)

Former English expatriate police officer Peter Clemmet also remembered the events of that night. He was directed to assist with riot duties after having only arrived on the island as a new recruit. "I arrived in Bermuda with 22 new recruits from the UK in October 1970 the day the riots broke out," Clemmet said, " we all disembarked and were immediately driven to Police Headquarters and outfitted with riot gear and plonked onto the streets of Hamilton. This went on for 12 days, working 12 hour shifts." (27)

Lord Martonmere had underestimated the level of violence that had caught the imagination of black Bermudian youths. He had also underestimated the popularity of the Black Berets amongst young people and did not take serious measures against them despite his concern they were a great danger to the security of the island. Within two days of the riot there were five attacks on businesses in Hamilton and two in other districts. Three incidents involved arson. The Governor expressed his fears that such incidents of violence played into the hands of the Black Berets.

On the night of October 3rd 1970 the Acting Government leader Sir Edward Richards delivered a speech, broadcast on the Bermudian television network, in which he called the incidents of violence and lawlessness, "purposeless and meaningless" and that they were attacks on the "whole community". He warned that the "consequences for those responsible will be severe indeed." (28)

The attacks continued despite Sir Richard's pleas. By October 7th the government had discovered, through police informants, that the Black Berets were coordinating events. However, the Berets had failed to incite the striking workers to violence. According to a police intelligence report, "Members (of the Black Berets) in cars, clever enough not to carry incriminating evidence, were involved last night (October 3rd) and Police Special Branch reports that at suitable opportunity Cadre plans to attack Police Operations Center (Police HQ). Police have today been placed at Security Stage Amber which means 12 hour shifts and more men on the ground."(29)

By October 8th the incidents of violence and arson were spiralling out of control. The headmaster's office at the Berkeley Institute had been set on fire and the Chesley White department store in Hamilton was also set ablaze and the fire destroyed most of the building. The Government responded by calling up the police reserves and the Bermuda Regiment was placed on stand-by although a state of emergency was not called. (30)

The firebombing attacks continued and on October 12th Sir Edward Richards issued a statement addressed to the people of Bermuda. Sir Richard said that "…the government recognises that the objective of those responsible for these acts of uncivilised conduct and wilful destruction of property are to destroy the economy, impoverish the community and disrupt the functioning of government. They are designed to terrorise and intimidate the public and create a state of anarchy". Sir Richard said that the Government was taking all measures necessary and he was determined to ensure law and order. The Bermuda Reserve Constabulary was placed on duty and the Bermuda Regiment was embodied at 3.30am that morning. (31)

Renee Webb, a future member of the 1998 PLP government, was a participant in the riots. She remembers being present when tear gas was sprayed. "When you are a teenager it's exciting" she recalled, "You don't understand the effect it is having on the economy. All you know is black people are fed up and they are burning. We were running into it to see the action. We weren't afraid. Then they started bringing out the guns and there was a ship stationed outside. A lot of people in power now were in the throes of that, at that time". (32)

Alarmed at events on the island that were spiralling out of control the Foreign Office seriously considered cancelling the Prince's visit. However, Foreign Secretary Sir Alec Douglas Home acquiesced to Lord Martonmere's advice when the Governor said he was satisfied there was no threat to the prince and no evidence to connect recent disturbances with the visit. He said the "situation" was contained for the time being. (33)

Nevertheless, arrangements were made to rapidly deploy troops to Bermuda should the violence reoccur. Three frigates were near Bermuda, one of which carried a platoon of Royal Marines that could be sent to the island if the authorities became aware of any threat to Prince Charles.

Gradually the unrest subsided and by the time of the prince's two day visit to the island security arrangements had been heightened and the police, assisted by Royal Marines, a naval helicopter and hand-picked men from the Bermuda Regiment were in control of the island. The visit attracted large and enthusiastic crowds and he was given a warm welcome although there were a number of minor incidents which caused alarm. In the capital city of Hamilton demonstrations by black radicals were organized and paint had been thrown on the walls of City Hall and St Theresa's Cathedral shortly before the royal motorcade passed en route to Parliament. However, there had been no serious threat to the Prince's life. (34)

The 1972 Elections

In 1972 Lord Martonmere retired and the British government appointed a new Governor of Bermuda. His name was Sir Richard Sharples, a former Conservative Party MP and close friend of the Prime Minister, Ted Heath.

The 1972 Bermuda elections were held a few months before the arrival of Sir Richard. Lord Martonmere had cabled London that the run up to the elections were proceeding without any trouble or violence. In his memo he said, "The most significant result (of the UBP primary elections) was the adoption of a black candidate, Mr John W. Swan, in Paget East, probably the most conservative of the predominantly white constituencies. Although Mr Swan is a highly respected and wealthy businessman, I doubt that such a result would have been possible at the time of the last election in 1968 and it is an indication of the long way the UBP has moved towards becoming a genuine multi-racial party."

On June 14th 1972, Lord Martonmere informed the Foreign Office that the June 7 election had been held "… in an atmosphere of calm with the minimum of abuse or political mud-slinging (by either party) …Activity of the Black Beret Cadre (throughout the election) is at a lower level than ever and there are no signs of the organization being re-activated…the internal situation is calm and likely to continue so…". (35)

In the coming months, however, the governor's assessment of the of the Black Berets' 'activities' was to prove sadly premature.

POLITICAL TARGETS

"(In the early 1970s) we were going to buy arms and shoot every politician in this country because justice was not being carried out."
Former Black Beret Cadre member Dennis Bean testifying before a commission of enquiry into serious crimes - August 2000.

GEORGE DUCKETT WAS born at St Anne's-On-Sea, Lancashire, on 1st December 1930.He was educated at King's School, Chester from 1941-1949, was chosen as a school prefect and captained the school cricket, tennis and football teams. After leaving school he enlisted in the Welsh Regiment as a national serviceman and served in the Royal Army Educational Corps as an instructor at the Headquarters of the British Army on the Rhine.

In 1951 Duckett joined the Colonial Police Service and attended courses at No 4 District Centre, Mill Meece, and at the Metropolitan Police College, Hendon. On the 20th November 1952 he was appointed Assistant Superintendent of Police in Nigeria and served as an Assistant Superintendent at Lagos. In 1957 he served with the United Nations Forces as the officer in charge of one of the Nigeria police contingents in the Congo, an effort by the international body to quell disturbances in that troubled nation.

Duckett was promoted to the rank of Deputy Superintendent in 1959 and transferred to Northern Nigeria where he served as Commandant of the Northern Police College. He quickly earned promotion to Superintendent in 1960 and Chief Superintendent in 1962. Two years later he was promoted to the rank of Assistant Commissioner and took up duties as commandant of the Southern Police College where he was responsible for officer training. In 1965 he was awarded the Nigeria police medal for Meritorious Service and was made an officer of the Order of the British Empire in the 1966 New Years Honours. A week before his death in September 1972 he was awarded the 'Colonial Police Long Service Medal'.

On 1st December 1966, prior to his retirement from the Nigerian Police Force, George Duckett served as Acting Deputy Commissioner, Capital Territory, Lagos. Coincidentally, Duckett served with the Acting Police Commissioner George Robbins who he was later to succeed as Bermuda's Police Chief. Robbins was appointed Bermuda's Deputy Police Commissioner in 1960 and Commissioner in April 1961.

In 1967 Duckett was appointed by the Ministry of Overseas Development to head the British Police Training School in Jamaica.

George Duckett arrived in Bermuda in December 1969 on a five year contract as Police Commissioner. He had been interviewed for the job in New York by Governor Lord Martonmere and was sworn in to office on December 30th. Duckett had been hired to affect a number of changes in the Bermuda Police Force, one of which was to encourage as many Bermudians as possible, both black and white, to join the force. He was also responsible for training Bermudian members of the police force for senior posts. The Bermudian Government believed he had accomplished his mission in the three short years he was Commissioner.

Duckett was, by all accounts, a fearless police officer who was determined to stamp out the 'hooligan-type' offences which were becoming a common feature of black youth on the streets of Hamilton. He was a big man standing over 6' 4" tall and described himself as an "blunt (English) North Countryman". (1). According to his men, "his bark was usually worse than his bite" and he took "a keen interest in the welfare of his men". (2) Duckett had a habit of defending his officers and always spoke out against unwarranted criticism. He also preferred to command his force "on the ground" rather than "behind a desk". (3)

Duckett's courage was well known and this earned him the respect of the Bermuda Police Force and many members of the island's community. *The Royal Gazette* characterized him as "bold and courageous…" (4) and "… not a mincing courtier, fawning on those who might criticise him. He is outspoken and blunt – and there have been many times in the past when the police service has desperately needed this kind of a spokesman." (5) During one minor riot in Hamilton Duckett personally confronted a gang of young men who were involved in the disturbances. He also frequently went to the notorious 'Devil's Hole' district of Bermuda, on one occasion personally confronting a criminal who was causing an affray.

According to former Bermudian police officer Territt Cabral, "One of the pertinent reasons why George Duckett was (a target) was because he took a first hand role in the disturbances, and high profile threats against civil disorder." Cabral said the force at this time was called 'Duckett's Raiders' and they "made their mark" by confronting unruly youths in the Court Street area of Hamilton and 'Devil's Hole'. At Devil's Hole Duckett had "rocks and bottles thrown at him. He was more involved in policing than he was on the Administration side. I think he took it to heart that his boys were being sought after. He needed better (political) leaders with resolve than he had back then." (6) Former police officer Nick Bolton said, "Many of the local thugs hated Mr Duckett because he wouldn't put up with their crap. He was an old style Colonial Policeman who was not frightened to mix it with troublemakers. Duckett was also known for taking chances with people….and of course did a lot to help Buck Burrows." (7)

Over thirty years later a number of other former Bermuda Police Officers recalled working with the Police Commissioner. One former officer, Alan Armstrong (*pseudonym*) said Duckett was "a really nice man from the North of England, like me. ….he recruited me because he thought I might be a good addition to his police rugby team. I'm also sure my career in the Bermuda Police would have been different if he had survived…..the force took a spiral down from there on…..George Duckett, who I really admired, had sent two of us off to Florida not too long before the (1972/73) murders to attend the US Naval Diving School. We trained with the seals….." (8)

George Duckett's no-nonsense policing methods made him many enemies. During his time in Bermuda he was threatened numerous times but he brushed them off as boastful braggadocio. He was also warned that some of the criminals he put away were out to 'get him'. As the *Royal Gazette* editorialized after his murder, "Often criminals swear 'to get' the man who got them. More often than not such threats are just boastfulness or made in the heat of the moment. But there have been cases where criminals have been determined and have succeeded in getting their revenge."(9)

In 1971 Duckett had assisted Scotland Yard detectives Chief Superintendent William Wright and Detective Sergeant Basil Haddrell when they investigated the murder of 24 year old Jean Burrows, a British journalist from Chatham in Kent who came to the island to work. She had been found floating in three feet of water at the edge of Hamilton Harbor. Duckett conducted the original enquiry and called for a Scotland Yard team who came out to the island on July 28th. When they arrived they were told that on the night of July 3 Jean, her husband and two other journalists had dined at Hoppin' John's, a restaurant on Hamilton's Front Street and had left in the early hours to go to Burrows' house for coffee. However, Jean did not arrive home.

Burrows' naked body was found by the water's edge at 4.30 in the morning, her only clothing a dress around her waist. She had suffered severe head injuries and an attempt had been made at strangulation. When Dr Wenwyon, the pathologist at the King Edward VII Hospital, examined Burrows it was discovered she had been raped before being knocked unconscious by a heavy blow on the head. She had then been drowned by having her head pushed under the water.

Bermudian police officers searched the area around the murder scene. Her wrist watch and her shoulder bag were found in a mangrove swamp nearby and on the opposite side of the road they found her earrings. Her sunglasses and briefs were found near the sea wall and her moped was hidden three hundred yards away in long grass.

When the Scotland Yard detectives arrived the forensics evidence was sent to London and a house to house enquiry was set up in the area where her body was found stretching back to the Hoppin' John's restaurant. Soon the name of 28 year old Paul Augustus Belvin was brought to the detectives' attention as he had previously been observed in the area watching female sunbathers and swimmers. He was characterized by people who knew him as 'weird'.

Belvin was approached by the Scotland Yard detectives and, as he related a lot of information surrounding the circumstances of the murder, Chief Superintendent Wright decided to play a ruse and asked him if he would like to play detective and help police reconstruct the murder. Belvin was pleased to assist and they drove down to the harbour. When Wright asked Belvin if he would like to make a guess at how the murder had happened the itinerant white Bermudian related in great detail how the killer would have hidden behind palm trees, knocked Jean Burrows off her moped, then hit her and raped her. He also said the murderer had probably used a metal pipe to bludgeon Burrows and that it had probably been thrown into the sea. When he was asked how he thought Jean Burrows had died he stood in the water, knelt down and acted out a strangulation scene.

Wright took Belvin to police headquarters as he was convinced he had the killer. Only the killer would have known the details of the murder which had been privy only to the detectives and the forensics experts. Later that day US divers from the nearby US Naval Station retrieved the iron pipe from the spot Belvin pointed out. Later, tests on his suitcase full of clothes proved he had had contact with the dead woman. More than 100 fibres were found to match those from Burrows' dress. On 1st September 1971 Belvin was charged with the murder. He was later found guilty, sentenced to hang but his sentence was later commuted to life imprisonment.

George Duckett and the Scotland Yard detectives were mutually appreciative of one another. They kept in touch and when Duckett visited London the following year the detectives met up for dinner. It was the last time Wright and Haddrell saw George Duckett alive.

*

Richard Sharples was born in England in 1916 during the First World War. He was educated at Eton and later attended the Army's elite officer training establishment at   Sandhurst. He became a Second Lieutenant in the Welsh Guards in 1936.

Sharples met his future wife, Pamela Newall, in 1940 when she was 17 years old. She was the daughter of Lady Claud Hamilton. Pamela had many admirers and at first Richard was at a disadvantage in courting her as he "… was not a good dancer". She also considered him to be 'spoilt'. (10) However, she quickly changed her mind and they began seeing each other regularly despite the intervening war years when Richard was, like most young men of his generation, often serving abroad. During the times he returned home on leave they would meet and enjoy nights out together. During the Second World War Pamela became a member of the Women's Auxiliary Air Force.

During the Second World War Sharples served in France, Italy and the Far East. He won the Military Cross for his courage during the evacuation of Calais in 1940. In 1944 when he served in Italy under General Mark Clark he was wounded in battle and was awarded the American Silver Star. During his service in the Far East he accompanied another officer to accept the surrender of Japanese forces in Bali. Expecting resistance the two officers were amazed to find the Japanese lined up on the beach with their arms on the ground in front of them.

When Richard Sharples returned to Britain in 1946 he became engaged to Pamela and they were married in July 1946. Eventually, they had four children - David, Christopher, Fiona and Miranda who were born between 1947 and 1954.

In 1948 Sharples was chosen as one of two Army officers to attend a course at the Royal Naval Staff College, Greenwich. A classmate was the Duke of Edinburgh and they both enjoyed a formal friendship during their time there. Reminiscing about his time at the college Pamela Sharples recalled how her husband and the Duke took a single taxi to a pub crawl in the Irish Republic along with a dozen or so fellow students.

Following the course at Greenwich Field Marshall Viscount Montgomery of Alamein asked Sharples to become his assistant at Supreme Headquarters Allied Powers Europe (SHAPE). He was promoted to major and appointed as Monty's military assistant. Sir Richard's home in Hampshire was not far from Monty's and they remained life-long friends. Following Sir Richard's murder a friend said, "It is sad to think that Monty, to whom he paid a filial visit shortly before going to Bermuda, should now be mourning his savage and untimely death." (11)

Sharples left the Army as he was convinced his future lay in politics. As Lady Sharples wrote, "Monty and SHAPE was really a political set up, so that presented Richard with the ideal opportunity to enter Parliament and being picked for Sutton and Cheam (Surrey) was ideal." (12)

In the year before his election to Parliament Sir Richard spent a year working in the economic section of the Conservative Research Department and received the O.B.E. In 1954 he won election to the House of Commons as the Conservative party's candidate. Two years later he left the backbenches and was appointed Parliamentary Private Secretary of State for Foreign Affairs. A year later he was appointed to the same position with the Home Secretary R.A.B. Butler. He held this position until 1959.

In 1960 Sharples became Assistant Government Whip and then held a number of posts for the following four years including Joint Parliamentary Secretary, Minister of Pensions and National Service and Parliamentary Secretary at the Ministry of Public   Buildings and Works. He left Government following the election of the Labour Party in the 1964 General Election. Sharples had been re-elected as the Sutton and Cheam MP with a strong majority of 12,696 votes. He spent the next four years as an opposition MP. According to Lady Sharples her husband, "… helped Ted Heath with Prime Minister's Question Time when in opposition."(13) In 1968 Richard Sharples was appointed Vice Chairman of the Conservative Party in charge of candidates, a position he came to enjoy.

When Edward Heath and the Conservatives won the 1970 General Election Sharples returned to government as Minister of State at the Home Office. He was instrumental in drafting the tough Misuse of Drugs Act of 1971. Speaking in January 1973 he told a Canadian television reporter, "I was directly concerned with the drug problem in the United Kingdom as Minister of State at the Home Office. I put through the misuse of drugs act in the United Kingdom and the act which has very recently been passed here (Bermuda) is almost word for word the same. That is a coincidence, but I have a very direct interest in this problem. I think the main problem here is marijuana. I don't think we have a large hard drug problem as yet, and I'm very keen that it shouldn't arise. As far as my own responsibility is concerned I want to crack down very hard on the pusher, the person who is making money out of this beastly traffic. And that is the whole essence of the legislation I started in England, and the legislation I brought in here." (14)

Sharples supported Edward Heath's position that Britain's future lay with the European Union. He also supported capital punishment and, during the 1964 House of Commons debate on the subject, he strongly opposed the abolition of hanging. According to The Times newspaper Sir Richard, "… though not of the first political rank – his final appointment in London was that of Minister of State at the Home Office – was an influential well-liked and respected figure in the Conservative Party throughout his 18 years in the House of Commons." (15)

Richard Sharples' outside interests included managing his vast estate at the 2,500 acre   farm, Southfield, near Alton in Hampshire. He was a lover of animals and cherished his dogs. In fact, it was Sharples' intention to devote himself fully to farming when he completed his three year term as Governor of Bermuda. He was also a keen yachtsman and owned a 53 foot ketch, '*Alaunt of Corfe*'. He often participated in yachting events with his friend Edward Heath and both politicians had been members of the Royal Yacht Squadron, Sir Richard since 1960. Heath, who became leader of the Conservative Party in 1965, frequently acted as a crew member aboard Sir Richard's yacht.

Although choosing a profession in which outgoing qualities were a necessity, Richard Sharples was described by many as, "an extremely shy and self conscious (man)". The political correspondent for the British newspaper, *The Daily Telegraph*, knew him and said his reserve, "…militated against his success as a Minister - a speech in the House or cross-examination at Question Time was for him a severe ordeal. Nor was he greatly at ease with journalists. As one who gained his confidence and friendship, I can testify that his sole aim in politics was the betterment of his fellow men, which in his opinion was most likely to be achieved through the application of Conservative principles…….Despite, or perhaps because of his self-effacement, Sir Richard was an excellent judge of character. Quite a number of Conservative MPs owe their entry to politics to the fact that, as vice-chairman of the Conservative Party, particularly concerned with the selection of prospective candidates, he discerned their merits." (16)

In April 1972 the Prime Minister announced that Sharples was to be the next Governor of Bermuda to succeed Lord Martonmere. Later, as he was about to embark on this new stage in his life, Sharples was given a private briefing by the Caribbean Department of the Foreign Office. During the briefing he was told his Aide De Camp should always carry a pistol.

Traditionally, the Governorship of a British Colony was reserved for those politicians whose careers in government had been winding down. As Lady Sharples observed, "18 years (in Parliament) was long enough and the offer of the post in Bermuda, what with the children grown up, seemed ideal." (17) Sir Richard was surprised he had been chosen. A friend said, "In a long talk a week or two before he left for Bermuda, he told me he had been genuinely surprised to be offered the Governorship but that, having accepted, he was determined to do all he could to maintain the stability and prosperity of the Colony while helping to steer it along the path of constitutional advance." (18)

The Governor's role was essentially to act as the Queen's local representative. He was appointed by the Queen after nomination by Britain's Prime Minister. It was always assumed that the Prime Minister would consult with the Bermudian Government before nominating a candidate. Bermuda's government was therefore given a de facto veto power over the nomination.

The Sharples sailed to Bermuda aboard the liner Oriana. So unassuming were they that their cabin steward, Roy Emory, believed they were just another English couple on their way to Bermuda for a holiday. (19)

Sir Richard first stepped foot on Bermuda's shores when he disembarked at Albouys Point on October 12th 1972. As he surveyed the scenery around him he expressed his delight at the beauty of the island. Dressed in full morning suit he told reporters he wanted to change the aloof image of a colonial governor whose usual dress was full regalia uniform with plumed headdress. He was accompanied by his butler, Latino De La Torre and his wife. They had worked for the Sharples family for four years. They described the Governor and his wife as "good people" and "excellent employers".

Shortly after he arrived Sir Richard met with the local press and told them he and Lady Sharples wanted to, "…take as much interest in everything as we can do .It will involve a heavy programme…. (I) just want to be as accessible as possible always bearing in mind the constitutional position that I must not involve myself in any way in the responsibility of the elected people in government." (20) He said his principle role was to act in accordance with the wishes of the people through their elected representatives and he was aware that a proportion of Bermudians wanted independence. However, he was also aware that until that political preference was adopted he had to carry out his duties as a colonial governor and oversee the defence and international position of the island and to liaise with the British Government. He told a Canadian television reporter, "I have been actively involved for the last eighteen years in politics in Britain and first of all, one has to remember that one is no longer a party politician and those things don't play any part here. I've got certain reserve subjects which are my responsibility and my main subject is responsibility for the elected assembly and the government of Bermuda, and I work very closely with them."(21)

Like Princess Diana a generation later, Sir Richard was determined to act as the 'people's representative'. According to a television journalist, Leighton Rochester, Sir Richard was, "…aware of the times and of the island life. He wanted to meet people from all walks of life in Bermuda. He had a job to do and he was doing it as best he could. He didn't want people to have that 'up on the hill' attitude towards him – he wanted to be one of the people." (22)

Alarmed at the distance previous governors had kept from ordinary Bermudians he wanted the people of the island to know him. He said that "…as far as my own life here is concerned and my own relationship with the people of Bermuda is concerned, I tend to favour …rather a less formal approach than some of my predecessors. I think this is a tendency that has been going on successively. I don't say I started this, I'm carrying on possibly where my predecessor left off…..Bermuda is moving towards a more modern approach and I think my own feeling is, that the role of Governor should be more up-to-date than in the past." (23)

The Sharples soon settled in to their new roles and many Bermudians were pleased they did not act like royalty but adopted a 'common touch' to their affairs. On arrival in Hamilton Lady Sharples told the press that she had always, "…done my own shopping in England and I propose to continue the practice here. I do this because I like to know the price of things and I have a better idea of values." Lady Sharples was often observed pushing a trolley in the local supermarket. Like his wife, Sir Richard strolled around the streets of Hamilton and was often described as 'approachable'. On one occasion he was seen driving an electric car around Hamilton. One of the first outings was to hire two small motor bikes and tour the island in the style of the average tourist.

Sir Richard also announced there would be less formality at Government House. Instead of large dinner parties there would be receptions and buffets. One of his first decisions as Governor was to move the visitor's book to the lobby of Government House and invite islanders to visit the mansion and sign it. (24) He also refused to wear the traditional uniform on the occasion of the state opening of Bermuda's Parliament. He was aware that the unreality of the pomp and circumstance was good for the tourist trade but a provocation to young Bermudians.

Sir Richard refused to subsidize his position as governor with large amounts of cash. The previous governor, Lord Martonmere, subsidized his office to the tune of $62,000 a year but he was married to an American heiress and could afford a lavish lifestyle. His wife used to order £200 worth of imported exotic blooms for Government House every other week when her favourite flowers were in season. She paid for them personally. Sir Richard, however, limited his contributions to $15,000. He said, "Although I've got a large farm in England the majority of money I have is invested in it and I can't go out and sell a cow or something." (25)

In his short five months as Governor Sir Richard made a favourable impression on most Bermudians. He was described as 'charming', 'approachable', 'sincere', and 'pleasant'. (26) Member of Parliament, William M. Cox of the United Bermuda Party, said Sir Richard was "pleasant, outgoing and informal". He characterized him as, "a Christian gentleman." (27) Most Bermudians believed Sir Richard when he said he wanted to be "close to the people of Bermuda". According to a Foreign Office memo, "… Sir Richard made a start at playing things in a lower key – to the distress of the older expatriate element but to the delight of the politically sensitive. I know he felt that Government should look for a more modest Government House. There are good reasons for this on security grounds alone. There are equally compelling political reasons, for it is now out of keeping with the scale and way of life of this island and sets the Governor apart from the rest of the community…" (28)

Lady Sharples concurred and later wrote, "In the first place, in our first month here we started wondering – from the practical and entertaining point of view – whether another house DOWN the hill could be found. The mere fact of 'them up here and us down here' is a physical fact and often mentioned. This place is out of all proportion with today's thinking." (29) Later, in a letter to the British Prime Minister discussing the circumstances of her husband's murder, Lady Sharples said, "When Richard told me you had asked him to come here I had great reservations - selfish I admit. Since that initial reaction, which was very short-lived, we have loved this island and ALL its people. I suppose I met many more than Richard as I was able to go around completely freely to fishermen, shopping in all areas, and I NEVER, never met other than friendliness and more from EVERYONE." (30)

However, there were some Bermudians who were unable to accept this 'very English Governor' and soon after his arrival a 'storm in a teacup' arose. It centred on the Governor's Great Dane, Horsa.

Horsa had become a 'celebrity' on the island. When the Governor and Lady Sharples drove around the colony in their official limousine Horsa went too – sometimes completely hiding the Governor and his wife because of its size. Sir Richard once described Horsa as a 'first class watch dog' with a 'blood-chilling growl'. But the animal was normally docile and gentle, especially with children. In his Christmas Day broadcast in December 1972 Sir Richard told his viewers that on Christmas Eve he had a visitor, a "tiny black Bermudian boy", who had trudged all the way up the hill to Government House and knocked on the front door. Sir Richard himself opened the door as he usually did on holidays, and the boy simply said, "Where's the dog?" (31)

Controversy about Horsa developed when questions were asked in the

British Parliament on the subject of a "7th birthday party" for the Great Dane. The controversy began when Sir Richard gave an interview to a Bermudian newspaper and made tongue-in-cheek remarks that Horsa would be seven that week and they would be holding a birthday celebration. "We will be holding a birthday party for Horsa" the Governor reportedly said, "who is sure to be in rare fettle that day. However, I do not think Horsa will have many friends at this celebration because there aren't a lot of Great Danes about". The humor had been missed by many who thought the idea of a birthday party for a dog was pure English eccentricity and decadence. (32)

Following the interview two Great Dane owners contacted the Royal Gazette and intimated they would like to attend with their dogs. The result was that the 'joke' became a reality after Lady Sharples arranged the 'birthday party'. Governor and Lady Sharples thought the idea the idea would be rightly seen as simply a publicity stunt to help provide 'color' to their lives at Government House, entirely harmless but also humorous. However, following the party and a photo array in the local press, one critic was provoked into writing an angry letter to the paper concluding with the question, "Why does such an educated man take the trouble to give the dog a birthday party?"

Lady Sharples decided to answer the critic with humor. In a letter to the newspaper, signed by Horsa, but believed written by Lady Sharples, she replied: "(The critic) must have forgotten that his allotted span is 70 years whereas I have only about seven more birthdays at the most to look forward to. Does he really grudge me the little bit of fun we had, with my picture in the paper? Or could he be just a little bit jealous of the publicity that always seems to surround me since I came to Bermuda? If I were not owned by a very special master and mistress I would suggest that he should see a vet or wear a flea collar. There seems to be something biting him." (33)

However, the letter did not quell the controversy and provoked some Bermudians to once again question Bermuda's colonial status. This feeling was not confined to anti-colonial Bermudians, however. A conservative peer in the British House of Lords took the opportunity to advance his career by publicizing the event in the British press. He called the affair 'undignified'. However, many British politicians dismissed his remarks and accused him of using the debacle as a way of raising his limited profile.

Despite the controversy over his dig the Governor had more real concerns about the workings of the Bermuda government.. After six years as the government auditor, D.H. Owen had left the island frustrated that "wastages and fraudulent practices involving public monies" were hidden from the public. (34)

Sir Richard, contrary to claims made later by Bermudian newspapers, was extremely worried about the growing violence in Bermuda. His concern was heightened by the discovery in 1972 of a plot to assassinate Sir Edward Richards. Sir Richard was also aware of police anxiety over threats to kill senior members of the Bermuda Government. The threats led to the placement of special police bodyguards outside Sir Edward's home.

Governor Sharples, however, was unconcerned about his own safety. In fact, he joked about it in one of his last public speeches. Addressing a dinner given by the Speaker of the Bermuda Assembly on February 2nd 1973, he recalled disputes between previous governors and speakers over the past 350 years. He singled out, "the offer by Mr Speaker Hinson, made at the parade in St George's in 1749, in the hearing of several persons, of £10 to a soldier if he would shoot the Governor in the head. If...I see you fumbling in your pockets I shall know it is time to look for cover." (35)

In February 1973 Prince Charles, who was carrying out his duties as Royal Navy sub-lieutenant, made another visit to Bermuda. It was an unofficial visit as Bermuda was the headquarters of the British Navy's West Indies Squadron and a regular calling point for British navy ships. His ship, the 2,500 ton frigate 'Minerva', captained by Commander John Garnier, made the stop-off at the beginning of the ship's tour of the Caribbean. During his short stay Prince Charles called on Governor and Lady Sharples and took a walk in the gardens of Government House following the same route the Governor and his aide would take a month later when they were confronted by armed black power militants. The heir to the British throne was due to return to Bermuda at the end of the tour as the frigate needed maintenance at the Old Dockyard on Ireland Island which was near Casemates Prison and the Prison Officers' Mess. The visit was cancelled following the tragic events in the weeks ahead.

*

The final week of Sir Richard's life was altogether uneventful. On Sunday March 4th 1973 Sir Richard and Lady Sharples took part in the Bermuda Hunt. They were both keen foxhunters and had enjoyed this mutual interest since their early days as a couple. Hunt Master, Durham Stephens, said Sir Richard was always very polite and wanted the group to feel he was just an ordinary member. (36)

On Monday March 5th the Governor paid an official visit to the ZFB television studios. On Tuesday he went to the weekly Executive Council meeting. On Thursday Sir Richard, accompanied by Lady Sharples, visited Warwick Camp, home to the Bermuda Regiment, for a cocktail party. The party had been arranged for the officers of Britain's First Parachute Logistic Regiment which was in Bermuda for training purposes.

On Friday Sir Richard, in his capacity as head of state, met with the Captain of the visiting Norwegian Royal Training Ship, Haakon VII at Government House. Sometime during Friday, Sir Richard's friends, Mr and Mrs Waddington, arrived in Bermuda for a short stay at Government House. On Friday night the Governor opened an extension of the Coral Island Hotel and went on to attend the Berkeley Education Society Concert at City Hall.

On the morning of Saturday 10th March 1973 the Sharples were looking forward to entertaining guests at a dinner party in the Governor's mansion. Six local people were invited along with the Waddingtons, Sir Richard's Secretary Moraig Valentine and the Governor's aide-de-camp, Captain Hugh Sayers. Sayers was the son of Colonel and Mrs C.L. Sayers and came from Newbury in Berkshire. His father was the yeoman Usher and Deputy Sergeant –At- Arms in the British House of Lords.

Captain Sayers had been educated at Sandhurst Military College then saw service in Germany and Northern Ireland before he was appointed aide de camp to the Governor in October 1972. He was due to return to his unit in October 1973. He was described by Baroness Sharples thirty years later as, "…a delight and very popular with everyone." (37) Like his boss, 27 year old Hugh Sayers was in the Welsh Guards. He also had another connection to the Governor. His grandfather, Admiral Sir Ralph Leatham, was Governor of Bermuda in the 1940s.

The local guests arrived between 7.45pm and 8.15pm. At around 10pm Lady Sharples complained of feeling unwell with a 'bad back' and retired to her bedroom. Sir Richard and his guests adjourned to the drawing room where they stayed until 11.25pm. The Waddingtons and the other dinner party guests remained talking for a further 15 minutes before Sir Richard announced he was going to bed. He then called his dog Horsa over with the intention of exercising it before he retired. As he took Horsa out the front door he passed the duty police officer, PC Deallie, and told him he was going for a short walk. A minute or so later Captain Sayers followed Sir Richard and closed the front door behind him.

Some two or three minutes later Officer Deallie heard a number of shots fired, followed by a cry for help. He saw Sir Richard dragging himself towards the house from the direction of the terrace steps and Captain Sayers lying prone on the lawn immediately in front of the steps. Both men were dead.

In the following 48 hours the island was in the grip of panic, fear and a deep sense of shame as news of the Governor's assassination sent shock waves around the world, especially in the United Kingdom. The British press was typical in its characterization of the island as being in the 'grip of fear'. *Time* magazine suggested a political motive and stated, "The closest thing to a militant organisation is the now defunct Black Beret Cadre, which flourished briefly from 1968 to 1970. At least two former members of the Cadre were being held this week in police custody. Compared with their black-bereted counterparts in the US, however, Bermuda's militants have little cause for complaint. In contrast to America's ghettoed cities, Bermuda is close to a paradise; there are no slums; there is, even today, no visible tension on the streets either by day or night. There is no official discrimination in employment, and blacks are represented in all enterprises on the island. In the legislature both the majority and minority leaders are black." However, PLP leader Walter N.H. Robinson disagreed and told *Time* reporters, "This is a bigoted place. There is racial discrimination here, as subtle as it is. Everything is open – in the civil service and private business

– but there is still a white attorney general, a white commissioner of police, a white chief justice and a white senior magistrate."(38)

At 2pm on the Monday following the shootings Sir Richard's daughters Fiona and Miranda flew in from London and were met at the airport by Lady Sharples. It was the first time the Governor's wife had been seen in public since the murder of her husband. Their sons, David and Christopher, had sailed the Governor's yacht into the Brazilian port of Salvador on Tuesday and had been told of their father's death. They flew to Rio de Janeiro then on to New York and finally down to Bermuda.

At noon on Tuesday 13th March Lady Sharples issued a statement to the press. It was read by the Acting Governor I.A. C. (Ian) Kinnear. "I am deeply disturbed to read some of the exaggerated reports of unrest on the Island" she said, "We have been so happy here, and had already met a large proportion of the island's people. I can only think that this is a temporary madness. If the assassination was in any way political or the person or persons concerned felt that (Sir Richard) would have stood in the way of the wishes of the people of the island they have made a terrible mistake." (39)

At 5.30pm that day the world's press met Lady Sharples at Government House. She was accompanied by members of her family and family friends, David Gibson-Watt and Sir Clive Bosom, who had flown in for the funeral. Also present were the Acting Governor Ian Kinnear and Sir Richard's private secretary Moraig Valentine.

Lady Sharples told the visiting press of how her husband loved Bermuda, how she used to go shopping in the local supermarkets and how friendly the Bermudian people were. "I have never been happier anywhere", she said, "It was the most glorious experience of most of our lives". (40)

*

Following the Governor's assassination the British Press came under attack from Bermudian officials worried the newspaper reports would harm the tourist industry. Although the *Bermuda Sun* had correctly assumed the assassination was, "…a bloody climax to five years of Black Power agitating and unrest on the island." tourism director W. James Williams said the UK press reports were 'erroneous' and 'exaggerated'. (41) Williams told reporters, "I can't believe that anyone would write such things, they must have very active imaginations." (42) The *Royal Gazette* opined the strategy and planning behind the assassination was, "clearly... the work of well-organised killers. This was the work of experts." (43)

In fact, the general thrust of news reports by Bermudian newspapers and government officials was to downplay the racial angle. Leading politicians were also eager to give some other motive to the assassination. PLP leader Walter Robinson said on a Canadian radio programme that the murders were an 'outside job', that in some strange way they were the work of foreign terrorists, Irish Republican Army terrorists or drug dealers.

However, their musings were criticised by a 'high British official' who wrote, "......People in Bermuda who are still bemusing themselves with vague ideas that this is really not their problem must be bombed out of their cloud cuckoo land. The sooner the general public know the true facts, swallow the cathartic truth and face up to their responsibilities, the sooner Bermuda can start to settle down into the new world of reality in which we must all live."(44)

Since that time the 'myth' that Bermuda's black militants had nothing to do with the actions of the Governor's assassins became the 'official' line. Little effort was made to fully investigate the allegations that a black power group had a hand in the Governor's death and an independent official government enquiry was never considered.

However, the British press did indeed correctly deduce the assassins were likely controlled by black militants. At the time of the assassination *Daily Express* reporter Ivor Key said that 'Black Power' could be responsible for the murders. Key wrote that, "...for years outsiders have been agitating that they should rise up and drive the white population which holds the economic power back to America and Britain. In a part of the world where independence is the cry of the island...it sticks out like a sore thumb." (45) The *Daily Express's* Chapman Pincher told readers the assassinations were the result of "the Black Power Movement". (46)

The *Daily Express* also correctly placed the blame on the island's politics and said Black Power could be responsible because, "... this British colony...

is a symbol of imperialism hated by the Black Power leaders of America and the Caribbean…..for years outsiders have been agitating that (blacks) should rise up and drive the whole white population which holds the economic power back to America and Britain…..it was Bermuda which American Black Power leader Roosevelt Brown chose to hold a conference in 1969. …..there is a possibility a hard core of black militants are on the island who eye the land owned by the whites, including many Americans, with envy. A policy of terror could have been conceived to whip up some feeling on the island. Many terrorist campaigns have begun with the assassinations of high Government officials like Sir Richard and the police chief. Both were appointed by Britain and were constant symbols of British Rule on the island….. for if Black Power is responsible this vulnerable island could be heading for years of terror." (47)

The British newspaper, *The Birmingham Post,* also correctly stated that the rise of the Black Power movement in Bermuda was to blame for the assassination. The newspaper stated, "One sign of the growing crisis is the rise of Black Power in many Caribbean states. An international Black Power conference was held in Bermuda in 1969, and left its mark on the host country. In the same year mass demonstrations were held in the streets of Trinidad and Tobago under the umbrella of Black Power slogans, and in 1972 the trial of Michael X, alias Abdul Malik, led to a rising of the political temperature. However, the eruption of organised violence can be traced further than that. In 1960, a now largely forgotten insurrection took place in Jamaica; fighters were imported from New York under the supervision of a black American policeman and two English soldiers lost their lives. In fact, the primary source of revolutionary ideology, at least in the Commonwealth West Indies, is the United States. Black militants, such as Stokely Carmichael, have exerted a powerful influence in recent years. Jamaica, which used to ban only subversive literature from communist countries, is now having to turn its attention to material coming from the United States mainland." (48)

The Daily Telegraph concurred stating, "Bermuda's tranquillity has been upset by Black Power two or three times in the past few years. Among those questioned …were people who were close to the small 'Black Berets' movement dedicated to the overthrow of white rule." (49)

The *Daily Mail's* reporter Dermot Purgavie experienced first-hand the resentment of some black Bermudians towards white Englishmen. When Purgavie visited the offices of the Black Berets, Bermudian blacks on the street shouted, "We don't want your kind round here." Purgavie said a Scotland Yard detective had told him, "…there were more guns on this island than Chicago". (50)

The Guardian reporter thought the islands' 'sleepy atmosphere' was 'deceptive'. "In the past five years", the newspaper opined, "there have been two major outbursts of rioting, plus a number of unexplained violent crimes…..the sleepy paradise, in fact, masks an island where political and racial tensions are bubbling in a very ugly fashion just below the surface… Bermudian business prospectuses and tourist pamphlets continue to proclaim that the island is a political rock, a haven of tranquillity. But as the days go by, it is becoming increasingly difficult to ignore the tension and strains that threaten to ruin this holiday paradise."(51)The newspaper also believed that politics was certainly the motivating factor in the murders. The Guardian's Simon Winchester wrote, "Most people tend to link (the murders) all to politics and to black grievances. A few are bold and implicate the Black Berets directly; a few even wonder where Roosevelt Brown was on Saturday night (the night of the Governor's assassination)." (52)

In fact the only British newspaper that engaged in sensationalist speculation was *The Sun* although it did correctly conclude the assassination was the result of the island's racial problems. In an article dated 13th March 1973 the newspaper said, "A squad of hired assassins are thought to have been smuggled into Bermuda to kill the British Governor and his aide….. They are probing a clue that black fanatics hired the killers…..Detectives think the death squad were whisked out of Hamilton and off the sun-soaked island a few minutes after carrying out their 'contract'…..a policeman said, 'It takes an iron nerve to kill like that, the nerve of a professional'…officials fear an uprising among militant blacks." (53)

THE BLACK BERETS
1969 – 1970

"Idealism Kills"
Friedrich Nietzsche

"The question of violence is not a question among the oppressed; the only questions are tactical and practical; how to exercise what kind of violence with what kind of preparation and for what ends...."
Black Panther, Kathleen Cleaver.

"The Cadre's Liberation classes are now attended weekly...with the chanting of anti-white slogans, the indoctrination of racial hatred is even more intense than hitherto and it is disturbing to contemplate the effect this will have on race relations in years to come. Even today it is an unhappy thought that these children are not waifs and strays collected from the streets but are attending the classes with the full knowledge and consent of their parents."
Lord Martonmere.

THE FORMATION OF the Black Beret Cadre had its origins in a Black Power conference held in Bermuda in 1969. Participants came from the United States, Canada and Caribbean nations. The conference was organised by the Progressive Labour Party's Dr Roosevelt Brown, (now Dr. Pauulu Kamarakafego), the PLP's 'resident extremist' as the *Guardian* newspaper called him. (1) The newspaper also said that Roosevelt Brown was, "...the representative of much that has gone wrong or may yet go wrong in Bermuda's otherwise tidily self-assured village life." (2) Brown was disliked amongst the white minority in Bermuda. He looked upon himself as a young black Che Guevara and was a self-styled Marxist, a former member of the House of Assembly, a youth leader and a black militant who frequently visited Cuba.(3)

However, amongst Bermudian youth there was some discontent with the PLP's 'Youth Wing', led by Roosevelt. It was seen by many as 'too liberal' in its approach to the problems of black Bermudians. Accordingly, a group of young blacks, led by John Hilton Bassett, decided to form their own radical organisation. It soon gained the respect of many black youths and succeeded in attracting financial support from many members of the black community. It also received financial aid from Cuba, according to British intelligence sources. The Berets were supported by a number of the PLP's radical members who opened up unofficial channels of communication with the Cadre. The connection was low-key enough to provide some politicians with a certain degree of plausible deniability if the group was implicated in any crimes.

Bassett modelled his group of black militants on the American Black Panthers, a black Marxist militant organisation. The Black Panthers also became a model for other groups around the world such as the Black Panther Movement in the UK, the Black Panther Parties in Australia and Israel and the Dalit Panthers in India.

The US Panthers attracted worldwide attention as party members travelled abroad to lecture and raise money. They were inspired by the writings and speeches of Malcolm X and the Nation of Islam, commonly called the Black Muslims.

The Black Muslims were led by Elijah Mohammad who frequently made violent pronouncements against Jews, whites and Christians. In fact, the teachings of Elijah Muhammad were based on exactly the same kind of racial hatred espoused by Southern white supremacists. According to Muhammad's teachings, white people were invented six thousand years ago by a mad scientist named Yacub in a failed experiment to dilute the blood of the original human beings, who were black. The experiment produced morally tainted 'white devils' that God planned to destroy when Armageddon arrived. Malcolm X never abandoned these beliefs even though he was expelled from the organization.

The Black Panthers were just one manifestation of the growing militancy that many African Americans developed during the 1960s. As the idea that African Americans should use non-violent methods to further their cause waned, new black heroes like H. Rap Brown and Stokely Carmichael and Black Panther Party leaders like Eldridge Cleaver, prophets of violence and separatism, became popular amongst America's black youth. The new 'civil rights' groups advocated separatism and espoused anti-white rhetoric. According to Panther apologist professor Charles Pinderhughes in 2002, "If you are not a Marxist-Leninist you cannot be in the Black Panther Party." Pinderhughes also said that Mao and Stalin never ran 'death camps' calling them 're-education camps' instead. (4)

In 1966, some months before the founding of the Black Panthers party, Student Non-Violent Coordinating Committee (SNCC) leader, Stokely Carmichael, had raised the call for black power in the United States, thereby signalling a crossroads in the civil rights struggle. Increasingly uncomfortable with Dr King's resolute non-violence, he sensed a shift in the direction of black separatism among some younger black members of his organization.

In June 1966 Carmichael addressed a crowd of 3000 in a park in Greenwood Mississippi. When marchers set up camp Carmichael was arrested. Frustrated, Carmichael told the crowd, "We have been saying 'Freedom' for six years. What we are going to start saying now is 'Black Power!' The crowd quickly took up the phrase and the cry was repeated in cities across America. Adverse reaction was immediate. It troubled many black leaders who thought it sounded anti-white, provocative and violent. After the integrationist speeches and sermons of Dr Martin Luther King Jr and others, few white Americans were prepared for the uncompromising demands of black militants who rallied to Carmichael's cry. Newspapers deplored the term and editorials warned of 'reverse racism'.

Contributions to civil rights groups from sympathetic whites fell after Carmichael's speech. Voting results in the November 1966 US elections reflected a white 'backlash'. Dr King called it an unfortunate choice of words and said it was an example of 'the raging of race against race'. National Urban League Director Whitney Young said, "Anyone can arouse the poor, the despairing, and the helpless. That's no trick. Sure they'll shout 'Black

Power', but why doesn't the mass media find out how many of those people will follow those leaders to a separate state or back to Africa?"

However, Carmichael explained the term as, "…a call for black people in this country to unite, to recognise their heritage, to build a sense of community. It is a call for black people to define their own goals, to lead their own organizations." However, his speeches became more provocative. In one speech Carmichael said, "When you talk of black power, you talk of building a movement that will smash everything Western Civilization has created". When America's cities rioted in 1967 and 1968 Carmichael's cry became associated with riots, guns and lawlessness. Instead of young people singing 'We Shall Overcome' black youths in their thousands were wearing black berets, raising clenched fists and carrying guns. As well as cries for social justice young blacks called for separatism and black power within a larger black nationalism.(5)

The American Black Panthers were probably the most violently racist of all the black groups in the United States. Although its leaders advocated self-help and keeping drugs out of the black communities across the United States, the Panthers combined militant Black Nationalism with Marxism and advocated black empowerment and self-defense, often through confrontation. During its heyday, members of the Black Panthers murdered more than a dozen law-enforcement officers. Today Eddie Conway, H. Rap Brown, Ed Poindexter and David Rice are among their alumni serving life sentences.

The Black Panther founders were Huey Newton and Bobby Seale who had been students together at a community college in Oakland, a largely black working class area across the bay from San Francisco. The new party quickly attracted members, among them Bobby Hutton and Eldridge Cleaver. Many members were also sympathetic to the urgings of Malcolm X, who had been assassinated a year and a half earlier who said that the struggle for black rights should be carried out 'by any means necessary'.

The Panthers first made headlines on 2 May 1967 when some 40 members invaded the legislative chambers of the California State Capitol Building in Sacramento, carrying loaded rifles, shotguns and pistols. The alleged purpose of the invasion was to discourage the State legislature from adopting more stringent gun control legislation. Six of the Panthers, including Chairman Bobby Seale, were eventually sent to jail with sentences of three months each. (6)

By the late 1960s the Black Panthers had chapters in more than two dozen cities. In the early 1970s members were feeding poor children free breakfasts across America. They issued a manifesto, the *'Ten Point Program and Platform – What We Want, What We Believe'* which was a mixture of black liberation, anti-colonial solidarity and anti-capitalistic rhetoric which became a model, they claimed, for the 'liberation of oppressed people'. Part of the Party Platform railed against the 'racist society' they alleged existed in the United States. It included exhortations to commit crime in the name of rectifying past injustices. The manifesto stipulated:

We want education for our people that exposes the true nature of this decadent American society. We want education that teaches us our true history and our role in the present-day society.

We want all black men to be exempt from military service. We believe that Black people should not be forced to fight in the military service to defend a racist government that does not protect us. We will not fight and kill other people of color in the world who, like black people, are being victimized by the white racist government of America. We will protect ourselves from the force and violence of the racist police and the racist military, by whatever means necessary.

We believe we can end police brutality in our black community by organizing black self-defense groups that are dedicated to defending our black community from racist police oppression and brutality. The Second Amendment to the Constitution of the United States gives a right to bear arms. We therefore believe that all black people should arm themselves for self- defense.

We want freedom for all black men held in federal, state, county and city prisons and jails. We believe that all black people should be released from the many jails and prisons because they have not received a fair and impartial trial. (7)

In particular the Black Panthers targeted the 'racist' US police forces for attack. In an article from the *Black Panther*, May 4th 1968 entitled *'Credo for Rioters and Looters'*, the party's organ stated, "America, you will be cleansed by fire, by blood, by death. We who perform your ablution must step up our burning – bigger and better fires, one flame for all America, an all-

American flame; we must step up our looting – loot, until we storm your last boarding place, till we trample your last stolen jewel into your ashes beneath our naked black feet; we must step up our sniping – until the last pig is dead, shot to death with his own gun and the bullets in his guts that he had meant for the people…We know that there are those amongst your people who are innocent, those who were brainwashed and manipulated out of their own humanity, out of their minds, out of their lives. We know who these are. These will help us burn you. These will help us loot. These will help us kill you…." (8)

Eldridge Cleaver summed up the Panthers' attitude toward violence by stating, "There are enough people in Babylon to kick pig ass from the Atlantic to the Pacific and back again. We can kick pig ass for days if we all start doing it…in times of revolution…I love the angels of destruction and disorder as opposed to the devils of conservation and law and order…we are either pig killers or pig feeders…" (9)

The ideologists of the Panthers made no effort to hide their Mao-style left-wing radicalism as evidenced by an article for the *Black Panther* newspaper in April 1968 which used language familiar with students of Chinese communism. The article called for, "The capitalistic, imperialistic, doggish, pimping of the People" to cease or "perish like Babylon. The People shall smash the glutton roaches running this decadent society and, along with the directing of the Black Panther Party, halt these running dogs and gain true liberation for all. We cannot depend upon the present government to fulfil our wants and needs. Thus more and more programs shall be set up to suffice the desires of the People and destroy the dictatorship of the bourgeoisie (ruling class) and its lackeys."(10)

Most of the Black Panther leaders had a criminal background. Newton and his friends would strap on guns and carry law books and drive around neighbourhoods on weekends shadowing police officers on their patrols through the ghetto. In a May 1967 article in the *Black Panther* the police were described as 'The Pig'. "A Pig is an ill-natured beast who has no respect for law and order", the article stated, "a foul traducer who's usually found masquerading as a victim of an unprovoked attack."(11) At the height of their fame the Panthers liked to outrage their white supporters by referring to

Martin Luther King as 'Martin Luther Coon'. (12)

Black Panther founder, Huey Newton, had spent most of his youth as a burglar attacking homes in the wealthy Oakland Hills district and his first criminal conviction was for stabbing a black man repeatedly with a steak knife at a party (13) In his autobiography, *'Revolutionary Suicide'*, Newton bragged that he hung out in hospital parking lots to pull off 'strong-arm robberies'. After the Black Panthers were founded Newton shot and killed a 23 year old Oakland police officer named John Frey after the officer pulled Newton's car over. Newton pleaded self-defense, got off with a conviction for voluntary manslaughter, and served less than two years in prison. He was re-tried a number of times but each case resulted in mistrials. He was finally acquitted in 1971. He later boasted about how he had 'offed the pig'. He also later admitted he had 'murdered' police officer John Frey. (14)

According to journalist Holland Cotter, "While the Rev. Martin Luther King Jr was quoting Jesus and Ghandi, Newton read Marx and Malcolm X. The idea of blacks taking what was theirs by force was ever-present on the horizon. King didn't go there; Malcolm X went, and then pulled back; the Panthers went and stayed." (15)

To many Americans the Black Panthers were simply a group of angry young African Americans determined to fight police brutality and create self-help programs in the ghettoes. To others they were a terrorist group acting outside the law. It would be decades before the truth about the Black Panthers emerged, allowing the American public to discover the types of crimes they were involved in, including murder.

When Panther accountant Betty Van Patter discovered that the leaders were misappropriating money from their 'breakfast programme' she was murdered. (16) Other murders carried out by the Panthers included Jimmy Carr, George Jackson's former prison mate, and Fred Bennet, a Panther who was killed after dating Bobby Seale's wife. In 1974 Newton fled to Cuba after murdering a teenage prostitute and viciously pistol whipping a black tailor who had come to his penthouse to measure him for a suit. He also beat two women in a bar for 'sassing him'. Additionally, the Panthers were guilty of extreme acts of brutality including turning female members into prostitutes if they broke a Panther rule. (17) Newton died in 1989 after being slain by a drug dealer outside a known crack house.

Another leading member of the Panthers was Eldridge Cleaver who had served almost 12 years in prison on a variety of assaults with intent to murder, drug, rape and theft charges. Cleaver once claimed that violating white women was a political act and brought about demoralization of the dominant race, exposing its inability to protect its own women from the worst kinds of deprivation.(18) Cleaver wrote, "I became a rapist. To refine my technique and modus operandi, I started out practicing on black girls….and when I considered myself smooth enough I crossed the tracks and sought out white prey. I did this consciously, deliberately, wilfully, methodically…rape was an insurrectionary act. It delighted me that I was defying and trampling upon the white man's laws, upon his system of values, and I was defiling his women." (19)

When Cleaver heard the news about Martin Luther King's assassination he ordered his party members to 'assassinate' police in 'retaliation' for King's death.(20) After a gun battle with Oakland police in April 1968 he fled to Cuba. He later admitted to writer Kate Coleman he wanted to 'kill police officers'. Cleaver and his wife eventually took up residence in Algeria in 1969. He continued to lead the international wing of the party during his exile and made trips to North Korea, North Vietnam and the Soviet Union, China and the Congo as representative of the party. His trips provoked the FBI into organizing surveillance of the party's members. Many years later, in his last television interview before his death, Cleaver acknowledged the criminality of the Black Panthers and his own role in the organization. He said that the United States had been remarkably good when compared to others and that people like he had benefited from American society. Cleaver said, "If people had listened to Huey Newton and me in the 1960s, there would have been a holocaust in this country." (21)

Today the Black Panthers are glorified by many black groups and black activists around the world, especially Bermuda. Many, like the Bermudian writer Quito Swan, view them as 'freedom fighters' and 'heroes in the cause of equal rights'. However, to those who have researched the history of the organization and the crimes they committed his descriptions of the organization are clearly ludicrous. In fact, a torrent of articles and books, many written by former sympathizers, has carefully documented the Panther reign of murder and larceny within their own communities. According to former Black Panther supporter, Sol Stern, Newton and his colleagues were nothing but, "….psychopathic criminals not social reformers…no one but a left wing crank could still believe in the Panther myth of dedicated young blacks 'serving the people' while heroically defending themselves against unprovoked attacks by the racist police." (22)

The chorus of vitriol directed against the Panther legacy has gained support from another Panther leader, Bobby Seale. In April 1968, while awaiting trial on the charges incurred on May 2nd 1967 when Panthers tried to enter the California State Capitol Building in Sacramento, Seale was arrested and found guilty of carrying a gun near a jail – a felony. He was given three years' probation on the charge. (23)

Bobby Seale admitted in a 2002 newspaper interview that the Panthers were indeed criminals. He said the Panthers were responsible for many murders and were effectively a criminal gang no better than the Mafia. Seale made reference in his interview to the work of David Horowitz who had written about the crimes the Panthers committed and he credited Horowitz with revealing the truth about the organization. (24)

David Horowitz, a former Black Panther supporter, believes the Black Panthers were "…just as the police and other Panther detractors said at the time – a criminal army at war with society and with its thin blue line of civic protectors…..The story of the Panthers' crimes is not unknown. But it is either uninteresting or unbelievable to a progressive culture that still regards white racism as the primary cause of all ills in black America, and militant thugs like the Panthers as mere victims of politically inspired repression….. the existence of a Murder Incorporated in the heart of the American left is something the Left really doesn't want to know or think about……They were attempting to launch a civil war in America that would have resulted in unimaginable bloodshed." (25)

Horowitz, a friend of the murdered Panther secretary Betty Van Patten, began to recognize that totalitarian and ruthless means were being advanced "to build the fantasy of an earthly paradise". The revolutionary vanguard of his socialist dreams, Horowitz said, became a criminal fraternity extorting money from Oakland's bars, night clubs, pimps and drug dealers. Horowitz cited an admission by Huey Newton in making his claims that the Panthers were a criminal group. Newton confessed that one of the most revered of all the Panthers 'good works', a programme collecting for sickle -cell anaemia was a 'con'. He said the Panthers set up fraudulent 'dummy corporations' and embezzled government social programme money. The money poured in to keep the Black Panther leaders in lavish lifestyles. (26) According to Kate Coleman, "(If anyone wants to know)… the real legacy of the Panthers…. they should pore over the cold statistics showing the huge spike in drive-by-shooting deaths and gang warfare that took place in Oakland in the decade following Newton's and the Panther's demise. The Panther fetish of the gun, worshipped by young , impressionable black males, maimed hundreds of black citizens in Oakland and other tough city ghettoes more surely than any bully cops ever did." (27)

*

John Hilton Bassett was a 26 year old electrician for Bermuda's Universal Electric Company. He had spent some time in the United States and become enamoured by the Panther's aggressive style in fighting alleged police racism. Bassett had the idea that a similar organization in Bermuda could attract a lot of supporters. After forming the Black Beret Cadre he adopted 'Dionne' as his revolutionary name and the group's motto was, "*Peace if possible, compromise never, freedom by any means necessary.*" The Berets' name was taken from the French beret which resistance fighters wore during World War Two in their struggle against German occupiers.

On 12 February 1970 the Berets held their first meeting at the YMCA on Cedar Avenue, Hamilton. John Brandon, a minister of the Allen Temple AME Church, was the keynote speaker. Brandon said, in a startling departure from the principles of his faith, "If violence must be used to smash the barriers that separate black people from the abundant life that Christ talked about, then under God there will be violence."

Alvin Williams, a future reporter for the *Royal Gazette*, was present at the first meeting. According to Williams, the Beret's presence and presentation was "nothing less than electrifying". Williams remembered the "young black

Bermudians in their black leather jackets and black berets pulled to one side". He said Bassett had told the meeting he had, "…spent some time in the United States" and that even though the group looked like a Bermudian version of the Black Panther Party in America, "it was strictly Bermudian". Williams said that at the meeting "…it was explained that the Black Berets would resist what they considered to be Bermuda's racist power structure. The first meeting was something Bermuda had never witnessed before and I must say, those of us who were there were spellbound."

To many black Bermudian youths the Black Berets filled the vacuum caused by the demise of the Youth Wing of the PLP. Alvin Williams remembered that young people at the time had "…common heroes like Malcolm X, Ho Chi Minh, Fidel Castro and writers like Franz Fanon who chronicled the anti-colonial struggle in the Third World". To Williams and many others in Bermuda the struggle for equal rights was, "a war and some of us remember the battles and conflict that took place on Bermudian streets and were very rarely reported on by the media". (28)

The Black Berets stated that they were not aligned to any of the established political parties but wanted to be a 'catalyst for political change'. Like their American counterparts the Black Berets believed the prevailing political parties were not radical enough and called some mainstream politicians 'reactionary'. They also believed that Bermuda's politicians, including some members of the PLP, were in league with the 'power structure' whose central aim they said was to keep the wealth of the country in the hands of the rich white establishment. For their part the Bermudian government believed the Berets, "…had no political aspirations: its philosophy is simply to control everything, first by destroying what exists and then by rebuilding in its own mould." (29)

According to a British newspaper report the Black Berets information officer, Mel Saltus, confirmed reports that the Black Berets had links to Black Power groups in America. (30) Williams admitted he had been influenced "…by the revolutionary precepts of the day, just like our black counterparts in America, who it could be said were involved in a real war in America's cities. At the time both America and Britain were reaping the whirlwinds of their racist and colonial pasts and thus were taken aback by the Black Power revolt and the emergence of groups like the Black Panthers and the Black Berets in Bermuda." (31)

A former Bermudian government cabinet member held a different view of the growing crisis between black and white Bermudians. He characterized the Black Berets as an organization influenced by, "…a half-assed guru in Canada, a lecturer at Carleton University in Ottawa which was then a hotbed of militant, leftist agitation." The former cabinet member said the lecturer, "flew in and out of Bermuda and they visited him in Canada". The Black Berets were, "…gangsters first, radicals second… highly conspicuous, wandering around in their trademark berets, military-type camouflage jackets and paratrooper boots, wearing these huge sunglasses like they were refugees from the Ton Ton Macoutes… they were always getting into trouble – spitting on tourists, marching on Parliament, burning the British flag on the steps of City Hall, occupying the dining room at the Mid Ocean Club and organising a string of mini-riots that kept breaking out in the late '60s and early '70s in and around Hamilton." (32) The 'half-assed-guru' was likely a Trinidadian Black Panther who visited Bermuda. He had incited violence in Canada during student demonstrations and called himself a 'revolutionary'. In an interview with the *Royal Gazette* the Trinidadian promoted violence against Canadians who vacationed in Bermuda.

At the time of the first Black Beret meeting the relationship between the youth of Bermuda and the Bermuda Police was at its lowest level. Clashes between black youths and police, mostly in the Court Street area of Hamilton, were frequent and on most weekends there were minor disturbances in Hamilton.

According to interviews given by former members of the Black Berets and the information supplied by police informants the Black Beret membership never went beyond 100. At its apex it never attracted more than a following of 200 out of a black population of some 40,000. Often only 50 or so members attended the meetings. However, its influence was greater than the sum of its parts. The organisation attracted the kind of attention the American Black Panthers garnered even though both groups were relatively small in numbers.

The key theme with both organisations was *'freedom by any means necessary'* which was taken by members as an acceptance of violent methods.

Taking their cue from the Black Panthers, whose primary aim was to bait the 'racist cops', the Black Berets exhorted its members and all Bermudian youth to confront the 'English racist police'.

During this period the Bermuda Police Force was made up of approx 45% UK expatriate police officers, approx. 45% black Bermudians and West Indian officers, and around 2-3% white Bermudians. According to former Bermudian police officer Territt Cabral, "…all the senior officers were white ex-pats except for William Sykes Smith and Frederick Colbert Bean." (33)

Following the formation of the Berets, Bassett soon found a headquarters for his group. It was situated in the Bassett Building on Court Street in Hamilton. They held rallies and meetings and a 'council of war' debated how and when their organisation would confront the 'power establishment'. It was in the basement of the Bassett Building that the Berets also ran a 'Liberation School' for children aged between 8 and 12. Its purpose was to indoctrinate young black Bermudians in communist revolution and the ideology of 'Black Power'. Another purpose of the school, the Berets said, was to teach 'African Unity and African History'.

However, the school's true aim was to indoctrinate children to fight capitalism, hate police officers and unite black Bermudians in overthrowing the government. According to an intelligence report sent to the British Foreign Office from Governor Martonmere, "The (Beret's) Liberation classes are now attended weekly…with the chanting of anti-white slogans, the indoctrination of racial hatred is even more intense than hitherto and it is disturbing to contemplate the effect this will have on race relations in years to come. Even today it is an unhappy thought that these children are not waifs and strays collected from the streets but are attending the classes with the full knowledge and consent of their parents." (34)

After reading Martonmere's report, British intelligence officials concluded that the Berets were using, "…crude but nevertheless effective indoctrination techniques, equal parts propaganda and brainwashing." They concluded that the Berets methods were, "…not a healthy development at all when young children are involved….it's an attempt to sow the seeds of violent revolution in the nursery bed of the future." (35)

The Black Berets began publishing their revolutionary newspaper "*Voice of the Revolutionaries"* in March 1970. Many of its articles were simply re-writes that appeared in the Black Panthers' newspaper. The Black Berets' periodical incited Bermudians 'to rise up against their colonial masters' and the 'tyrant white power structure'. Between 1969 and 1971 the Black Berets were relatively successful in attracting support.. Its Black Power literature also succeeded in encouraging young black Bermudians to confront the police and in recruiting youths who had a criminal background.

The Black Berets became well funded locally and may have received financial aide from Cuba. According to British Intelligence sources, "The establishment of a Cadre community centre...poses the question of the source of funds: on the face of it, it seems unlikely that the members actively involved will be subscribing the kind of money which is required to keep an operation of this kind going." Intelligence officials also believed that some of the Black Beret membership had received training in revolutionary warfare and the likely suspect was Cuba. British Intelligence believed that the Black Berets' "... (Incitement of) violence without personal involvement would suggest that experienced hands are at the helm." (36)

The suspicions the Berets' were closely involved with Cuba were echoed many years later by a former cabinet official who told the *Royal Gazette* that, "At one time (they) wanted to send one of their members to Cuba for training at one of Castro's para-military schools – at the time there were kids from all over Europe, South America and Asia being trained by Castro so they could go back home and stir up trouble along the lines of his Cuban revolution. But the Berets could never figure out a way to get one of their people into Cuba". (37)

The Black Berets were surveilled by police and reported on both openly and secretly. The orders for the surveillance were probably handed down by Governor Lord Martonmere who took his reserve powers seriously regarding internal security. Additionally, he had operational control of the police. It was not until the 1980s that effective control of the Police Service was ceded to the Bermudian government (although overall authority still remains with the Governor of the day). The informants who reported to the security branch of the police service were drawn mainly from black expatriate police officers from the Caribbean, according to former Beret supporter Alvin Williams,

"Not too many Bermudians," Alvin wrote, " if they were in the Police Force, would be willing to play the role of mole. Thus it was mostly officers from the Caribbean who were used in this way...." (38)

On February 21st 1970 the Government gave the Black Berets permission to hold a rally in Victoria Park, Hamilton, to mark the 5th anniversary of the assassination of Malcolm X. The meeting included prayers, poetry readings and speeches from Beret members. During the meeting the Berets re-named the park 'Malcolm X Memorial Park'.

In the following months the Berets began to target schools in a move to incite black youths. Disturbances occurred at two schools in early 1970 and a sit-down demonstration was organised at the Mid-Ocean Golf Club in Tucker's Town. On March 21st an arsonist, believed by police to be a PLP Member of Parliament, attempted to set fire to the chamber of the House of Assembly which the Berets had publicly threatened to attack. The MP was never charged. Later in the year the Black Berets attempted to take advantage of civil unrest sparked by labour union disputes at the airport and a car dealership. Confrontations with the police occurred regularly as Bermudian youths, incited by the Berets, engaged in mini riots, most of which occurred in the Court Street area of Hamilton.

In March 1970 the British Government received the first notification that a Black Power group of militants were embarking on a policy of violence designed to destabilize the Bermudian Government. A confidential telex between the Commander of HMS Malabar (a permanent structure which was used as the headquarters of the Senior Naval Officer West Indies (SNOWI), situated near Casemates maximum security prison) to the British Ministry of Defence stated, "Youth organisation has in last few days provoked disorders on two school sports fields and achieved sit-down demonstration at Mid-Ocean Golf Club. There was also an arson attempt in the Assembly House. Culprit not yet found but Black Berets have previously threatened to burn this building." In response the Foreign Office informed the Governor three warships were near the island and carried Royal Marines and sailors who had been trained in anti-riot duties.

On March 29th 1970 the Berets became the prime suspects for the firebombing of the Old Devonshire Church. Keith Adderley, a Beret supporter, was eventually charged with the offence. He was found guilty at his trial and sentenced to seven years in prison. During this period there was also an abortive attempt to burn the House of Assembly chamber.

Following the arson attack the Governor Lord Martonmere became fearful that the Berets were, "…rapidly becoming a serious threat to security. With purely racist motives it is challenging authority, apparently with the intention of provoking government reaction and using this as an excuse for violence". He was also concerned that the Berets were encouraging young people to bait white teachers and hold demonstrations in the schools. "More recently", he said, "there has been growing evidence that the cult of black separatism among young people is being actively promoted; the movement is apparently becoming better organised and more effective".

The police were also keeping the Governor informed about demonstrations being planned for the Easter holiday. As it turned out, the demonstrations did not take place due to the increase in police surveillance and the presence of a British frigate. However, Bermuda's second oldest church was firebombed and destroyed. The police suspected the Black Berets were responsible for the arson attack. The Governor believed the destruction of the Church indicated a "new phase of bolder and more determined attacks against authority." (39)

Martonmere believed that the Black Berets did not have the support of older Bermudians. However, he was concerned that Bermudian youth were quickly becoming attracted to the Berets' revolutionary rhetoric. Martonmere pointed out that segregation had existed only ten years previously and that the ruling UBP were remiss in not taking into account "the simmering resentments which still resonated". (40)

Following a summer of minor disturbances in which police clashed with unruly black youth, there developed a major outbreak of violence in October 1970 which had their origins in an incident that took place on Friday 7th August 1970. Several Black Beret members held a demonstration in front of City Hall, Church Street, Hamilton, denouncing arms sales to South Africa. Beret leader Bassett delivered a speech then burned the Union Jack flag. He was assisted by Beret member Mel Saltus. The Bermuda Police made no arrests during the demonstration but later, on the 15th August, Bassett was questioned at Central

CID by Chief Inspector Clive Donald and on Tuesday the 6th October Bassett and Saltus were charged with offensive behaviour and contempt of court. They pleaded not guilty and represented themselves. The magistrate, Richmond Smith, gave them six months in prison. Later that evening, at 11.45pm, a 15 year old boy was arrested for throwing a petrol bomb.

On October 4th 1970 Calvin Weeks, a leading member of the Berets, along with his brother, were among a crowd at City Hall. Both men threatened a police officer. They also exhorted the crowd that had gathered to split into two groups, one group to attack the police station nearby and the other to prepare firebombs made with gasoline. The crowd responded and mayhem ensued. (41) The police blamed the Berets for the arson attacks and riots. "It is now known", a police report stated, "the Black Beret Cadre is directing these attacks. Members in cars clever enough not to be carrying incriminating evidence were involved….and (Bermuda Police) Special Branch reports that at suitable opportunity Berets plan to attack police operations centre. Police today have been placed at Security Stage Amber, which means 12 hour shifts and more men on the ground." (42)

The violence and rioting spread out over eight successive nights – 25 arsons, 13 malicious damage offences, two shootings and two malicious telephone calls were recorded when a hoaxer threatened to burn down City Hall and St Theresa RC Church.

Police Chief George Duckett, who had recently been appointed, in part to deal with youth unrest, was seen by many blacks as an example of 'white police repression'. He held the view that civil unrest must be confronted head on lest the unruly element in society gain a foothold which would lead to a higher crime rate. His views were no different from those prevailing in the UK and the US whose police forces had been learning valuable lessons during race-related riots in the 1960s. Four decades later the British Police force would learn that valuable lesson during the 2011 London Riots.

However, no amount of rationalizing could dissuade Bermudian black youth that the efforts of Duckett and his force were designed to protect the citizens of Bermuda. According to a Black Beret supporter of the time, "I still see in my minds eye the infamous flying squad, comprised of six Land Rovers, each carrying eight policemen in full riot gear. These were protected by a light steel mesh which covered the vehicles (against) rocks and bottles. It was just like a Northern Ireland in the middle of the Atlantic. The idea was to have a mobile unit able to respond quickly to gatherings of young people and to hold the line until a larger unit could be called to assist."(43)

On the evening of October 8th/9th an arson attack destroyed the Chesley Building on Reid Street in Hamilton. The damage came to over $250,000. As firemen struggled to control the fire arsonists attempted to torch a furniture store on the same street. By the evening of October 9th the civil unrest subsided. The Black Berets were anxious to appear uninvolved fearing Bassett's appeal against his six month prison sentence, which he received for the flag burning incident, would be compromised. However, Beret leaders did instruct their members to, "Do their own thing – and this means meeting in twos and threes each night to arrange and perhaps participate in arson and damage" (44)

The short lull in violence did not last long. On the night of October 10th/11th the Bermuda Regiment was mobilized to deal with full scale rioting. The trouble began around 8.45pm. In Hamilton City centre Bermuda police officers requested a crowd of youths to remove their motor cycles which were causing obstruction on the pavement. The young black Bermudians refused and began to swear at the police officers. When the officers attempted to arrest one of them for his aggressive behaviour a large crowd of around five or six hundred people gathered and began to pelt them with bricks and bottles. When the officers threw tear gas the crowd disbursed but it later reassembled and built road blocks to the entrances to Court Street.

For the next seven and a half hours the police battled the rioters who ran created mayhem destroying cars and firebombing shops. On three occasions police were fired on, once by an automatic weapon but no one was injured. The police had difficulty in controlling the crowd and removing the barricades because demonstrators had destroyed the street lighting in the area around Court Street. They were also hindered by the tactics of the crowd which repeatedly dispersed and then reformed. However, police were eventually able to restrict rioters to an area around Court Street. (45)

One week later in a speech at a church hall in Southampton on October

18th 1970, a Beret member told the audience his group of black militants were willing to, "make the supreme sacrifice to bring about changes and to ensure our children get what they should. We feel if the Government believes it is all right for arms to be sold to South Africa which practices open discrimination against black people, then they would feel all right to destroy this system of injustice which has been placed on us by our British colonial masters. We might have to break unjust laws to accomplish this and even if it hurts the tourist industry we must be willing to pay some price to get the right people in the right places to run this country." The Beret then invoked the name of Christ who, he said, 'died for the struggle'. "We must do the same", he said, "We are not joking about this. We are very serious."(46)

Government officials were extremely worried about the security situation following the riots. Prince Charles' visit to Bermuda was only weeks away. In response to these fears Lord Martonmere ordered riot police to be on stand-by. However, in consultation with Government members, he advocated that heavy-handed tactics be avoided at all costs as he believed this would provoke riots. As it turned out, the Prince's visit occurred without any major disturbance.

On October 27th a meeting was arranged by the Berets attended by around 60 non-members. During discussions it was decided to hold a demonstration on Hamilton's Front Street for Saturday, 31st October. There was talk of burning effigies, forming a procession along Front Street and alternatively lying down to obstruct police or running away from police in order to create confusion and mayhem. The Berets told their supporters that the main object of the demonstration was to protest against unfair discrimination in court sentencing and in particular to protest the prison sentence handed down to Beret leader Dionne Bassett. Before the march Berets distributed a leaflet entitled 'Reasons for Demonstration' in which they protested the sentencing system, the jury system, high prices, press 'censorship' and Police 'Gestapo' tactics. The Royal Gazette was fined $5000 and one of its assistant editors $1,250 for contempt of court after publishing on the paper's front page a statement issued by the Black Berets following Bassett's imprisonment.

The planned rally took place at 4pm. A crowd of around 70 people gathered at the Flagpole on Front Street bearing placards. However, there was no attempt to form a procession to march. After milling around aimlessly for a while the crowd moved off towards City Hall. Police acted to prevent disorder by arresting six ringleaders. Although the police believed the crowd was going to assemble in Bernard Park it soon disbursed.

The government concluded that the rally on Front Street had been "an abject failure" and by November the government were beginning to believe the Black Berets were failing to attract support for their cause. (47) However, a few months later, in early 1971, Lord Martonmere was having second thoughts. He believed the Black Berets were taking the initiative owing to PLP 'quiescence' in constitutional social and economic matters. Martonmere wrote, "…the Cadre appears to be the only organisation effectively fighting for so-called justifiable grievances and, whether or not this is the reason, there is no doubt that the middle class and even some of the intelligentsia are increasingly sympathetic." However, Martonmere also believed that if the Black Beret Cadre resorted to overt violent tactics its support amongst middle class Bermudians would diminish. He expressed dismay that the Berets were supported by some PLP members who were on the radical wing of the party. (48)

In effect the PLP were quietly supporting the Black Berets' efforts to stir up discontent among black Bermudians in the hope this disgruntlement would turn into party support at the polls. Martonmere called the PLP/Black Beret connection an 'unholy alliance'. And he believed the central figure in this association was Roosevelt Brown. Martonmere also believed the Bermuda Regiment had been infiltrated by Black Beret members in order to gain access to weapons and training. He described the activities of the Berets as 'terrorist' in nature and was disappointed that some Bermudian government officials were unwilling to proscribe the organisation or take action against it. He wrote, "It is one of the less satisfying aspects of the Bermuda scene that some members of the community, including senior civil servants, are reluctant to be seen to take action which might make them unpopular with the more militant youth. This is partly the consequence of living on a small island but it is also a reminder of the influence that a small but subversive organisation like the Black Beret Cadre can exercise through fear." (49)

FOUR

THE BLACK BERETS
1971 – 1972

"Despite prison sentences meted out to two of its leaders and their absence in prison, the organisation has remained intact and continued with its meetings and propaganda and with the 'Liberation School' classes which are attended by increasing numbers of schoolchildren whose parents either do not wish – or are afraid – about the indoctrination of their children." **Lord Martonmere, Government House memo to the Foreign Office, 5 March, 1971**

"The (Royal Gazette) stories are being written from documents recently declassified and released by the British Government. The sources for the Black Beret Cadre article were, therefore, impeccable" **Gavin Shorto, Royal Gazette, June 17, 2003**

B Y 1971 THE British Foreign Office was satisfied that Bermuda had made important strides in building an integrated and equal society. The Foreign Office noted that employment opportunities for black Bermudians had improved considerably over the period of the previous few years and that black Bermudians had been acquiring employment in Bermuda's banks, insurance offices and other areas of employment that had until now been restricted to Bermudian whites and British expatriates. However, the Foreign Office added a cautionary note, observing that the new opportunities needed to be broadened and encouraged if multi-racialism was to be successful. The Foreign Office also noted that a racially fair society could not succeed, "…if the racialist doctrine of Black Power and its derivatives become firmly established in Bermuda. The substantial black middle class are more or less immune and it is among young people that the danger lies…." (1)

The Foreign Office also advised the Bermudian government to counter the growing importation of black power literature which advocated hatred of whites, allowing that it was not easy to carry out the ban. "It is hard to imagine anything more poisonous to the young mind", a Foreign Office memo stated, "...the cold-blooded murder of three (American) sheriffs appears in a Black Panther magazine as 'Three Pigs Executed'....Black Power is not indigenous to Bermuda but it is a rub-off from the United States". Foreign Office officials reasoned that it was doubtful Black Power could flourish in an affluent society like Bermuda, "without sustenance from the outside. It may be necessary to be much tougher with trouble-makers who come on visits etc." (2)

During January 1971 the Black Berets held an average of three meetings per week. A typical meeting would include discussions about political indoctrination and the purposes and tactics of 'revolution'.

Dionne Basset, anticipating he would be imprisoned for the 'contempt of court' offences he had been charged with, announced at a public meeting on the 5th January that members with leadership potential would be considered by the 'Central Committee of the Berets' and a number of members were encouraged to volunteer. He told the audience these measures were necessary to ensure the survival of the Berets, "despite pressure from the police and courts".

On the 12th January 1971 Black Beret members were informed that Bassett and Saltus had been sentenced to a term of imprisonment. They both received nine months in jail. Angered their leaders had been sent to prison, a demonstration was organised for 16th January when members could show their displeasure at what many perceived as a perversion of justice. However, a number of members voiced disapproval of the impending demonstration as they feared reprisals from the police. They were also concerned that the 'community' were "getting tired of being inconvenienced by (the demonstrations)". The Berets were split down the middle on the issue. Consequently the plans for the demonstration were abandoned. (3)

Although three Beret leaders had been imprisoned of late there was no indication that the increased attention which the Berets had received from the courts and the police was having any effect on the organization's activities or morale. The Berets were in the process of consolidating their position and the government feared they would gain more middle class support due to the ineffectiveness of the PLP. The Bermuda government's intelligence committee noted that the Berets', "... propensity for inviting violence without personal involvement would indicate that experienced hands are at the helm. The establishment of a community centre poses the question of the source of funds; on the face of it seems unlikely that the members actively involved will be subscribing the kind of money which is required to keep an operation of this kind going." (4)

Shortly after Bassett and Saltus were imprisoned reports reached the police that the two Berets, along with Black Beret 'chief ideologist' Phil Perinchief, were allowed 'special privileges'. The three convicts shared the same cell and police voiced their concern that they were allowed to receive 'any type of literature'.

Phil Perinchief was imprisoned on 20 November 1970 and was graded as a 'star prisoner'. He was given the responsibility for the library and on 21st January 1971 he was allowed by the prison authorities to organise Mathematics and English classes for prisoners. A police report described him as being, "held in high esteem by the other prisoners" who called him "teacher or sir". The report also stated that Perinchief settled a dispute over prison conditions. Perinchief's central aim in prison as far as his leadership role in the Black Berets was concerned, was to indoctrinate his fellow prisoners with Black Beret 'aims and principles'.(5)

Although prison officials had given Perinchief the role of prison librarian, the Warden of Prisons, John Bull, expressed concern that the prison library contained books dealing with revolutionary techniques and that, "Perinchief was in a position to choose additional publications". (6) The Bermuda Police Intelligence Committee voiced its concern that, "Not only should this type of literature not be allowed in the prison but steps should be taken to prevent it entering the colony". (7) The Committee said there was reluctance amongst politicians to ban Black Power (literature) but noted that it was, "a similar initial reluctance which resulted in the deplorable state of affairs in America whereby the authorities now have no control over publishers."(8)

The Intelligence Committee expressed concern over a particular book,

"The Revolutionary's Cook Book" (*Author's note: the correct title is 'Anarchist's Cook-Book'*) which they described as 'an encyclopaedia of sabotage'. It recommended the prison library be purged of 'undesirable literature'. Moves were made to review the library stock by the Permanent Secretary for Education and the Warden of Prisons. It also recommended that the Government ban books of a 'seditious nature'. (9)

The Intelligence Committee was also highly critical of Casemates Prison. It was reported that of a total of 112 prison officers, only 12% were white and that most of these officers were at Prison Headquarters in Hamilton. In particular, Casemates Prison had only two white officers out of a compliment of 40. There was also concern that during evenings and weekends only eight officers were on duty and at night as few as four. Particular concern was given to the fact that, "…some 40% of the warders and 75% of the prisoners are either like-minded or under the influence of Perinchief and the Cadre". (10)

The government also considered segregating Beret members but concluded it was impossible and "psychologically inadvisable". If Beret members were housed separately the problem of "unreliable staff" would remain and if the prison authorities treated the Black Beret members differently it would, "inflate their egotism and sense of martyrdom". The government was also concerned that the incarceration of Beret members was "potentially dangerous" because they "are in a position to organise civil disturbances in Hamilton to coincide with rioting in Casemates". In February 1971 they also believed, "the situation in Casemates Prison is alarming and poses a serious threat to security". (11)

Lord Martonmere advised the Foreign Office that the Berets were now in a position to, "cause trouble as and when they will. The Government Leader and the member responsible are aware of the position and urgent consideration is being given to rectifying it."(12)

This report likely prompted prison authorities to recruit more prison officers from Britain. In November of 1971 a contingent of 12 British expatriate officers, known amongst themselves as the 'Dirty Dozen', arrived and most of them were sent to Casemates Prison. The report had recommended that the only long term solution, "not easy to achieve", was to introduce "more reliable staff". (13)

On 22 January 1971 the Berets held a public meeting at Devonshire Recreational Club. It was attended by political activist Roosevelt Brown and the issues for discussion were identified as "education and the judicial system". The police called the meeting "a new tactic" and stated that the Berets were "sheltering under a new name (*The Concerned Four*)". The meeting was attended by approximately 35 people. Criticism was levelled at the government for not proceeding swiftly with integration in the schools and participants also expressed anger that the courts were allegedly giving out harsher sentences for black Bermudians. A reference was made to "… Bridges and Smith, both white, who allegedly were only fined after being convicted of motor manslaughter". The intelligence report noted this allegation was a lie and that Smith's offence was only "driving in a manner dangerous to the public". (14)

A second meeting under the guise of '*The Concerned Four*' was held on 20th February 1971. It was billed as a '*Revolutionary Seminar*' and '*Black Arts Festival*' and was held at Bishop Spencer School. The attendance averaged between 150 and 200 people. The meeting included African music, dancing, a fashion show, plays, karate demonstrations and recitals of 'revolutionary poetry'. Children who attended the Liberation School recited poetry which was described by the police as 'racial'. The event was attended by PLP activists Roosevelt Brown and Lois Browne-Evans. (15)

During the early part of the year three further 'Liberation' classes, with an average attendance of 12, were held. The Berets also reissued their 'manifesto' and members were warned against distributing it on the streets in case they were arrested. The Berets completed the process of establishing a community centre in the basement of the Bassett Building on Court Street immediately below its existing headquarters.

Despite the imprisonment of Beret leaders Basset and Saltus for disorderly behaviour and contempt of court the organization grew in popularity throughout 1971 although the membership remained stable at 45 or 50 (16) Plans were made to send a group of Berets to Cuba for training in revolutionary doctrine and guerrilla methods. Lord Martonmere expressed alarm at the idea the Berets were sending members to Cuba. "A (leading member of the Berets) explained his interpretation of revolution, reform, socialism and communism. At one stage the possibilities of going to Cuba were discussed. (The Beret) explained this could be done by going through Canada, but that such visits would attract police attention." (17)

The Government was also concerned about the infiltration of the Bermuda Regiment by Beret members. However, the authorities were pleased that as a new chain of command had been introduced in the regiment it meant that officers, NCOs and men would remain together for three years and would be in a better position to judge each other's 'abilities and loyalties'. "This closer rapport will make for a more accurate assessment of the Regiment's reliability", a report stated, "even though it must be appreciated that, apart from an annual fortnight's camp, meetings are restricted to forty short periods per year". Despite these new procedures authorities were concerned that "two – and presumably more – members of the Black Beret Cadre" were now part of the Regiment. The report said that the government were unable to, "unearth all undesirables" but that "careful security checking of the 1971 intake has resulted in a greatly improved morale and enthusiasm." (18)

By early 1971 the Black Berets were meeting on average three times per week. The Government were still extremely concerned about their activities because the organisation could, "...operate in a manner it is virtually impossible to prevent. Neither clandestine persuasion nor intimidation is rarely, if ever, likely to be reported." (19)

When Basset, Perinchief and Saltus were serving their time in Casemates Prison the Beret leadership roles were taken on by two ex-convicts, one of whom, in March 1973, would become the 'third man' involved in the assassination of the island's Governor. (*Police believed a 'fourth man' had been involved and, although they had a long list of suspects, they were unable to produce any evidence as to his identity.*)

The 'third man' had a hair-trigger temper and a long criminal record. On 14th March, 1971 at King Edward Memorial Hospital he threatened to kill Detective Chief Inspector John Sheehy. The 'third man' was arrested and appeared in Hamilton Magistrates' Court on 14th May, 1971. He was found guilty of the offence and sentenced to a period of corrective training.

He appealed against this conviction and on 25th June, 1971 the sentence was reduced to a fine and he was bound over to keep the peace for 12 months. In August 1972 he was arrested in Berlin, Vermont and charged with breaking and entering a Sporting Goods store armed with a .22 rifle. He was allowed bail but returned to Bermuda before he could stand trial and never returned to the Vermont town to answer the charges against him. It had a debilitating effect on his father, according to a Foreign Office report. (20)

During this period the Berets concentrated on developing an 'intelligence and security' unit. During their meetings the militants continued to discuss 'revolution' and 'detailed explanations of the Black Beret Cadre manifesto'. However, the central subject in their discussions was the role of the Bermuda Police force which they believed was 'in control of the community'. The new leadership called for intense 'revolutionary training' and the use of violent methods, but they understood that police surveillance of their activities would hinder their training program. (21)

After the two ex-convicts took control of the Black Berets the organization resumed its normal routine and regular meetings were now attended by up to 40 members. Classes on physical fitness, karate and first aid were introduced on a weekly basis and the first edition of the Beret's newsletter appeared on Saturday 20th February 1971. It was prepared in prison by Phil Perinchief. Although it was considered by Bermuda's Attorney General to contain seditious material, the authorities backed off from prosecuting Perinchief, allowing the police to collect further evidence against him. The newsletter had a circulation of around 2,000 copies, the probable limit imposed by the Beret's production capacity. Black Beret Cadre membership gradually increased to 100. Police believed the 'hard core' numbers remained below 20. (22)

The Berets secured the cooperation of the Bermuda Industrial Union most likely because a leading Beret member had a close relationship with the union leader, Ottiwell Simmons. The aim of the joint effort was to raise money for the Simmons family whose home had been destroyed by fire in January 1971. A leaflet printed by the BIU urging financial support for the family was attached to copies of the Black Beret Cadre manifesto. The BIU and Black Berets also joined forces on 15th February 1971 to organize a cocktail party to raise funds. It was held at the Hamilton Parish Workmen's Club. However, an intelligence committee report cautioned, "There is no evidence to suggest that the BIU leadership wishes to be closely associated with the Black Beret Cadre". (23)

Still concerned about the growing popularity of the Black Berets and their links with the PLP Governor Martonmere informed the Foreign Office that the expansion of the Berets' membership and sympathizers was 'inexorable and irrepressible'. The Governor noted that the Progressive Labour Party had been careful to "remain reasonably aloof from the Cadre". However, he did believe that the "aims and ambitions" of the PLP were "… sufficiently similar (to the Black Berets) to be almost …an unholy alliance between the two. It is a matter for conjecture on the dog-wag-tail principle, whether, to their own advantage, the (PLP) can harness the Cadre or whether the Cadre will assume an independent role. Even at the moment the Party has no control and can only hope, probably with good chance of success, to influence the Cadre through the efforts of (Cadre supporter and black militant) Roosevelt Brown." (24)

The Bermuda Police were described as "the enemy" at Black Beret meetings. Photographs of police officers were shown to members and orders were given for the Berets' intelligence and security unit to collect information about every police officer. The 'security and intelligence' section of the Berets was created in May 1971. It was made up of the more militant members. Their brief was to move across the island at a moments notice committing acts of arson and violence. The unit had six members with provision for increased numbers depending on demand and circumstances. It was split up into cells of two and each cell had a specific responsibility for communications, information, and what was referred to as 'mobility'.

Each cell member was issued with a list of instructions and responsibilities which included the provision of security for all Beret equipment and property, guarding public or private meetings and functions, guarding Black Beret Cadre headquarters against police raids or patrols, obtaining information and the maintenance of weapons which included machetes, clubs and knives. Members were shown paragraphs from the '*Mini-*

Manual of the Urban Guerrilla' by Varlos Marighella. They were headed *'characteristics of the Urban Guerrilla Technique'* and *'Desertions, Divisions, Seizures, Expropriations of Arms, Ammunition, Explosives and Sabotage'.* However, there was less than complete enthusiasm for the security unit. According to a police intelligence report, "there appears to be a decided lack of interest on the part of its members. The group has held only one meeting since its formation and on that occasion only three of its members turned up...." (25)

The intelligence and security units were also instructed to note the personal appearance of every police officer they saw, especially those police officers in Special Branch and the Criminal Investigation Department, how many officers were on duty at any given time, the number of available police cars and riot trucks and any other information they deemed useful. Senior Police Officers later expressed concern that a Beret member had been seen at police headquarters taking the vehicle numbers of officers' private cars.

Black Berets were told that the members of Special Branch and CID should be watched "at all times". Members were also advised that should trouble erupt the Berets' "secret cells" would be called on to "attack the individuals concerned and their homes". Berets were exhorted to use guerrilla tactics to "scare the government into agreeing to Black Beret demands". However, these orders were challenged by Calvin Weeks who said it would be a mistake to instil fear in the people "as the government would then bring in more forces and intensify the existing 'police state'." (26)

During this period the Black Berets exhorted their followers to support the 'revolution' by adopting more violent methods in ridding Bermuda of 'the white power structure'. Police Chief George Duckett was described as a, "mercenary and a killer who has virtually a free hand in suppressing black people and who, despite being a mercenary, was efficient and planned his moves in advance". (27)

The Bermudian government responded by using 'counter subversion' efforts which were co-ordinated by Lord Martonmere. However, these efforts were largely confined to public relations exercises because the Governor had accepted the advice of the Foreign Office to take a low key approach, avoiding large scale confrontations with 'Black Power' activists and advocating compromise and a commitment to improving the life of ordinary working class Bermudians. A Foreign Office advisor consulted Lord Martonmere about how the Bermudian Government could prevent the spread of Black Beret influence among Bermuda's youth. In a May 1971 memo the advisor wrote, "If trouble in paradise is to be averted it seems to me that the following considerations might help: that the Bermuda Government should come out firmly in favour of multi-racialism and social progress. The Black Berets are racialists feeding on latent discontent against an allegedly unprogressive part-time government by rich men…Bermuda's short-term problem, as I see it, are to frustrate the growth of trouble in paradise by policies and measures which will frustrate the efforts of the main racialist trouble-makers."(28)

The government acted on the advice and swiftly introduced government programs to expand black Bermudian entry to the civil service. The Foreign Office advice was also heeded by events within the ruling United Bermuda Party. By the end of 1971 UBP leader and Premier Sir Henry Tucker had been replaced by Sir Edward Richards, a black Bermudian. His appointment persuaded many Bermudians that the government was making real progress in building a bi-racial and equal society.

Despite exhortations by the Foreign Office to take a low-key approach the Governor was becoming increasingly anxious about the Berets' activities and he thought the situation was becoming dangerous. He said the Black Berets' methods were, "…more purposeful" and that they were organising "cool, systematic, well planned operations" He said efforts to discredit the police were "well thought out" and that there was a danger "that these might have far-reaching effects if the internal security should deteriorate". The Black Berets efforts to infiltrate the prisons and schools gave the Governor "cause for particular concern" and he recognised that sympathy for them was "now fairly widespread". He believed racial tension would "likely escalate to flash point unless urgent action is taken by the Bermuda Government."

The situation was considered so serious by the Bermudian and British Governments that the British Foreign Secretary, Sir Alec Douglas Home, held a meeting in May 1971 in which the Black Berets were discussed including ways in which to counteract the black militants' activities.(29)

However, by the summer of 1971, the police were pleased to learn from their informants that tensions had emerged within the Berets and their meetings were now characterized by heated arguments about the direction in which the organisation was heading. The Berets had always been a mixture of radicals, self-styled 'revolutionaries', progressives and moderates. They also had their 'criminal element' who were attracted to lawlessness and violence. Reflecting this mixture of styles, members were beginning to disagree on the tactics employed by the leadership and the direction of the Berets' 'revolution'.

During this period a meeting of the Berets was called to discuss the future of the movement. It resulted in a "near fist-fight", according to an intelligence report. The membership was split on the issue of whether or not the Berets should pursue its 'revolutionary agenda' through violence or instead work within the political system. The executive committee promoted the 'violent route' but some members vehemently disagreed. The relationship between the Black Berets and the PLP was also discussed. Some members were resentful of having to play "second fiddle" to "armchair revolutionaries" in the PLP. (30)

The PLP was severely criticised by some Beret members. At one meeting a leading Beret member highlighted his criticisms by reading passages from a book by Frantz Fanon. He then said that the PLP should attempt to discover the "needs of the masses instead of sitting on the fence while the Black Beret Cadre did all the work". He also said that while the PLP had some talented people they were too busy becoming 'capitalists' while others were only active during election time or when a situation they could exploit came about. As an example he praised PLP Member of Parliament Freddy Wade as a "worker" but criticised Roosevelt Brown for "taking trips" or "just driving around all day". (31)

By July 1971 police believed the morale of the Berets had been affected by the apathy of its members. The Beret member who had co-ordinated the security units had expressed dismay and disgust when none of his members turned up for a pre-arranged, second meeting. He was also upset at the apparent general lack of interest amongst the members. He called a special general meeting to discuss and determine why this state of affairs had come about. When Berets were told they could talk freely accusations were made about the superior attitude of the executive committee. After some members critized the treatment of the rank and file the meeting developed into a shouting match and two Berets stated their intention of resigning. Another member accused Beret leaders of distorting the manifesto and selling falsehoods to the public. He later apologised for this statement but his allegations appeared to receive some support. (32) In his determination to act with decisiveness the security units' organizer formed a second group of six members, known as the 'Guerrilla Force'. He told the group they would be subjected to an intensive training course to condition them for their revolutionary role.

On the 10th July 1971 Dionne Bassett was released from Casemates Prison and he was welcomed back into the fold. Despite his release police were under no illusions that Bassett had changed. He was still a man who embraced "violence" as "part of his plan" and still "impatient for change". (33)

When Bassett met up with his colleagues he expressed dismay that the Berets had deteriorated to the point of "being almost useless" and that members had "apparently lost direction and dedication towards achieving its goal". (34) Bassett then gave a speech in which he praised revolution and the part it had played in the development of Third World countries. He reminded members that it was "the responsibility of vanguard organizations such as theirs to condition and prepare the people for revolution". He made reference to Cuba as a good example of how a small band could condition the people and eventually taken control of the country. According to Foreign Office files the 'third man' reminded the audience that if a small band operated with equal dedication in Bermuda they could ruin the economy of the island but "the masses would have gained freedom from exploitation". The third man said the Berets had, "nothing to lose but everything to gain from revolution". (35)

During the meeting Bassett was challenged by a member of the audience who reminded him that "this type of reckless action would kill the tourist industry, the people would be homeless and jobless and frustrated and

Bermuda would become a jungle". The objecting Beret member went on to say that the political and economic education of black Bermudians was a more acceptable way of bringing about change. Bassett was also told that, "those who live by the gun die by the gun". Although Bassett acknowledged the logic of the argument he replied that it would take black Bermudians "300 years to accomplish their aims by this method". He urged his audience to take specific action to form security patrols in their areas to observe police activity and "attack them if they were seen to harass the public". He said the patrols should actually incite trouble and create incidents which would lead to, "…guerrilla tactics with the express purpose of destroying… targets which represented the power structure". (36)

Bassett's ideas were a direct imitation of US Black Panther tactics. In the summer of 1971 the Beret leader acquired a shotgun and said it should be used by members acting as guards at Beret headquarters during meetings. Around this time the Berets also 'penetrated' the St George's Youth Club which was run by the government's youth service. Its new assistant manager was believed to be a Beret supporter. The police were concerned it would become yet another meeting place for the organisation. (37)

A new edition of the Berets newsletter was circulated on 17th July 1971. Police believed it had been prepared by Bassett during his time in Casemates. The contents were "somewhat different from recent issues", a police report stated, and probably written with "some legal advice". The issue lacked the usual photos of weapons and did not contain any direct incitement to violence. A police report stated that it was "more moderate in tone" but "in variance with Bassett's known views". (38) The newsletter also reported a meeting held on June 25th with the BIU and the PLP to draw up a new constitution to put to the people. The report also stated, "It would be in the Cadre's interest to see a PLP victory at the next election (1972) and while they may wish to seek to influence the PLP to adopt a militant black policy, they will be an embarrassment to the Party so long as they openly advocate violence and revolution". (39)

The leader of the BIU, Ottiwell Simmons Sr, had expressed an interest in politics when he returned from a workers' union course at the on his return from Ruskin College in England. The college was a bastion of left wing radical ideas. On his return Simmons told his union members they should support the PLP. He also told them that 'workers control', meaning industry owned and run by the workers, was a long term project for the BIU. Although these views were left-wing in nature it appears that Simmons wished to distance his union from the radical Black Berets. (40)

By the end of 1971 the Black Berets, like their American counterparts, the Black Panthers, appeared to be weakening. Their efforts to infiltrate the schools and recruit new members were met with derision by many students. The Berets' efforts to recruit new members in Casemates Prison also appeared to have failed. The Foreign Office was pleased to hear that the Berets were involved in internal strife. Their hope was that the non-violent faction would win the day. However, despite this lack of success the Berets still engaged in political activities. On the 5th November 1971 and 26th November 1971 dances were held at Crawl Workmen's Club to raise funds to assist a Beret member in his appeal against a prison sentence. Both functions were described as 'successful'. (41)

The Liberation School continued to indoctrinate the children of Beret members and supporters. Classes now held up to 30 children at a time and it was believed the school had a total intake of 35-40 children. Black culture and black history were central to the curriculum. A police report noted that, "… recent teaching has concentrated on promoting racial hatred and violence in the minds of very young children. To this end, nursery rhymes are being distorted so that , for example, Mary no longer had a little lamb but instead 'Mary had an M1 gun'….. 'Mary had an M16 (machine gun). Its barrel as black as coal …'".

The government was also disturbed that the term 'pig', used to describe police officers, had been introduced into the children's vocabulary and was being used as a prefix to surnames whenever a person representing authority was mentioned. The government was aware that the parents of the children must have known about the racist content of the literature as the children took their 'song sheets' home with them. "So far there have been no complaints from parents", a police report stated, "They may not be fully aware of what their children are being taught but it seems more likely that they either condone this particular Black Beret Cadre activity or are afraid to complain. Although the classes are held out of school hours at Black Beret Cadre headquarters and do not appear to have had any effect on schools where the situation is quiet at present, the Committee recommended that the Commissioner of Police should compile a report on these classes for submission to the Attorney General and to the Permanent Secretary for Education so that they could decide whether the existing law was being infringed or whether amendment to the law was needed." (42)

The Governor expressed disgust at the teaching methods and content of lessons at the Berets' Liberation School. In a despatch to the Foreign Office dated the 15th February 1971 he said the Berets had, "increasing success with 'Liberation Classes'. They are now held weekly and attended by twenty-five youngsters between the ages of eight and twelve. With the chanting of anti-white slogans, the indoctrination of racial hatred is even more intense than hitherto and it is disturbing to contemplate the effect this will have on race relations in years to come. Even today it is an unhappy thought that these children are not waifs and strays collected from the streets but are attending the classes with the full knowledge and consent of their parents." (43)

A young female Black Beret member was believed by police to be the most successful of the school's teachers. She taught the children racial and violent songs and slogans and handed out posters of Bassett, Weeks and Phil Perinchief to the children, telling them to hang the posters over their beds. She also warned the children in her care not to talk to policemen but to walk away if they were approached. Whenever she mentioned a 'person of authority' she used the pre-fix 'pig'. A police report noted that "(She) is clearly a continuing source of concern." (44)

The female Beret was certainly an uncompromising 'revolutionary' who believed "the violence of the system (could) only be challenged with violence". During Black Beret debates which considered the future direction of the movement she invariably sided with those members, particularly the executive committee, who advocated the violent overthrow of the Bermudian Government. At one meeting she suggested the Berets begin a campaign of burning down Bermuda's hotels as this would frighten tourists from the island and cause economic hardship. She said that unless the Berets adopted such hard-line tactics it would take "300 years to achieve its objectives". The young revolutionary advocated a "guerrilla campaign" that would put the Bermudian "system" out of business for a few months. The Berets would then "be in a position to dictate terms", she said. (45)

The idea of bringing the island to its knees through violent guerrilla activity was not without its critics within the Berets' ranks. She was challenged by a moderate member who asked her how his grandmother would be able to pay her mortgage if the hotel where she worked was burned down. He said the Berets were now in a position to influence the policies of both political parties and had the potential to be a force for good. He told her that items in the Beret manifesto relating to affordable housing and Bermudianization (*Author's note: a policy of giving English expatriate jobs to Bermudians*) were already being implemented by the government and that such programmes would probably be accelerated under a PLP government. He argued that the Berets could achieve all its aims by stepping up its propaganda activities and eschewing violent methods altogether. His comments were, however, derided by the hard line faction of the Berets and he was told to "shut up and sit down". (46)

The government appeared to be helpless in controlling the Liberation School. The Race Relations Council made contact with the teachers but there is no evidence they had any effect. In fact the Council wrongly believed the Black Berets had turned away from violence to a "more constructive attitude". (47)

By late 1971 the Governor's Intelligence Committee, which included Police Chief George Duckett, believed the Black Berets had failed in much the same way the PLP Youth Wing ran out of steam in the late 1960s. The Berets had ceased holding regular meetings and stopped the publication of their newspaper. However, police intelligence reported the Berets were still active and, although the organization was disturbed by public apathy, they nevertheless were determined to pursue their revolutionary agenda. According to a November 1971 report, the Black Beret Cadre, "...has continued to remain quiet and relatively inactive ....It was also mentioned that the public did not seem to be relating to the Black Beret Cadre programme... 'Dionne' Bassett (is) reported to have suggested that guerrilla warfare was the only answer. For the first time Bassett has shown some reaction to the general apathy of the group and the lack of public interest in its activities. Bassett is probably aware of the appeal that violence has to the youth of the island and could possibly be advocating guerrilla warfare to stimulate interest among the members." (48)

The Bermuda Intelligence Committee believed a small group of the more militant members went "underground" during 1972 and the police were "unaware of their activities".(49) The collapse of the Black Berets came about, they concluded, partly because the PLP did not give enough support to the group and the PLP- dominated workers' trade unions kept their distance.

Bermudian writer Jonathan Kent believes there were 50 or so members remaining at this time (50) By September 1972, after Beret leader Dionne Bassett had left the island, only a small group of hard-liners remained. However, unlike US law enforcement agencies, the Bermuda Police did not conduct an 'FBI COINTELPRO- style' programme to destroy the organization. Instead, the approach was to ignore what remained of the Berets as far as possible believing that tactics such as internment and a banning order would create martyrs for the cause. (51) Four days before the murder of the Police Chief, Acting Governor Ian Kinnear told an intelligence committee meeting, "The name 'Black Beret' is hardly ever heard now. The Cadre seems to have folded up in the same way as the (militant) Progressive Labour Party Youth Wing in 1970" (52)

However, throughout 1972 the remnants of the Black Berets had begun to compile a 'hit-list' of the Bermuda 'pigs' they intended to 'execute'. They also began to stockpile weapons including pistols and shotguns which were to be used when the time was ripe for 'revolution'. (53)   And in late 1972, ignoring the infighting amongst the Berets, the 'third man' became determined to revive the organization after the Berets' leader, Dionne Bassett, fled the island following the murder of the police chief. The police noted that the militant Beret had been, "restless recently, has changed his job a number of times and has caused his father a good deal of worry. His interest in re-establishing the Cadre may be an outlet for his leadership ambitions in the absence of Bassett from the island (on September 30th)." (54)

*

Even after the police chief's tragic death in September 1972 the acting Governor Ian Kinnear, who took office after Lord Martonmere retired, was telling the Foreign Office that the Berets were not a real threat. In a December 1972 Government House memo to the Foreign Office Kinnear wrote, " (The third man) has indicated that he is interested in reviving the Cadre…he has held informal meetings with a select few of its previously more staunch supporters and has suggested the first task should be to raise funds to send someone abroad for training in guerrilla warfare…He has met with a good deal of apathy, however…Those he has contacted have financial problems of their own and it seems unlikely, at this stage, that he will be able to rekindle any interest in the Cadre." (55)

Although the Bermudian Government believed the Black Berets harbored no real threat to the security and well-being of the island the British Government had no such illusions. The Foreign Office were concerned that 24 Bermuda Regiment rifles had gone missing. They were part of a batch due to be demolished at the Bermuda Technical Institute then dumped out at sea. It was also suspected that other weapons due for destruction had also been routed to Beret members. The arsenal included a Bren gun. The Foreign Office awaited the results of an enquiry into the missing weapons. (56) It was later discovered Dionne Bassett had been responsible for the theft of the weapons. He was charged with the offences but was released to await trial which was set for 9th October. However, aware that he was also a suspect in the murder of the police chief and no doubt convinced that the police could make a strong case that he was responsible for the theft of the guns, he left the island never to return.

The Bermudian government's lack of action in dealing with the Black Berets came back to haunt them when the Police Chief and the Governor were murdered. There had been definite warnings that the Berets were ready to strike at government targets.

In December 1972, following Duckett's murder the previous September, Sir Richard Sharples suspected the Berets were responsible for the police chief's murder. His opinions clashed with those of most members of the

Bermudian Government who believed the crime was the work of either a madman or drug dealers. In a December 1972 memo to the Foreign Office Sir Richard wrote, "(Scotland Yard Detectives Wright and Haddrell's)... departure is an indication that no solution to the crime is in sight. Mr Wright is now inclined to discount any connection between the former (police chief's) murder and drug traffic. This leaves a grudge against Mr Duckett personally, or a political assassination as the most likely motives. Obtaining information about the activities of a small hard core of the Black Beret Cadre must remain a priority." (57)

In the last of Sir Richard's monthly memos to the Foreign Office regarding internal security, dated 6th March 1973, the Governor displayed a remarkable insight into the political implications of George Duckett's murder. Sharples said that the remaining members of the Berets, "a small hardcore" as he put it, "held a number of meetings during (February 1973)", and a leading member of the Berets, the 'third man', was becoming, "increasingly vocal and is understood to be planning to acquire a new headquarters for the group". The governor noted that this Beret leader was planning on re-organising the group and urging other members to gather weapons, "in preparation for the struggle". The governor was also aware that the Beret would be making arrangements to send a member to Cuba or Tanzania for guerrilla training. The governor wrote, "Although (his) previous attempt to revive the Cadre has met with little success, the present frequent contacts between certain members suggests that he could be more successful this time and a close watch is being kept on developments... (The reorganisation) of the hard core of the Black Beret Cadre and the possibility of further arms being in the hands of (members) is a disquieting development." (58) Four days after dictating this memo the Governor was dead.

It was not until the Governor was assassinated that the full implications of the Police Chief's assassination were recognized by the Bermudian Government. Now they could not ignore the role black militancy had played in the killings. In a report of May 1973 Acting Governor Kinnear, who once again took over the responsibilities of Governor, concluded, "(The Berets') attempts to gain public support failed and it ceased to function as an overt organisation in 1971. It now seems likely that perhaps half-a-dozen or so of the hard core of the organisation went underground at this stage and we lost touch with them. We do know, however, that they obtained a number of handguns from abroad at about the same time of the (Police) Commissioner's murder and it is significant that since these arms arrived on the island there have not only been five murders but a marked increase in the number of robberies involving the use of arms." The Acting Governor concluded that criminal elements had joined forces with the hard core elements of the Black Berets. (59)

What Kinnear did not know at the time he made his report was that some of the criminal elements he mentioned included 42 year old Bobby Leroy Greene, owner of 'Greene's Grill' on Court Street and self-styled 'Godfather', small-time criminal 'Buck' Burrows, Beret supporter and lifelong criminal Larry Tacklyn, a young man who harboured a virulent hatred towards 'whites'.

FIVE

THE MURDER OF BERMUDA'S POLICE CHIEF

"Having known these petty criminals personally, they would have never done these things without some type of reward offered or some thought of a gift or something down the road. The killers are the killers but the reasons they were picked is because those behind the conspiracy to change the Government used them".

Former Bermuda Police Officer, Territt Cabral

URDER WAS NOT a new phenomenon in Bermuda. In June 1934 Martha Annette Outerbridge was executed for the murder of her boyfriend, Herbert Leslie Lambert. She had struck him 119 times with a hatchet. In 1941 Harry Sousa was found guilty of the murder of Margaret Stapleton. In 1959 a vicious sex predator was at large and in seven months three women had been murdered, a fourth barely escaped. In March 1959, 71 year old Gertrude Robinson was attacked and murdered in Warwick Parish. Four weeks later, a second victim, 53 year old Dorothy Pearce was found badly battered in her cottage. In July of that year 53 year old Rosaleen Kenny was attacked while she slept but her screams frightened the killer away. In October 1959 a third victim was found, mutilated by sharks, floating in the surf off Southland Beach. She was a 29 year old office secretary named Dorothy Rawlinson who had arrived in Bermuda from London five months previously. Some Bermudians called the murderer the 'Moon Mad Killer'. (1) And, in early 1971, Scotland Yard detectives had investigated the murder of Jean Burrows by a white Bermudian, Paul Belvin.

However, beginning in late 1972 Bermudians were to witness an unprecedented level of violence which had never been experienced on the island.

*

Bermuda's police chief, 41 year old George Duckett, had become extremely unpopular amongst the island's criminal fraternity because of his hard line policing methods. But no one feared for his life even though authorities had received information from confidential sources he had become a target for assassination. According to a report by Scotland Yard Detective Chief Superintendent William Wright, "..........information was received that a Mrs. B, employed at the Research Station, overheard Mr. A. say to a group of people that if there was a Black Cadre revolution, the first to go would be Mr. Duckett. This was alleged to have been said some five weeks prior to the murder." (2)

George Duckett spent Saturday night, 9th September 1972, at his home Bleak House, watching television with his wife Jane Chalmers Duckett, known as Sheena, and his daughter 19 year old Marcia who was home for the summer holidays from boarding school in the UK.

'Bleak House', whose name was later changed to 'Tyne Bay House', was situated in an isolated area of Devonshire parish approximately a mile and a half from Police Headquarters in Hamilton. The house, which was near a disused railway station, was believed to have a sinister air about it. It was here during the Second World War that its owner, Colonel Mann was murdered. One of the roomers, Maureen Stapleton, a member of the Imperial Censors, was later murdered by Harry Sousa, a private in the Bermuda Rifle Corps. He was tried for the crime and executed in 1946. He was the last man to be hanged in Bermuda.

Bleak House was surrounded by trees and heavy undergrowth which allowed an unobserved approach from all directions. The house had a lounge, drawing room, three bedrooms and a kitchen which was partly divided by a wooden partition. The lounge was situated at the front of the house which overlooked North Shore Road, whilst the kitchen was at the rear facing the driveway. On this balmy Saturday night the kitchen and other lights were on but no curtains were drawn.

Some hours earlier, during the morning of the 9th September, George

Duckett received a telephone call from Acting Governor I.A.C.(Ian) Kinnear around 10:45 a.m. then attended a regular police officer's staff meeting at police headquarters. Following the meeting he had drinks with his fellow officers at the Officers' Mess and returned home at approximately 2pm. He was due to leave Bermuda on Friday 15th September with his wife and daughter. The trip was to accompany Marcia who was returning to her school in England and then Duckett and his wife were going on to an Interpol conference in Germany.

After George returned home he had lunch with his wife and daughter on the front veranda facing the sea. Around 3 p.m. they tidied up and Marcia retired to her bedroom for a rest. She had been feeling exhausted after a recent throat operation. George took his lounge chair to the front veranda by a redwood table along with a book and settled down to read. Sheena checked on Marcia to see if she was alright and mother and daughter talked about her time at school.

George too was feeling tired and told his wife he was going to bed to rest. Marcia and Sheena drove to Hamilton, parked by Archie Browns store, and enjoyed their short shopping trip. Around 5pm both women returned home. Sheena parked her car in its usual place, under the car port to the south of the kitchen. George's police car was parked by the backdoor steps.

George was still fast asleep when Sheena and Marcia returned. He awoke around 5.45pm and joined his wife and daughter. He appeared "quite cheerful" and was dressed in a sarong-type gown he wore when sleeping. At approximately 6-6:30 p.m. George and Sheena took their drinks out to the veranda and enjoyed the beautiful setting and approaching sunset.

At 7 p.m. George and Sheena went indoors to watch the news on television. They switched on the security lights on the back veranda and the security light outside the kitchen. The atmosphere was quite convivial. "We were all quite happy" Sheena said. "George was teasing Marcia about losing weight." (3)

Nightfall came at 7.36pm. The sky was overcast and the night air humid and still except for a slight breeze at eight knots as the Duckett family settled down to watch a favourite television show starring Lucille Ball. Later George tuned the television to ZFB television Channel 8 to watch a programme he had more than a little interest in - "The Fear Fighters", a documentary about new advances in criminal forensic science. The family ate their meal as they watched the documentary.

At 9pm, at the conclusion of the documentary, George assisted his wife with the dishes and they moved to the kitchen leaving their daughter in the living room to watch a Don Rickles comedy show. On the way to the kitchen he noticed a security light on the porch was out and he asked Sheena to fetch him a new bulb. Though Sheena suggested that he wait until morning, he insisted on doing it immediately. Unknown to Duckett, the bulb had been deliberately loosened. It later transpired that the person who had loosened it had known of the Police Chief's personal habits and that he would instinctively go outside and replace the bulb rather than wait until morning.

After Sheena Duckett handed the bulb to her husband he stepped out on to the porch and held the screen door open with his back. As he reached for the light fixture he must have realised at that instant that the light did not need a new bulb but instead the bulb he was about to change had simply been unscrewed. In an instant Duckett was confronted by a man who had stepped out from the shadows holding a pistol. The gunman fired one shot from his .22 Schmidt revolver, hitting Duckett in the back. "Suddenly there was a 'pop' noise" Sheena recalled, "I thought he had dropped the bulb. I turned around and saw him falling into the kitchen. He had blood on his side....I tried to turn him over but couldn't. I saw blood on his mouth and it started pouring out of his nostrils and mouth." (4)

George staggered into the kitchen and somehow managed to close the door behind him before collapsing on the floor. A pool of blood collected. Marcia and Sheena were stepping in the blood, slipping and sliding across the floor.

Sheena tried to telephone Police Headquarters but the phone was dead. She screamed at Marcia telling her to do something. Marcia responded by turning her father's head to one side. As Sheena rushed to the telephone to call for help she heard further 'pop' sounds. "About five", she said. Marcia had been hit in the chest by gunfire as she stood in the kitchen. "Mummy, I have a pain in my chest", she shouted. After shooting Duckett the gunman had moved to the back of the house, pulled himself onto the low roof of the water tank and fired five shots through the kitchen window. Police later concluded that the direction of two of the bullets, which struck a metal tray during flight, indicated the shooter was either trying to hit Duckett again as he lay on the floor or he had been deliberately firing at Sheena, who was at her husband's side. Police also concluded that the remaining three bullets were deliberately fired in the direction of Sheena and Marcia as they stood in the archway of the kitchen as Sheena attempted to telephone for assistance. Two of the bullets struck the wood panelling whilst the third one struck Marcia in the chest. It is likely the killer made a conscious effort to kill the wife and daughter as George's body was out of sight when he continued firing.

At first Sheena thought her daughter was having an asthma attack and she told her to sit down and be quiet. After telling Marcia she was going to get help, she "drove as fast as (she) could" to the Police headquarters at Prospect with her hand on the car horn. Arriving at the operations center she pleaded with officers for help telling them "The Commissioner is dying – get somebody to the house right away".

Police headquarters immediately contacted the hospital for an ambulance and issued radio messages to all police cars in the vicinity. An officer on duty drove Sheena back to the house and by the time they arrived the place was swarming with police who had been alerted by the radio call. As she passed her daughter on the steps of the house she saw Marcia was in a state of distress holding her chest.

At first Marcia had been unaware she had been shot and thought the pain she felt resulted from her recent throat operation. "I am shot as well", Marcia told her mother. (5) A few minutes later the ambulance arrived with Dr Matthew Shawcross. After a cursory examination George Duckett was pronounced dead.

Later examination of the scene of the crime revealed bullet holes in the top section of the kitchen window and the spent remains of four bullets were laying on the floor. The shooter had also cut the telephone wires at a point where the wire had crossed a Casuarinas tree some 15 yards from the south-west corner of the house. Below the tree police investigators discovered a Marlboro cigarette packet which contained five Marlboro cigarettes, a box of unused Camel matches, a packet of Rizla cigarette papers and a package containing a small amount of marijuana. Two pieces of loose bark on the tree revealed that someone had climbed the tree to cut the telephone wire. When officers inspected the police chief's official car they discovered the microphone wire had been cut. Investigators believed it had been a deliberate act to prevent anyone calling for help. Police believed it had been the killer's intention to kill everyone in the house but the plan had somehow failed.

Sheena and her daughter were taken to King Edward VIIth Memorial Hospital. Sheena was diagnosed with severe shock and was sedated. (6) Marcia was examined by Dr James King who found a small wound high up in the chest which had ragged edges and was bleeding slightly. Following an X-ray it was discovered that a small metal object was lying outside of the chest cavity "in the vicinity of the palpable mass". She was taken to an operating theatre where the small bullet was removed. (7)

After Deputy Police Chief 'Nobby' Clark had been informed of the shooting he drove immediately to the Acting Governor's residence on Montpelier Road, Hamilton to inform him of the incident.

The body of the Police Commissioner was sent to the mortuary of the King Edward Hospital where a preliminary examination was carried out by Dr C.E.M. Wenyon, the pathologist. Also attending the examination was Detective Superintendent Hammond.

The main autopsy was performed the following morning. The examination revealed there was a gunshot wound in Duckett's back and around the wound were several dark areas some of which contained metal fragments. It was later deduced Duckett had been shot at close range. On examination of the neck and thorax a bullet was found in the "right lower posterior portion of the right thoracic cavity lying free". Dr Wenyon concluded that death was the result of "a gunshot wound of the chest involving both lungs, the heart and aorta". (8)

*

Later inspections of the crime scene revealed footmarks in the soil around the water tank and the tank roof. Principal Scientific Officer John

McCafferty examined glass in a window frame removed from the house. He was able to establish bullets had been fired from outside the window in a downward direction and microscopic lead splattering on the glass indicated that at the time the bullets were fired, the muzzle of the gun was about one and a half feet from the window. (9) Ballistics experts established that the weapon used was a .22. Schmidt revolver which was one of a consignment of eight alleged to have been stolen during transhipment from West Germany to the USA via Bermuda and the Bahamas some time between 31st January and 25th February 1972. (10)

On the morning after the shooting Bleak House was cordoned off and off duty police officers in Bermuda shorts and open-necked shirts arrived to assist in the investigation. Divers searched for evidence on the North Shore within the vicinity of the house and police officers searched the grounds and surrounding areas looking for clues that might help the investigation. Roads leading to Bleak House were sealed off and a 'Murder Squad' was set up at Police Headquarters in prospect. Bermuda Police officers, Superintendent Frank Hammond and Chief Inspector John Sheehy took charge.

Acting Governor Ian Kinnear telephoned Scotland Yard. A team of detectives, headed by detectives Bill Wright and Basil Haddrell, were immediately despatched to assist in the murder investigation. The detectives had been specifically requested by Kinnear as they had prior knowledge of the island having investigated the murder of *Royal Gazette* reporter Jean Burrows in 1971. They flew to Bermuda on BOAC flight 409 and arrived on the Monday afternoon following the Saturday night shooting.

The Scotland Yard team began their investigation immediately and decided that it was imperative the government make available $10,000 to pay out to informants. However, they were aware of the problems police faced when investigating crimes on the island. Bermuda was a close knit community and islanders were extremely cautious in speaking to police officers. According to former police officer Philip Swift, "I suspect the Bermudian population did not like speaking to the Murder Squad detectives – they considered them outsiders who were worthy of contempt because they did not understand the island and its people....." (11)

*

Fearful that the murder of the Police Chief was a political act the authorities tried to quell fears by suggesting his murder was the work of a maniac or drug dealers out for revenge. The *Royal Gazette* concurred and editorialized, "….we are relieved…by the views expressed by the Acting Governor and the police that it appears to be an 'isolated' incident….the implication being that, so far as they can see, it is not part of any organized uprising…. His life was spent working against criminals and in upholding law and order, so it can be said that he was ever in the front line of battle…. In these circumstances he must have made many enemies, not only in Bermuda, but in his professional career in Jamaica and elsewhere. Often criminals swear 'to get' the man who got them. More often than not such threats are just boastfulness, or made in the heat of the moment. But there have been cases where criminals have been determined, and have succeeded in getting their revenge." (12)

Acting Governor Kinnear went along with the prevailing school of thought. He said he did not want to "prejudge" the outcome of the police investigation, but went on to say there was no evidence to suggest the murder was anything but an "isolated incident" and "without political implications". He appealed for the public to assist the police in their investigation of a crime that was "unknown in these islands". Kinnear went on to praise George Duckett describing him as "a highly experienced, professional policeman and a man of considerable courage". (13) Not one word was mentioned of the Black Berets whose hatred of George Duckett was known to the authorities and who had a clear intention of removing the Bermudian government "*by any means necessary*".

However, Foreign Office files have revealed that the Acting Governor had indeed been suspicious of the Berets all along but kept his suspicions outside public discourse. He was convinced a political motive was responsible for the Police Chief's murder and described some politicians' efforts to supply a personal or criminally-related motive for the crime as a, "…self-deluding exercise in wish-fulfilment". He said their comments would not help the island in the long term or safeguard the lives of other politicians who may have been targeted for assassination. In a despatch to the Foreign Office Kinnear wrote, "It would be imprudent to overlook the fact that a number of young men on the island have been indoctrinated in violence over the last three years through the activities of the Black Beret Cadre; it would be stupid to pretend that this has not rubbed off on some of them…While the Cadre has to all intents and purposes ceased to exist, there is always a possibility that some of the more militant members have gone underground and that we have been unaware of their activities." (14)

Kinnear wrote in a further report his belief that the Black Berets considered the elimination of the Police Chief as "a blow against the 'invisible' (colonial) government against which it used to rail. For a criminal element, a blow against law and order, probably with political overtones, for the hardcore criminal element is black on an island where the police are 75% expatriate and white." (15)

Following George Duckett's murder Kinnear thought it ironic that after the Intelligence Committee met on September 4th 1972 and made an assessment of "no obvious signs of trouble ahead" that Duckett, a member of that committee, would be brutally murdered a few days later. Kinnear wrote, "It is over a year since the Black Beret Cadre stopped putting out its publication; it has held no (regular) meetings for almost as long and there has been no evidence recently to suggest that there is any organised body on the island bent on violence, let alone killing…It would be imprudent, however, to overlook the fact that a number of young men on this island have been indoctrinated in violence over the last three years through the activities of the Black Beret Cadre. It would be stupid to pretend that this will not have rubbed off on some of them. While the Cadre has to all intents and purposes ceased to exist there is always the possibility that a small group of the more militant members have gone underground and that we have been unaware of their activities." (16)

Although the Bermudian government had been trying to quell fears by telling islanders there was no evidence that the murder of the police chief was organized by black militants, Dionne Bassett and other Berets became prime suspects. Bassett was interviewed by Detective Inspector Swan on the 11th September, 1972 but apart from giving his name, he refused to answer any questions. Bassett was also visited at a Prospect job site by Police Constable Patrick Hamlett on September 11, 1972. "I approached Basset, introduced myself . . . then said to him, 'Mr. Bassett, we are making inquiries surrounding the death of the late Commissioner of Police, Mr. Duckett'", Officer Hamlett wrote in his report of the interview. "Bassett, voice heavy with sarcasm, replied, 'Yeah, I heard all about it on the radio and I am deeply grieved'". Basset refused to answer any questions. However, he did give officers permission to search his Woodlands Road home for the Duckett murder weapon. (17)

Bassett's apartment was searched for firearms but with negative results. At that time he was on bail awaiting trial at the Supreme Court commencing 9th October, 1972 on a charge of receiving stolen firearms, but on the 30th September, 1972 he left for Canada and the USA and failed to return to Bermuda to stand trial.

Police were also aware that another suspect, a fanatical member of the Berets, had been interviewed "on several occasions and flatly refused to answer any questions". (18) Six months later he was identified by Scotland Yard detectives as the 'third man' in the conspiracy to assassinate the new Governor, Sir Richard Sharples.

*

In the days following the murder, Acting Police Chief L.M. (Nobby) Clark had delegated an ex-convict, 28 year old Erskine 'Buck' Burrows, a handyman - janitor at Police Headquarters in Hamilton, to clean up the blood at Bleak House once Police forensics investigations had been concluded.

Burrows knew the house well. One of his work assignments was to look after the gardens and paint inside the house. He also cleaned the Duckett family cars. When he completed his chores he would telephone headquarters and his transport would arrive to collect him.

In 1971 Burrows had even worked at 'Bleak House' when he was serving a jail sentence after confessing to a series of break-ins at police officers' homes in Prospect. Police Chief Duckett had helped to arrange his participation in a day-release work programme. Sheena Duckett said the Duckett family trusted Burrows implicitly and that he was frequently left alone at the house when she and her husband were out.   Scotland Yard detective Basil Haddrell, who arrived in Bermuda on the 11th September, recalled seeing Burrows and another man cleaning up the blood from the kitchen floor. (19) Later Burrows attended the funeral of the police chief. The funeral was held on September 14th. The burial took place at the Military Cemetery in Prospect which overlooked the Duckett home. Police officers remembered him standing by the coffin for some 20 minutes, head bowed, paying his respects to the man who had given him a second chance following his release form Casemates Prison.

During their investigations police officers discovered Burrows' fingerprints around the Duckett home but dismissed them when they learned that Burrows was the Police Chief's handyman. They believed he was above suspicion and wanted to clear him from their inquiries so they could focus on more 'realistic' suspects.

*

Buck Burrows came from a considerably impoverished environment and had spent many years in prison for various offences. He was born on 15th March 1944 in Friswells Hill. He was the 5th of nine children born to Viola Burrows who was divorced when Burrows was born. In 1951 the seven year old Burrows was sent to a school on Happy Valley Road and was there for a year before he transferred to a school on Court Street. As a nine- year- old Burrows attended his first formal school staying there until he was 12 when his mother died. At school he was said to be slightly below average ability. He was characterized as a poor attendee and a regular truant.

Following her mother's death Burrows' eldest sister could not cope in looking after her siblings so Buck and the four youngest children were sent to an orphanage, the Lady Cubitt Compassionate Association. Lady Cubitt was the wife of the then Governor and founded the association in 1932 for underprivileged families. Later, Burrows transferred to the Sunshine League home for children where he stayed for about a year. Burrows ran away from the home and lived rough. At the age of 13 he was employed as a golf caddy at Ocean View Golf Course in Devonshire. After his 14th birthday he went to live with his sister.

After schooling Burrows' work history consisted of a large number of irregular types of work with much unemployment in between. Burrows began working at the Bermuda Mineral Water factory, stayed for 6 months, then left. After returning to his employers and asking for work he was re-hired but stayed only a short time, around 9 months.

As a young man Burrows spent a great deal of time in custody either at the training school for young offenders or, as an adult, at Casemates Maximum Security Prison. Since the age of 15, and during the few brief periods he was not in jail, he had lived like an animal – in the open, in and under trees, in dense bush. On each occasion when he was arrested various items he had stolen were found in polythene bags buried in the ground near his lairs. In 1961 he was arrested for stealing and was sent to prison for one year. In 1962, shortly after his release, he was arrested again and was imprisoned for three and a half years for breaking, entering and stealing. He was released in September 1964. Two months later he received a three and a half year prison sentence for robbing a bank clerk of $3000. During Burrows' time in prison he enjoyed listening to country and western music as it was the only music that was on at the times when he was allowed to listen. Unusual for a black Bermudian, he became a fan of Country and Western singer Dolly Parton. (20)

Lance Furbert, a friend of Burrows and fellow black militant, said Burrows was a "man of dignity", a "Robin Hood" who would steal from the rich and distribute it among the residents of Middletown, a poor black neighbourhood. When Furbert met him he had "unbelievable amounts of money", he said. "He would go to Middletown and just hand it out. He was a clever thief", Furbert said, "(He was) …a hero to young black men… a friend of mine, although we only knew each other over a short period of time. He stayed with me when the police first started to look for him (following the murders)."

Furbert believed Burrows was a, "…victim of this society – he spent most of his life in jail. I remember asking him if he'd ever considered going straight, and he said 'yes' on a couple of occasions.... One time he told me he was walking down the street and the police told him to get in the car. They took him to prospect (Police HQ) and threw some jewellery on the table and said 'you stole this'. I asked him why he didn't protest and he said there was no point, that he had already been labelled. I think he accepted in his own mind he was an outlaw." Burrows told Furbert he had been beaten as a child and could not tolerate injustice. (21)

According to former police officer Neville Darrell, "(Burrows) was a self-taught individual. He had done a lot of reading, probably in prison. He was a shrewdly intelligent individual (and) he was very quiet spoken. If you knew him you could not help but like him, he always had a smile." (22) Without any hint of shame, Darrell also characterized him as having "... decisiveness in political action (which) displays strength of character, which is lacking in most politicians." (23)

However, according to a Government House report, Burrows loathed whites and officials guessed it had something to do with the fact that his mother died whilst giving birth to the child of a white father. (24)

According to former Bermuda police officer Nick Bolton, "Burrows was a strange case. He was basically considered non-violent. He was a hand-bag snatcher and I believe he also used a rod to 'fish' in people's homes and lift out wallets, bags and such like. He rarely spoke and spent a lot of time running. You would see him on the railroad track or the back roads with a transistor radio pressed to his ear just running along, he would go for miles." Bolton confirmed the allegations made by a number of sources who said Burrows had been beaten up by police officers. "There was a rumour that a change came over him after he was beaten by two police officers," Bolton said, "it was rumored not to be a minor beating...." (25)

Territt Cabral was a young white Bermudian police officer who joined the force in 1967 as a cadet. During this period Cabral, who was born in Bermuda to a Portuguese family, met "...two trustees. One was named David and the other Erskine 'Buck' Burrows. Burrows had the run of the place, headquarters' offices, Criminal Records, narcotics. He was very polite and one could take a liking to him. He gave the impression of being sorry for his past ways." (26)

Cabral also confirmed the suspicions many police officers held that Burrows and his friend Larry Tacklyn had been severely beaten by two rogue police officers. Cabral said that the incident leading to the beatings occurred in 1971 and began with the Cycle Squad checking riders on Glebe Road. It was a typical handbag snatch incident, Cabral said. Burrows and Tacklyn rode up to a victim on their cycles snatched a handbag and "ran like hell". Cabral said they were caught 100 yards away on a school field. "I was with the purse and cycle", Cabral said, "After the chase, they were beaten horribly by my associates. I mean I was aghast, horrified. When they were brought up to the truck and handcuffed, the beatings continued. I even asked them to stop. It went on, even when we got to the station a few blows were handed out. Yes, Larry (Tacklyn) and Buck (Burrows). I will never forget that, and this is the first time I have ever mentioned it. I worked with these guys but I never thought they would react this way. That's why they were easy prey for the Black Beret Cadre, and the PLP through back doors. Career criminals with a grudge…. (Burrows) liked George (Duckett) but he was easily led, as was Tacklyn. (27)

On the 17th January 1967 Burrows was released from prison but was arrested for stealing and given a nine month sentence. In January 1968 he was sentenced to six years for burglary and assaulting a police officer. During this period he was characterized as "a very manipulative person". In 1969 a psychiatrist, Dr T.G. Tennent, described him as a man who revealed "a great deal of attention seeking behaviour". (28)

During the latter part of his prison sentence Burrows was made a 'trustee' and allowed out of prison to work at Police Headquarters in Hamilton. He had the free run of the grounds and at 4pm each day he was returned to Casemates Prison. Police Chief Duckett befriended Burrows because he felt some compassion for him. Duckett was also aware that Burrows had lived a life of extreme hardship. It is also likely, according to a former police officer source, that Duckett knew that the charges against Burrows, which resulted in his most recent six year sentence, were false. Duckett's sympathy for Burrows was the result of information he received from some of his officers. He was told that two rogue officers had beaten Burrows up and tortured him into signing a confession.

Before completing his sentence Burrows was released on the 31st December 1971 and Duckett gave him a job cleaning Police Headquarters. He was given a free room in the Police Betterington barracks which was situated next to the police headquarters building. His duties included cleaning the Officers' Mess, the Single Officers' rooms and the headquarters' offices. He also cleaned the cars of the Police Chief and Deputy Chief. Following his release from Casemates Burrows performed all his duties without direct supervision.

Notwithstanding the trust Duckett placed in Burrows there was some unease amongst senior police officers who thought Burrows had not changed and was continuing to commit crimes after he had served his prison sentence. Nevertheless, many police officers and civilian staff at Police Headquarters trusted Burrows, so much so that a number hired him as a babysitter at weekends so he could supplement his janitor's salary. Former expatriate police officer Peter Clemmet remembered Burrows as a "small, affable man" who didn't appear to have "attitude". When Clemmet was in the traffic department he had occasion to drive Burrows from Police Headquarters to Casemates Prison when the inmate had completed his cleaning duties. He said Burrows would "clean officers' cars for cash and smokes". (29)

Burrows also frequently visited Bleak House in the course of his duties. He had knowledge of the grounds and house and the surrounding area and knew the habits of the Duckett family. He also knew about the police radio in Duckett's car, having cleaned it on many occasions, and the fact that there was no other form of communication with police headquarters inside the house other than the telephone. Crucially, Burrows knew the difference between the telephone cable and the electric power cables that all led to the house. They had to be closely observed in daylight to be differentiated. (30)

After his release from Casemates the Black Berets took an interest in Burrows. Impressed with their flattery he adopted the nicknames "*The Cuba Kid*" and "*Cuba*" after the Berets began to teach him the organization's philosophy and revolutionary aims. (31)

Even though police knew that Burrows had worked at the Duckett house and felt he was above suspicion they were still obliged to question him as to his whereabouts when the police chief was murdered. Burrows said he was in his room at Police Headquarters until about 7.45pm on the night of the shooting. He said he walked to Court Street at 11pm and was surprised to hear the police chief had been murdered. Burrows said he sat on a wall talking to a number of people who appeared happy that Duckett had been killed. Burrows also said he visited his friend "G. Wilkinson", a career criminal recently released from Casemates Prison and who now cared for the animals at Eve's Farm – the property immediately adjacent to Bleak House. Wilkinson had come to the attention of Police in the early days of the Duckett murder probe. Burnt clothing was found in his backyard oil-drum incinerator. The clothing was forensically examined and found to contain flecks of paint from the floor mats of George Duckett's car. Burrows had painted the mats in his capacity as Duckett's handyman.

Following police questioning Wilkinson was unable to explain why the clothes had been burned or why they contained traces of paint from the car. Police later concluded that Burrows hid out at Eve's Farm after murdering Duckett and it was his clothes that had been set on fire in a failed attempt to dispose of potential evidence. Scotland Yard detectives characterized Wilkinson as an extremely vicious man.

*

One of Burrows' accomplices in crime was his long-time friend and former prison cellmate, 20 year old Larry Tacklyn. Tacklyn was a young fair-skinned black Bermudian who came from a troubled background and spent his youth as a petty criminal, securing convictions for theft, assault on police and possession of marijuana. Tacklyn's personality was different from Burrows', according to prison officers and police officers who knew him. Tacklyn had a hair-trigger temper and a surly manner as opposed to the mild–mannered and affable Burrows. (32)

John Henry Williams, a career criminal who resided at Mount Hill, Pembroke, had known Tacklyn since childhood because he had once dated his mother, Lois Tacklyn. Lois had moved to the United States when Tacklyn was five or six leaving him in the care of an elderly woman, a 'Miss

Lottimore' who cared for him at her home in Parsons Road, Deepdale. Tacklyn, Williams remembered, had a troubled adolescence and had been sent to the old Junior Training School on Paget Island because of his involvement in petty criminal activities. As a young adult, Tacklyn had been in and out of Casemates Prison for various criminal offences. Williams said Tacklyn "did not like white people". (33)

Former police officer Nick Bolton also knew Tacklyn and said he was "…an unpleasant character well known to police. No one liked to deal with him…. in cells he was a pig. He was typical of the violent, unbalanced type of Bermuda criminal….. (Tacklyn was) the opposite (to Burrows). He was a known to be violent, but he was small time. He was the one who, when locked in the police cells, used to throw excrement at passing police officers or try to get it through the window into the parade room." (34)

*

The head of the Government of Bermuda, black Bermudian Sir Edward Richards, issued a statement following the murder of the Police Chief which read, in part, "The news of the death of the Commissioner by an assailant's bullet has come as a profound shock to everyone of us in this community. Mr Duckett was a dedicated and fearless police officer devoted to his men and in particular was interested in their participation in community life. By his death, a cowardly blow has been struck against the forces of law and order – against the security of all law-abiding and peace-loving citizens of these islands. Wandering among us today is a person or persons whose hands are stained with blood and it is the duty of us all to assist the police in their investigations so that the culprit or culprits may be brought to justice." (35)

The Royal Gazette editorialised, "Many events have occurred in Bermuda's long history, but none so tragic, perhaps, from a national point of view, as the shooting this weekend of Police Commissioner George Duckett. For this act…falls very near to the category of 'assassination' – a description normally applied when heads of state….are killed by a gunman's bullets…It is a new dimension of crime here, for there is nothing in the records to show that Bermudians or non-Bermudians are in the habit of carrying firearms, and shooting them off, even when engaged in crime." (36)

The Police Gazette voiced the views of most of the Bermuda Police Force and called the murder, "a terrible act – when the victim is an unarmed police officer, relaxing at his home with his family, it takes on a more serious and sinister aspect in that it strikes not only at the victim's family and colleagues, but at society as a whole. The brutal and senseless shooting of our Commissioner… shocked and outraged the community, the shooting and wounding of his 17 year old daughter, Marcia, further compounded the seriousness of the cowardly act which deprived the Force and community of a dedicated and fearless Commissioner. The written word cannot adequately convey the feelings of his family and colleagues, the former have lost a loved one and the latter a friend and comrade. He was a policeman above all else, police work was his life and he lived it to the full. His main objective from the day he assumed command of the Bermuda Police on 29th December 1969 was to give Bermuda a police service of which it could be justly proud. In his short tenure of command he realised much of his mission, especially that part in which his men involved themselves in community and, more particularly, youth activities. As a police officer, he faced and accepted hazards which do not ordinarily confront the average citizen – he was a 'big' man in every sense of the word and took all obstacles in his stride. His courage and fearlessness were well known and earned him the respect of friend and foe alike." (37)

George Duckett was buried at the old military cemetery in Prospect on September 14th 1972. Following a funeral service at the Anglican Cathedral in Hamilton, hundreds of Bermudians and tourists lined Church Street as his flag-draped coffin was taken to the cemetery.

SIX

THE ASSASSINATION OF BERMUDA'S GOVERNOR

"I was not alone when I went up to Government House to kill the Governor but I shall never reveal who or how many others were with me…. One week before the Governor and his ADC were killed I went up to Government House and as I hid in the bushes which were to the right of the front doorway facing North I saw the Governor and his ADC and his dog Horsa come out of Government House, walk across the terrace and go down the steps. I was glad to see this because it revealed that the enemy was to be delivered right into my hands. The following week I again went up to Government House…."

Erskine 'Buck' Burrows in a handwritten letter witnessed by Casemates Prison Divisional Officer Dean.

"…. also with (a leading Beret member) I conducted at least four reconnoitres of Government House and its grounds……(He) made sketches of the grounds and buildings including positions where police and other persons could be found and where vehicles were parked….I know that all information gained from these and similar reconnoitres was to be passed to Mel Saltus…."

Bermuda Police, Statement of Witness, Sylvan Musson Jr, 23 May 1976

SYLVAN MUSSON JR had begun to attend meetings at the Black Beret Cadre headquarters in Court Street before he submitted an application for membership in 1970 shortly after the Union Jack was burnt outside City Hall, Hamilton. He was accepted as a member by the Central Committee. At the time he joined Dionne Bassett was the Chairman and five Berets formed the Central Committee. At some point in his career as a Black Beret, Musson became a police informant but the police files do not indicate exactly when.

The aims of the Berets were "towards Marxism and Communism", Musson said. He also said that it was common knowledge within the Berets that "certain persons holding important offices in Bermuda" would have to be removed "by any means necessary, including as a last resort by killing those individuals". Musson also informed his police handlers that the Berets actually had a list of targets for assassination including politicians, policemen and members of the Judiciary. The Governor, the Commissioner of Police, and the Premier were all 'high on the list'.

Soon after joining the Berets Musson became an active member and participated in   'surveillance of the enemy' which included reconnoitring the private houses of individuals on the 'hit list', including the residence of George Duckett. He was also given instruction on the use and care of firearms and shown literature on how to make explosives from common and easily obtainable ingredients. Musson said the firearms instruction was usually given by Dionne Bassett. During one period of instruction Musson was shown a Walther P38 and other revolvers, one of which was, "black in colour and it was a .38, in good shape". Musson was never allowed to actually fire a gun but he knew that some of the senior members of the Berets "actually practised by firing bullets". He believed the target practice took place in a "disused fort". (1) Former police officer Nick Bolton said the Black Berets had a "shooting range at Fort Langton........it used to have underground passages and powder storage rooms that Larry Tacklyn and Buck Burrows used to conduct target practice." (2)

During the time Musson reconnoitred the 'enemy', which included visits to police headquarters and the residences of police officers and members of the Judiciary, he was accompanied by one of the leading members of the Berets,' the third man' who police believed assisted in the assassination of the Governor. On two occasions Musson and his fellow Beret entered Police Headquarters by way of Prospect Road. They had binoculars and noted the movements of police officers coming and going. They also noted the vehicle numbers of police cars and private cars, the locations of radio control and they noted the positions of the petrol pumps and ways of entry and exit. His colleague drew a sketch plan of the layout of buildings and vital points. (3)

However, the most disturbing job Musson carried out was reconnoitring Government House which he did, "on at least four occasions, three of them in the hours of darkness" and "the other was during the afternoon and daylight". The Governor at this time was Lord Martonmere, Musson said. On each surveillance trip Musson and the 'third man' entered the grounds of Government House from Bernard Park across Marsh Folly Road and then climbed a gate or wire fence. They went up concrete steps which led to the main driveway. Sometimes they crossed the drive and climbed the grass bank which led to the main entrance to the house. From there they could see into the house and observe what was going on. They made 'sketches' of the buildings and grounds including the positions of police officers guarding the Governor's residence. According to Musson, "We always left Government House by the same route we entered by and on these occasions we wore sneakers and dark clothing." (4)

*

24 year old Wayne Michael Jackson, a black Bermudian and petty criminal but described in court as a 'commercial fisherman', was a close friend of Larry Tacklyn. He was well known to the police as a burglar and robber and had often been accompanied by Tacklyn in the commission of his crimes.

On the 10th March 1973, around 6.30pm, Jackson arrived at his parents' house at Harris Bay. He knocked on the door then entered the downstairs apartment which had been rented to Tacklyn. As he entered Tacklyn said, "Close the door, quick". Tacklyn was sitting on a sofa chair talking to Erskine 'Buck' Burrows who was sitting on a bed. (5) He noticed Burrows examining a long-barrelled Schmidt .22 revolver which he had pulled out from under the bed. It was a German modification of the American Colt. The gun was later identified as the pistol used to shoot George Duckett.

Tacklyn was holding a .38 pistol. "This looks nice", Tacklyn said. (6) Jackson saw it was a dark-coloured revolver in good condition and that the rifling in the barrel had a right hand twist. Both guns were loaded and extra ammunition was contained in a plastic bag which was lying on the couch.

Tacklyn introduced Jackson to Burrows. "This is my man Buck, the guy that took care of Duckett" he said. As Burrows' burst into a large grin Jackson asked, "What's going on here?" Tacklyn beckoned Jackson to close the door (7) then handed his gun over asking Jackson to "feel it". Tacklyn said they were "planning a mission. We are going to take care of the man on the hill. We are going to take care of all those devils." (8) Immediately, Jackson realised that the person they were talking about was the Governor of Bermuda. Jackson responded by telling his friend he was "crazy". "We've got to do what we must do", Tacklyn replied. (9)

Jackson said he wanted to look at the pistol Burrows was holding. However, Burrows refused, telling Jackson that, "No one handles this gun but me. This is my personal weapon." (10) It was the gun that Burrows had used exactly six months earlier when he shot Police Chief George Duckett.

Throughout the investigation into the Duckett killing Burrows had kept his job at Prospect Police Headquarters and maintained an apartment in the building housing the Police Officers' Social Room. He had free access to the offices of the Police Chief and Deputy Police Chief – and also their files on the lacklustre progress of the Duckett murder investigation. He also knew that on the evening of March 10, 1973 only a skeleton Police presence would be on duty – it was the night of the Police Ball at the recently opened Southampton Princess Hotel and most of Bermuda's Police Force would be in attendance.

At approximately 7pm, after Jackson had prepared a meal upstairs, he saw that both men had left. Later that night he heard on the radio that the Governor had been shot and he immediately thought of "Larry and Buck". (11)

When Buck Burrows was later questioned by police as to his whereabouts on the night of the Governor's assassination he cited his friend 'G. Wilkinson' as his alibi. Burrows told police he arrived there about 9.30 p.m. by way of Prospect Road and the old railway trail only to discover Wilkinson was out. Burrows said he walked through the unlocked door, turned the lights and the radio on then read a Harold Robbins book, 'The Adventurers'. He then lay on Wilkinson's bed and fell asleep. Burrows said Wilkinson arrived home about midnight. They spoke for a while then Burrows asked if he could stay the night. (12)

*

Some weeks prior to March 10th, John Smith, a reporter for the UK's 'People' newspaper, interviewed the Governor at Government House. Smith was in Bermuda reporting on the Duckett murder enquiry. He was convinced the murder had political and racial motives. Sir Richard had invited Smith for tea at Government House and as Smith went through the gates he noticed that the only sign of security was "a police constable who opened the front door". (13)

Smith was served tea and chocolate cake in the drawing room. He immediately found that Sharples was a "friendly and rather shy man". Smith asked Sir Richard about the Duckett murder. "A terrible business", the Governor said, "but it seems to have been an isolated incident. We have no reason to believe it was a Black Power plot." Smith disagreed and told the Governor, "If Duckett's death was part of a planned political plot aimed at the British you yourself could be next." According to Smith, Sir Richard smiled and said, "I know you newspaper chaps like to write about the island of fear or 'murder in paradise' and that sort of thing. But Bermudians aren't militant. Any outsiders trying to stir up trouble will be disappointed. I don't think the people of Bermuda are Black Power fanatics. I get on well with them." (14) Clearly, the Governor was keeping his suspicions about the Black Berets to himself aware that any injudicious remarks might provoke further racial disturbances. His contacts with the Foreign Office revealed his true beliefs that the Duckett murder likely had political and racial overtones. (15)

A few weeks after Smith's visit, Saturday night March 10th, the Governor held an informal dinner party. Sir Richard told his 10 or so guests that he was looking forward to seeing his two sons, Christopher and David who were sailing slowly up to Bermuda from Rio de Janeiro on Sir Richard's yacht. He also spoke of his excitement in taking part with his sons in the Newport to Bermuda yacht race and that his two daughters, Fiona, 23, and Miranda, 21 were in England at Sir Richard's farm in Hampshire.

Saturday had been a bright sunny day. However, at dusk the skies became cloudy and the air was damp. Guests that evening at the dinner party included friends of the Sharples, Mr and Mrs Waddington, who were staying with the Governor, and Morag Valentine, secretary to Sir Richard. Sir Richard's aide de camp, Captain Hugh Sayers, was also present.

Government House is situated in its own grounds of approximately 36 acres bounded on the north side by North Shore Road, on the east by the area known as Government Gate, on the west by Black Watch Pass and Langton Hill and on the south end of the grounds (above Marsh Folly Road) facing towards North Shore. It has a superb view of the ocean across grounds planted with cedar, casuarinas, rubber trees and oleanders.

Lady Sharples believed the house was not suitable for a modern day Governor. She said, "This place, with 45 acres, is out of all proportion with today's thinking. …..this is not the right house for the job in the first place. It is resented by very many and that's easy to understand…." (16) It was estimated that the upkeep of Government House was approximately £78,000 per year and the costs were met by the Bermudian Government. (17)

The only protective wall around the building is a three-foot high grey stone fence behind which are planted thick oleander bushes. Public roads ran all around the perimeter and could be scaled by a small child. According to some Bermudians who lived in Hamilton the low fence was often vaulted at night by people eager to take a walk in the Government House grounds. (18)

The heavily wooded grounds provided considerable cover for any trespasser. A driveway covered the terrace area of the house bounded on its outer side by a lawn and a five foot stone wall broken by a series of steps leading to the grounds. The steps are bounded on each side by a stone balustrade supported by round stone pillars. The distance from the front door of Government House to the top of the steps is approximately 65 feet. The front door of the mansion was lit by two carriage lights attached to the wall. The area around the steps, however, was in total darkness at night.

Security around Government House was poor. Although the new Police Commissioner, 'Nobby' Clark, said the security arrangements had been 'sufficient', it was clear to many that the grounds were easily accessible. Gates remained unlocked and on a number of occasions a small boy had retrieved his football by simply walking through the front gate. There was only a 4 foot wall separating the grounds from North Shore Road and at Government Gate there was a door that had been broken for months. In fact, one Bermudian had been arrested for growing marijuana outside the grounds. Following the murders the British Foreign Secretary, Sir Alec Douglas-Home told the House of Commons he would investigate the security of the Governor's mansion which he described as 'abysmal'. (19)

A police constable was posted in the hall just inside the front door and he kept a record of everyone who entered or left the building. The duty officer also made frequent patrols around the exterior of the house.

Guests arrived between 7.45pm and 8.15pm.Some guests arrived after dinner, around 10pm. After dinner Lady Sharples complained of feeling unwell and went to her bedroom. The party guests then retired to the drawing room until 11.25pm when the party wound down and guests began to leave. Sir Richard, the Waddingtons and Morag Valentine remained talking for a further 15 minutes when Sir Richard told his guests he was taking his Great Dane, Horsa, for a walk in the grounds. It was a habit Sir Richard kept before retiring for the night. Two weeks previous he had taken the same night walk with Prince Charles. (20)

Duty security officer, Detective Constable Franklin Deallie, arrived at Government House at 10 p.m. for a shift that lasted until midnight. When he arrived he noticed four cars parked in the driveway in front of the building. Aware there was a dinner party in progress, Deallie contacted the Police Central Division Headquarters that everything was running smoothly. Carrying a flashlight, he patrolled the outside of the house for 15 minutes and saw and heard nothing unusual. At 10.40 p.m. he had a 'check visit' from Inspector Sheehan. At 11 p.m. Deallie sent the 'OK' signal to Police Headquarters and performed another patrol around the building, returning to the front of the house to find the Governor showing pictures of his yacht to dinner guests.

Shortly after 11.30 the Governor and Captain Sayers walked to the main door to see the dinner guests off the premises. When the guests left Deallie made an entry in his log and signalled to Headquarters. As Sir Richard left the house by the front door he told Deallie that he was just taking the dog for some exercise. A minute or so later Captain Sayers joined Sir Richard and closed the front door behind him. He had hurriedly gone to collect his .38 revolver which he stuck in his cummerbund. (21) The evening air was quiet except for the sounds of tree frogs and the quiet conversation of the Governor and his 23 year old bodyguard.

Erskine 'Buck' Burrows, Larry Tacklyn and at least one other accomplice, who the police later referred to as the 'third man', were dressed in dark clothing and positioned at the bottom of the steps leading to the terrace of Government House. Burrows had two guns with him, one to shoot the Governor and the other to be used against anyone who tried to prevent him from fleeing. The assassins had arrived at Government House at 10.15pm and positioned themselves to the right of the steps leading down into the grounds. After they had waited "for some time" they saw Sir Richard's guests leave the building and drive away in their cars. At one point the assassins believed the governor was not going for his regular evening stroll and considered leaving. However, Burrows insisted they stay a while longer. Soon they heard noise coming from the direction of the front of the house. Burrows looked through the opening in the balustrade and saw the Governor walking towards them followed by Captain Sayers who hurried to catch up. When they reached the top of the steps, nine feet away, the Governor and Captain Sayers stopped. Burrows heard them quietly conversing. Although there were carriage lamps on either side of the front door of Government House, the area around the staircase balustrade was completely unilluminated.

Burrows noticed Horsa come down the steps and approach the killers. It gave no warning barks. He thought about shooting the dog but realised he would alert his victims. He ignored the dog, "cocked the gun" in his right hand, aimed, and began to fire at the two men who were standing at the top of the steps. Sayers was hit first, Burrows said, then the Governor. Both men fall to the ground as Burrows turned his pistol towards the dog and fired, killing it instantly. (22)

However, there is compelling evidence, which shall be examined later, that suggests Burrows had not fired the gun which killed the Governor and Captain Sayers and that the shooter was actually Larry Tacklyn.

The assassins had struck at 11.45pm. Officer Deallie heard the shots - one shot, a short pause, then two shots - followed by a cry for help. He immediately activated an alarm system summoning police assistance and then ran outside where he saw Sir Richard dragging himself towards the house from the direction of the terrace steps. "I saw the Governor on the ground, crawling towards the front door", he said "He was on the edge of the grass with the steps behind him. He was dragging himself with his left arm, holding his right arm across his chest….I saw the dog stumbling towards the steps." Blood had been bubbling up Sharples' throat and running down his face and shirt front. Captain Sayers was lying prone on the lawn immediately in front of the steps and Horsa was lying by the wall nearby. (23) Deallie went back into the house to call for help.

Moments later Deallie was joined by Sir Richard's butler, Latino De La Torre, who had heard the shots from his room which overlooked the North Terrace. On hearing gunshots Torre's wife, Marion, looked out of their room and saw Sir Richard stagger a couple of steps towards the front door then collapse. Latino said that when he reached the Governor, Sir Richard tried to speak but couldn't. Torres placed a cushion under his head as the governor lay on the tarmac outside the front door. Shortly afterwards PC Deallie and Latino were joined by the Waddingtons. Morag woke Lady Sharples and told her that her husband had been shot. (24)

PC Kenneth John Van Thall, accompanied by other police officers, was the first on the scene as a result of the emergency call. He immediately examined Sir Richard and Captain Sayers but could find no signs of life. Shortly afterwards an ambulance arrived. Nurse Geraldine McPartland felt the Governor's pulse and tried resuscitation without success. She saw Captain Sayers lying face down with his hands still in his pockets. Horsa was lying by the terrace wall between two bushes about 9 feet away from Sayers.

Sir Richard was then taken by ambulance to the King Edward VIIth Memorial Hospital. As the ambulance was about to leave, Nurse McPartland was joined by Dr Hugh O'Neill. On route to the hospital O'Neill administered external cardiac massage to the Governor. When they arrived Sir Richard was taken to the Surgical Room where Dr James

King opened the left side of his chest and applied further cardiac massage to revive him. Dr King was unsuccessful. Hospital pathologist Dr Keith Cunningham pronounced Sir Richard dead at 2.30am Sunday morning. (25)

*

As murder detectives and forensics officers examined the crime scene they soon deduced the shots that killed the Governor and Captain Sayers had been fired upwards through the stone balustrade. There were powder marks on the stone, indicating the muzzle of the gun had been close to the first and second stone pillars to the right of the steps when it was fired. Three bullets had been fired from this position. A bullet later discovered by police deep in the ground near the bottom of the steps was established by police as having first entered the dog and then passed through it. A bullet had struck the wall of Government House. It was determined this bullet was the one that passed through Sir Richard's chest. Sir Richard had also been shot in the leg and the bullet passed straight through ending up in a tree nearby. The lines of trajectory and the blood trail indicated that Sharples and Sayers had been standing side by side facing outwards over the grounds when they were shot from a distance of some 14 feet. (26)

Investigators also concluded Sir Richard had not died instantly. He had been hit in the chest two inches from the mid line and there was a corresponding wound in the back. As he crawled towards the door the assassins had shot him in the right knee and the bullet passed through his leg. The cause of death was due to, 'haemorrhage, asphyxia and blood in (Sir Richard's) air passages and multiple wound injuries.' (27) Brian Arnold, a police scientific officer, later examined the Governor's clothing and reported that the size of the bullet hole indicated that "the bullets were .38 caliber and the absence of powder marks indicated that the weapon was fired more than two feet away." (28)

When doctors examined Captain Sayers' body they concluded he had been shot in the right side of his chest five and a half inches from his armpit. The bullet had passed through several internal organs. He had died immediately "from massive haemorrhage and multiple injuries due to a bullet wound". (29). At the time of the shooting Sayers had been armed with a fully loaded .38 Smith and Wesson pistol but had been unable to draw it from his holster as it had been concealed by the cummerbund of his dress suit. Sayers had been issued with the weapon by Chief Superintendent James McMaster following the murder of Police Commissioner George Duckett. McMaster was fearful that the Governor was also a target for assassination. (30)

It was later established that Sir Richard and Captain Sayers were killed by bullets fired from the same gun, a .38 revolver "by an assailant who was positioned behind the right balustrade of the terrace steps". The weapon was never recovered. (31)

*

By 12.30am in the early hours of Sunday morning, roads around Government House had been sealed off as police officers, still in their tuxedos, had been called from the police choir dinner dance at the Southampton Princess Hotel to help in the manhunt. The group included Police Commissioner L.M (Nobby) Clark. The maitre'd of the hotel had approached Clark and told him about the Governor's assassination. A large crowd was waiting for the police choir to sing but an announcement had been made that there had been an emergency and the choir would not be performing. Police Officers left the Southampton Princess and reported for duty at the nearest police station. A flight out of Bermuda to Heathrow Airport, London, was delayed. Bermudians were stopped and searched and police guards were placed at the homes of high government officials.

The Commanding Officer of the Bermuda Regiment, Lt Col. Michael Darling was   informed of the murders at 12.20am by Police Chief Clark and he immediately called a meeting of the Regiment's key officers. Clark requested that 20 or so soldiers should be stationed as a perimeter guard around Government House. A signals unit was also set up on the grounds of the mansion for direct communications between police headquarters and the Regiment's headquarters. By the next day 110 soldiers, mainly from Company B under the command of Major Douglas Roberts, had been in position ready for deployment by the Police Chief. William McPhee, the commandant of the Police Reserve was told about the murders about 1.30am and put his organisation on stand-by. HMS Sirius, a Royal navy frigate was due to leave on Monday but its departure was delayed. It was moored at H.M. Dockyard, a short distance from Casemates Prison.

Government leader Sir Edward Richards was informed of the murders by a police sergeant and a constable who arrived at his house around 12.30am. He was taken by police car to Police headquarters and met with the Police Chief. Shortly afterwards they visited the home of the Chief Secretary I.A.C. Kinnear who lived a short distance away on Montpelier Road. Sir Edward was concerned that the murders might spark off yet more riots by militants taking advantage of the political tensions. He was also concerned that he might have also been a target for assassination. On Sunday afternoon he announced a state of emergency.

*

Police brought in a tracker dog and established that the assassins had entered the grounds of Government House from a wall near St Monica's Road. The other side of the wall gave access to a housing estate and paths which led down to Marsh Folly Road. The grounds of Government House were also searched by police assisted by members of the Bermuda Regiment. The search lasted over two weeks but nothing of any relevance was found.

The police investigation did, however, establish that 43 people in the area of Government House heard the sounds of gunshots. Witnesses said a total of four shots were fired in succession. (32) Amongst the most valued witnesses in the area around Government House were Audrey Lorraine Armstrong, Glenford Augustus Allen, Gloria Claudine Hart, Barbara Francis and Ray Bascombe. (33)

Audrey Armstrong lived in a house on the ocean side of North Shore Road, Pembroke. The house was situated 75 yards east of the North Gate to Government House. She heard footsteps run past her bedroom window at approximately 11.30pm.

Glenford Allen had an apartment in a house situated on the ocean side of North Shore Road, a few yards east of the northern entrance to Government

House grounds. He heard the sounds of "four or five shots" fired in quick succession and about two minutes later he heard the sound of someone running past the east side of his apartment and slide down the banks to the water's edge. Gloria Hart lived in a house near a pathway running from the rear of Government House grounds to Marsh Folly Road. She heard a number of shots fired coming from the direction of Government House. Soon afterwards she heard the sounds of "two or three persons" running past her house along the track in the direction of Marsh Folly. (34)

Twenty-six-year-old Barbara Francis and her friend Ray Bascombe were at Bascombe's home at 13 Marsh Folly Road. Shortly after 11.45pm they left the house to go to the P.H.C. Club in Hamilton. As Bascombe walked towards his scooter Francis walked to the centre of Marsh Folly Road waiting for him to start the engine. As she stood in the road she heard the sounds of people "running". Within an instant, "a young man" ran in front of her, about five to seven feet away, from the direction of the path that led up to the side of Government House followed by another man running towards her. She noticed the second man was looking round and running fast. He was six feet away and she was able to "get a better look at this one".

Both men ran across Marsh Folly Road and turned left along the old railway tracks which give access to the Middletown and Court Street areas of Hamilton. They were still running fast and "the second man, the one I had a good look at", was looking behind him. When the men ran past her she wondered who they were running from. (35)

Francis described the first man she saw as "light coloured, about 25 years of age, height 5'7' to 8, wearing dark clothing and a dark woollen hat". The second man she described was "also light coloured, about 25-26 years of age, clean shaven with an Afro hair style". Francis said the first man was wearing dark clothes, a tan colored trench coat and a dark woollen hat. Bascombe said he only saw the side profiles of the suspects but nevertheless gave similar descriptions as Francis. Police believed Bascombe could have named one of the suspects but "was too frightened to do so". (36) However, Francis made a sworn statement identifying Larry Tacklyn as "one of these men".(37)

Police determined there were "at least three people who were involved in the assassination of Sir Richard Sharples and Captain Sayers, two making good their escape by way of tracks leading to Marsh Folly Road and the other in the opposite direction towards North Shore Road". (38)

Police rounded up the 'usual suspects' including those who had been involved in the politically-inspired riots of previous years. Four members of the Black Berets were arrested in early morning raids. Police assumed from the start that the murders were politically motivated. The assumption was bolstered by the knowledge that the Governor had been assassinated six months to the day following the Police Commissioner's murder, a coincidence the police were not ready to accept.

*

Armed police guards were assigned to leading politicians like the Deputy Governor and Sir Edward Richards. One policeman told *Royal Gazette* reporter Patrick Burgess that he was sent to Sir Richard's house, "…handed a handgun and told to shoot anyone that (entered) the yard on the night the Governor was assassinated." (39) Another officer said he had been assigned to protect Deputy Governor Kinnear, "I… got the job of protecting Lady Sharples.…Kinnear… he lived at 'Montpelier' near Prospect. He was scared to death and hid away for a while on Nonsuch Island with his family, and me. (It was) a very pleasant place to hide out." (40)

Ian Kinnear, Sir Richard's deputy, who once again became Acting Governor following the assassination, sent an urgent telex to London. The duty clerk at 10 Downing Street sent a message to Prime Minister Edward Heath informing him about the Governor's murder. Kinnear told the Foreign Office that the murder of Sharples and Sayers appeared to be an isolated incident on the same pattern as the murder of the Police Chief the previous September. He said he assumed the murders were 'political' but there was "no unrest and no - repeat no - indication of an insurrection". Kinnear allowed there might be some necessity in detaining "a number of people, including the hard core of the Black Beret Cadre. It will only be possible after the declaration of a (State of) Emergency". He said that Scotland Yard were sending a Murder Squad and that it was vital leave for Bermuda on that day's BOAC flight. He asked that if this presented some difficulty the British authorities ask contact BOAC and "make room for them by turning other passengers off." (41)

On the 11th March Acting Governor Kinnear declared a 'State of Emergency' in Bermuda to enable him to grant the police wider powers. On Monday 12th March Britain's Foreign Secretary, Sir Alec Douglas Home told the House of Commons, "The culprit or culprits have not yet been discovered. A team of Scotland Yard detectives are now assisting the Bermuda Police in their investigations and every possible effort will be made to bring the assassins to justice."(42)

*

In December 1972 Scotland Yard Murder Squad detectives Chief Superintendent Bill Wright and Detective Sergeant Basil Haddrell, who had been investigating the murder of the police chief, had returned to London for a conference. During the flight to Heathrow airport Haddrell learned he had been promoted to Detective Inspector but was to stay on the Bermuda enquiry. The two detectives returned to Bermuda in January 1973 for another six weeks of investigations into the police chief's murder but they failed to gather any substantial clues. Chief Superintendent Wright decided in February to call a halt and he and Haddrell returned to London. Local detectives were given strict instructions to pursue the investigation.

On the night of the governor's assassination Bill Wright was celebrating his wedding anniversary. Basil Haddrell was the night duty officer on the Murder Squad and was surprised to receive a telephone call from Police Chief Nobby Clark who told him of the Governor's murder. Clark asked Haddrell and Wright to return to the island. Haddrell booked tickets for a flight at 8am. Wright was at home having celebrated until 5 am. They met at Heathrow Airport at 7am.

The two detectives arrived in Bermuda at approximately 2pm Sunday 11th March and immediately set to work. A few weeks later the FBI and Canadian Police were enlisted to help in the manhunt for the killers. Bermuda Police believed the gunman may have slipped through and leave the island by sea or air. The Canadian Police and the FBI were asked to scrutinise the immigration records of their nationals who arrived before the murders. They were also shown a photographic record of half the island's population. Additionally, police photographers had taken photos at the funerals of the Governor and his aide and pieced them together to form a panoramic view. (43)

Haddrell and Wright were assisted by members of the UK's Regional Crime Squad headed by Commander John Morrison together with Chief Superintendent Gordon Powell. In all nine high-ranking detectives had arrived by Wednesday 14th March to assist in the enquiries. The team of detectives was the largest ever sent on a case overseas.

The 52-year-old Morrison was the senior officer in the investigation. He had been   Deputy Co-ordinator of the Regional Crime Squad in the UK since December 1972. He was previously Deputy Head of Scotland Yard's A1 Branch which investigated complaints against police officers. He was also a member of Scotland Yard's Murder Squad and both he and 52 year old Chief Superintendent Wright had visited Bermuda previously to investigate the Jean Burrows and George Duckett murders. Commander Morrison had received 17 commendations during his career.

Chief Superintendent Powell was also a member of the UK's Regional Crime Squad who had previously worked for the Murder Squad. Another member of the team was Detective Sergeant Nicky Birch who had narrowly escaped injury when a bomb blew up outside London's Old Bailey Courts a week before his trip to Bermuda. The 35 year old Birch had just parked his car behind the bomb car, planted by the IRA, when it exploded. The explosion hurled Birch across the street and wrecked his two week old Triumph sports car.

There were two 'scene of crime' officers, Detective Sergeant Colin Rumsby and forensics expert Arthur Sabine. The team also had a fingerprint expert, Detective Superintendent Sydney Draper.

By May 1973 Scotland Yard detectives had been working continuously since their arrival in March. (44) In the UK the Foreign Office voiced its fear that, "….there are almost certainly racial implications in the choice of the British Governor as the victim: it could hardly be otherwise in the absence of any more obvious motive for the crime. …. (Government Official) Duncan

Watson was in Bermuda for the funeral and found a wide range of views on the subject among expatriate officials. The Acting Governor's assessment, with which we would agree, is that despite prosperity and some recent progress in communal relations in Bermuda there may well be continuing resentment among some of the coloured community; but that there is not the state of general seething dissatisfaction which is the usual prelude to disorder. The most reasonable assumption would seem to be that there is a small 'revolutionary' cell which possesses arms and whose target might be described as the removal of symbols of colonial authority in Bermuda." (45)

*

On the night of the Governor's assassination Wayne Michael Jackson turned on the radio and heard the Governor had been shot. He immediately thought of "Larry and Buck".

At 8am the next day Jackson decided to wash his car which was parked in the driveway of his parent's house. Tacklyn approached him carrying a brown paper bag. He was "dressed clean" and had on a pair of dark flared trousers and an "army type of jacket". Jackson noticed that the night before, Tacklyn had "definitely been wearing blue jeans". After greeting Jackson, Tacklyn said, "Did you hear about it?" Jackson knew that Tacklyn had been talking about the Governor's murder and replied, "Yes, did you get rid of your clothing?" Tacklyn told him he had not only disposed of the clothing but the gun as well. Jackson said Tacklyn "appeared to be excited". (46)

Tacklyn went on to give a description of the shooting. He told Jackson about how, "… (The Governor and Captain Sayers) walked right across in front of us. I took care of them and one tried to run. You should have seen their faces. The dog, a big one, tried to get me and Buck took care of him. The police came so fast they were all over the place. I almost fell down a hole getting away. I didn't know Buck's mobylette (50cc motorcycle) was so fast." Tacklyn boasted, "We have got to get rid of *all* these devils". (47)

Jackson suddenly realised that the two friends had tied him and his family to a crime of enormous proportions. He asked Tacklyn to leave and told him he would see him later as he had to take his wife Carol to work.

When he returned to his house he saw that Tacklyn had left with all his belongings, except for a few items of clothing.

As the weeks and months passed both Burrows and Tacklyn continued to visit Jackson at his parents' home but neither man mentioned the murders. Jackson loaned Tacklyn $150 "so he could go to Canada". (48) A few months later, in August 1973, when Jackson was inspecting the plumbing of the basement apartment he found a brown paper package containing Tacklyn's gun and also a .22 revolver and a number of rounds of .38 and .22 ammunition. The type of ammunition appeared to be the same as those he saw at the apartment when he was introduced to Buck Burrows. (49)

Jackson gathered up the incriminating evidence, borrowed a friend's boat, and dropped the weapons and ammunition in the sea just south of Castle Point. Later a search by police divers in this area failed to recover the weapons and ammunition as the depth of the water varied from 80 feet to 240 feet over a broken rocky seabed. (50)

After Jackson dumped the guns he returned to his basement apartment and discovered he had left a further round of .38 ammunition behind which had apparently fallen from the package when he removed it from behind the pipes.

Many months later investigators were to conclude that, "…there can be little doubt (the .38 revolver) was the same revolver dropped into the sea by Wayne Jackson…..Similarly, there can be little doubt this weapon was used to assassinate Sir Richard Sharples and Captain Hugh Sayers. Jackson's description of the right-hand twist rifling in the barrel of the revolver held by Tacklyn on 10th March 1973 is corroborated by ballistic evidence indicating the murder weapon had rifling consisting of six right-hand twists". (51)

Scotland Yard detectives would later describe Jackson's statements to police as, "…corroborated by known fact. Tacklyn's admission that one of the victims (in the assassination of the Governor) tried to run away and that the dog, Horsa, was shot from the position used by the assailants to effect the murders is supported by blood trials and from the position in which the bullet responsible for killing the animal, was found." (52)

Tacklyn had confessed his involvement in the assassination to ex-convict

58 year old John Henry Hillgrove Williams. Williams had known Tacklyn since he was a child. When Tacklyn was on bail for the Master's Store robbery he visited Williams and "started talking of the murders". (53) Police deduced the time period would have to be between 5ᵗʰ and 9ᵗʰ July, the only period Tacklyn was on bail for this offence.

When Tacklyn arrived at Williams' house he "sat on the bed and drank… wine", Williams said, "…he struck me as a changed person from what I knew him as (because) I can say I've seen him grow up. He was talking about the Rastafarians and (other uncharacteristic) things…" Tacklyn seemed anxious to talk about the murders, beginning with the murder of George Duckett. He said he was "away at the time" but his "ace boy took care" of Duckett. Williams knew Tacklyn was talking about Buck Burrows as Buck was his close friend. Tacklyn told Williams he (Tacklyn) would have, "done a better job". Tacklyn added that "everybody in the Duckett house was supposed to have been shot" but did not reveal to Williams that "there was more than one person involved in the murder."

Next, Tacklyn told Williams about the assassination of the Governor. He said, "I did it; it was a clean job". Tacklyn said he went to the end of Dutton Avenue, near Government House and hid in the bushes. He knew there was a police dinner dance planned for that evening and the knowledge that police officers would be in short supply gave him the idea. "It was a good time to get him (the Governor)", Tacklyn told Williams. Tacklyn said that "some people (were) moving around (outside) Government House when suddenly the Governor and his ADC came near". Tacklyn said he shot the Governor first and the Captain Sayers immediately afterwards. Horsa was killed as the dog had approached Tacklyn.

Tacklyn went on to tell Williams that he left the grounds of Government House by running down a track and across Marsh Folly Road before arriving at his home in Deepdale. Williams said Tacklyn was, "talking about he didn't like whitey. He didn't mention anybody being with him but only that he had done the murders himself." (54)

The Scotland Yard detectives believed Williams had been telling the truth as the method described by Tacklyn was practically identical to what police knew occurred that night at Government House. "It must be accepted that

Williams, who was in prison at the time (of the assassination) was telling the truth", they concluded (55)

Police also believed that it was virtually impossible for anyone to relate the known events of the Governor's murder with so much accuracy unless, "that person was involved and had been present....for instance, where the dog had been shot was known only by a limited number of officers engaged on the investigation and it was never released to the press media. Neither was the fact that only one gun had been used that night....Tacklyn's description of how he killed the dog, Horsa, corresponds with known facts, in that the animal was mortally wounded from the position known to have been taken by the assassin of Sir Richard and Captain Sayers, ie behind the balustrade to the right of the steps.....the point where the bullet was found after passing through the animal, its obvious downward trajectory and trail of blood leading from the point of impact to where the dog died, clearly corroborates this...the route described by Tacklyn when he left Government House grounds after committing the murders is corroborated by the two witnesses, Miss Francis and Mr Bascombe, who saw two men run along down a track...other witnesses who heard footsteps of a person or persons running along this path further corroborates Tacklyn's account." (56)

This compelling evidence suggests that it was Tacklyn and not Burrows who murdered the Governor and Captain Sayers. Additionally, police noted that at Wayne Jackson's house Burrows had been brandishing a .22 which he referred to as 'his gun' and Tacklyn was seen handling a .38 - the type of weapon used to shoot Governor Sharples and Captain Sayers.

*

On the day of Sir Richard's funeral the Queen received a telegram from President Richard Nixon which read, "I want you to know how deeply shocked and grieved we are to hear of the tragic death of Sir Richard Sharples. All Americans, and particularly those who know and love Bermuda and its people, share with you the deep sadness which this event has caused you and your people." (57) Foreign Secretary Sir Alec Douglas-Home told the House of Commons on Monday 12th March 1973, "Sir Richard Sharples had a long, gallant and most distinguished career of public service, in recent years as our colleague in this House and as a Minister of the Crown. The knowledge of our respect for him and of our deep regret will, I hope, be of some comfort to Lady Sharples and the other members of his family at this time. I also extend the sincere sympathy of the House to the family of Captain Sayers, whose promising military career has been so cruelly cut short."

Lady Sharples decided her husband should be buried in Bermuda, "It would have been his decision,"she said,"He would have wanted to be buried where his duty was. This was his last duty and he always put duty first." (58)

The joint funerals of Sir Richard Sharples and Captain Sayers were held at St Peter's Church, St Georges on Friday 16th March 1973. The funeral began at the Bermuda Secretariat Building in Hamilton at 1.15pm. A massed band of the Bermuda Regiment and the First Parachute Logistics Regiment led the way down Front Street which was lined by soldiers of the visiting Parachute Regiment.

Thousands of Bermudians, expatriate British, American and Canadian workers and tourists packed Front Street to observe the gun carriages, pulled by land Rovers, carry the bodies of Sir Richard and Captain Sayers. Laid out over the Union Jacks which covered Sir Richard's and Captain Sayers' coffins were the medals Sir Richard had been awarded for valour in the Second World War the medals Captain Sayers had been awarded for service in Northern Ireland. Sir Richard's coffin also bore the plumed Governor's hat he never wore and an empty scabbard. Sir Richard's pallbearers, members of the Bermuda Regiment, walked alongside. Captain Sayers' pallbearers were friends from the Welsh Guards to which he and Sir Richard had belonged.

Behind the gun carriages were the cars which took family and friends to Number Five Dock in Hamilton where the coffins were carried to the stern of the frigate HMS Sirius. As the coffins were lifted from the gun carriages Sirius crewmen piped them on board.

As the ship slowly edged its way out into Hamilton Harbour, Lady Sharples and her family stood on the bridge, occasionally waving to the crowds. She was dressed in a white satin dress and a black hat. HMS Sirius was followed by a flotilla of small boats as the Royal Navy vessel made its way to St Georges.

HMS Sirius reached Ordinance Island, St Georges, at 4.15pm. The coffins were taken from the ship and placed on the gun carriages for the short journey to St Peter's Church for the funeral service. On the site where the church stands the first church was erected just months after Bermuda's first settlers arrived in 1612.It was in this church that Governor Nathanial Butler convened the new colony's first parliament in August 1620.

Hundreds crowded the harbour area as the procession moved past King's Square on its way to the church. Lady Sharples and her family walked behind the gun carriages as HMS Sirius fired a 17 gun salute.

As the coffins were laid in the aisle of the church Lady Sharples took her seat followed by Government leader Sir Edward Richards, the British Government's representative, Sir David Gibson-Watt, all the members of the House of Assembly and Legislative Council and former Government leader Sir Henry Tucker. Acting Governor Kinnear sat near Lady Sharples. As the service proceeded Sir Richard's son 27 year old Christopher, read from Corinthians 1 Chapter 13.

The service was led by the Bishop of Bermuda the Right Rev. Eric Trapp. At the end of the service Trapp led the way as the coffins and a few mourners were led to the graveyard at the rear of the church. As the church organ played, the mourners who remained in the church were startled by a sudden burst of gunfire – the volleys fired by the Bermuda regiment after the coffins of Sir Richard and Captain Sayers were laid in their graves at the western end of the cemetery where the graves of slaves and free blacks are situated. Two buglers in the tower of the church played the last post.

At the conclusion of the burial Lady Sharples joined the rest of the family and friends to make her way to the official cars that would take her back to Hamilton. As Lady Sharples walked down the steps at the front of the church she noticed the scores of floral tributes that had been placed on the ground.

In a letter to Prime Minister Edward Heath Lady Sharples wrote, "There was a feeling that although everything was quiet on the surface it might not have taken much to spark off trouble – but I don't think anything like this was anticipated. We took care to always vary our routine at night. Richard was the right man: he blossomed here with the obvious liking that everyone had for him...Richard could have made a real success here if only the madmen had had the sense to see it." (59)

For more than thirty years Lady Sharples would occasionally take a poem from her desk draw and reminisce about the tragedy and the short period if time she spent on the island with her husband, the 'happiest of times' she called them. It was written for her by a Bermudian poet:

"A light has been extinguished in our midst
And in the darkness shock and anger lurk
With ugly rumour doing its dirty work:
No one can walk in safety till the dawn.

On beach and ocean shines Bermuda's sun,
But violence and evil cast their gloom
Even where perfumed oleanders bloom:
Even where sails are leaning on the wind.

A light has been extinguished in our midst.
In shame and grief Bermuda bows her head.
Could kindliness and brotherhood be dead
Where golden kiskadees and blue birds sing?

SEVEN

THE UNHOLY ALLIANCE

"The Sixties defined itself by its efforts to delegitimize the police as an 'army of occupation' while also celebrating crime as a form of existential rebellion and the outlaw as a perceptive social critic. There was a numbing barrage against what was derided as 'law and order' seen in slogans such as 'off the pigs', in the insistence that 'all minority prisoners are political prisoners', and in the romanticizing of murderers like George Jackson who deserved to be locked deeper in the prison system rather than becoming international symbols of American injustice."

David Horowitz and Peter Collier, *Destructive Generation*

"I asked Tacklyn if he was also involved in the murders at the Shopping Center. Tacklyn replied, 'Yes, man. That Portuguese bastard hit me in the guts. That's the reason they both got shot'"

John Henry Williams, friend of Larry Tacklyn

LARRY TACKLYN AND Buck Burrows associated with a number of Black Beret members who had served prison sentences and who frequented Greene's Grill. The restaurant was owned and run by 42 year old Bobby Greene, the self-styled 'Godfather of Court Street', and was situated in Court Street, a geographical area of Hamilton that was frequented by Bermuda's criminal fraternity. The Berets likely saw in Burrows and Tacklyn a way to accomplish the organization's goals without risking themselves to any large degree.

A chain of circumstantial evidence established a link between Burrows, Tacklyn, the Bermudian criminal fraternity and the remnants of the Black Berets. The political/criminal *unholy alliance* was the operative term used by government officials to describe the Governor's assassins and the phrase was used by police investigators and the Acting Governor Ian Kinnear. Kinnear believed, "….this combination of revolutionary and criminal elements provides both the motive for assassination and the means to achieve it without outside assistance." (1)

Bobby Greene's restaurant was the centre for criminal enterprises on the island including drug importation and distribution and the planning of robberies. One witness at the trials, John Henry Williams, the life-long friend of Larry Tacklyn, said he knew that, "….Bobby Greene (was) behind a lot of (drug-related) stuff. I use Court Street a lot although I don't hang around there. I know for a fact that right now there are plenty of guns sold in Bermuda and I could get one quite easily."

Williams also said he knew there had been a small arsenal of guns imported into Bermuda in early 1971 from Jamaica along with a major shipment of drugs. "I never saw the guns", Williams told police, "but I heard about it when they arrived. They ended up on the Block (Court Street). Later that year I was locked up for receiving stolen property from a (burglary) at Stuart's. I got two years. I was released in May 1973. I was in prison when (the) murders took place. When I came out of prison I started work on my building at home. At that time I only knew what I read in the papers about the murders."(2)

The police knew that Greene was an active receiver of stolen property, dealt in drugs and organised robberies which he incited others to commit. Police also believed that in addition to being a criminal he was known to have extremist political views and made frequent attempts to "indoctrinate the (youth) of the Court Street area with his anti-colonialist ideals". (3)

Former police officer Nick Bolton recalled how Greene's Grill was a focal point of drugs, crime and fringe politics. Bottom line, Bolton said, Greene was in it for the "money and himself." (4) Acting Governor Kinnear described Greene as "a highly dangerous man". (5) In fact, Bobby Greene was so immersed in the drug culture he was smoking crack cocaine up until the time of his death in 2005. According to a source, whose grandmother lived in the same nursing home, "(He) was smoking crack 'til the end – even once or twice in Westmeath Nursing Home." Furthermore, Greene's notes (i.e. memoirs) "mysteriously disappeared after his death" Part of his memoirs included the revelation that he and others (most likely Black Berets) had "attempted to blow up Bermuda's Parliament". (6)

According to former police officers Bobby Greene was not only a powerful and violent drug dealer at the supplier level but he was a 'legend' in Bermuda. Former officers spoke of how, if they ever wanted to catch a drug dealer, they would stake out Greene's Grill. (7)

Bobby Greene was often referred to as 'Mr Big' by local criminals and there was talk amongst police officers of, "political influence above him…we always thought it was the PLP hierarchy (who protected him)". One officer described Greene as a, "thug who would take a knife or gun to anyone. He had his drones around him but he was not averse to doing it himself ……" Former police officers remember how difficult it was to convict Greene. One ex-policeman remembered him arriving at the airport to leave the island and being arrested. "The porters (were) falling all over themselves trying to lend him money so he could continue his journey", Nick Bolton said. (8)

Greene had also been arrested in England during the early 1970s on suspicion of carrying drugs. The case against him collapsed. Following his release he made a speech in which he said that on his return to Bermuda he would bring the country to its knees. According to Bolton, Greene was, "very anti-white and anti-establishment. I dealt with him a couple of times, he was most unpleasant. I gave him a ticket once and he told me quite seriously he would hate me for ever." (9) It was believed Greene financed the Black Berets as a way of distracting police from his lucrative and criminal drugs importation and distribution business. He was known to use Black Beret members to protect his illicit drugs business from competitors and to collect debts. (10)

The criminal fraternity that frequented Greene's Grill would sometimes go target shooting at Fort Hamilton. On one occasion before the murders, Larry Tacklyn, Wayne Jackson and a leading Beret member, the 'third man' involved in the Governor's assassination, took a .32 pistol to the old fort. The gun had been handed to the men by Bobby Greene outside Greene's restaurant and was to have been used in a robbery at Pitts Tobacco Company on Happy Valley Road. "(The Black Beret) fired it first", Jackson said, "then

Tacklyn and myself. The three of us later fired the gun at Harris Bay." (11)

*

In February 1973, approximately five months after the murder of Bermuda's police chief and one month before the assassination of the Governor, a group of criminals met at Greene's Grill to plan a robbery of Masters Ltd, a well-known Bermudian store in the Clarendon Building situated a short distance away.

Anthony Brown Mello, a former reserve police officer, worked at Masters. He was responsible for the distribution of stock from the warehouse to the various departments. He was also responsible for securing bags of money in the vault. The bags were brought up to the vault each day when the various departments closed for business. It was on the third floor of the building, had a large thick metal door with a five figure combination lock and gave access to approximately ten square feet of storage area.

At about 5.10pm on Saturday 24ᵗʰ February 1973 the last bag of cash was brought up from the builders' supply department and handed to Mello. He put it in the vault, closed the door then locked it. After checking the warehouse to see if everything was secure Mello put on his coat, lit a cigarette and left the building. He locked the door and walked across the loading bay which would take him down the steps to the main road. Suddenly, two men later identified as Larry Tacklyn and Dennis Bean, former school friends, rushed Mello and pushed him back into the loading bay. He saw that both men wore masks and both were carrying guns, a ".45" and a ".38". Bean said, "Look, we want the money".

Mello protested, told the robbers he didn't have any money and asked them to leave. After Bean called Mello a 'liar' he hit him with his gun. Mello's spectacles fell off and he dropped to the floor with blood running near his left eye. "Sit down on that fucking box", Bean said. Mello was then forced to take off his jacket and empty his pockets. As Mello's wallet was snatched from his hand he was kicked and told to "open that fucking (warehouse) door". (12)

Mello protested that he could not open the vault as he did not have the lock's combination. Each time he protested the robbers insisted he knew how to open the vault and threatened violence. "Don't fucking well lie to me," Bean said, "I know that you know how to open it." When Mellow repeated his protests they hit him over his eye again and started to kick him. Bean stepped back, put both hands on his gun, cocked it, and then said, "Now is your last chance. I know you know how to open it." (13)

Mello tried to open the vault but it was too dark and the blood in is eye was obscuring his vision. Tacklyn retrieved Mello's glasses and handed them to him and the store manager was given a towel to stem the flow of blood. When he had cleaned his wound he opened the vault. Bean stepped inside and told his partner to, "Keep him covered". They made Mello lie down with his face on the floor. Bean pointed a gun at him and threatened to lock him in the vault. When Mello told them he wouldn't be able to breathe the robbers relented and instead tied him up, dragged him into the toilets and closed the door behind them. Shortly before they made their escape Mello heard one of them say, "Let's get out of here. You got everything?" (14)

Mello waited for a short moment before freeing himself and then he set off the fire alarm as he couldn't reach the telephone booth. As he arrived at the front door to the warehouse he was met by a police officer.

Bean and Tacklyn had made their escape through the rear door, jumped from a wall on to the sidewalk and were seen by taxi driver Albert Cabral who had been driving along Par-La-Ville Road.

Cabral was born in the Azores in 1953 and came to Bermuda in 1968. He lived with his parents near Crawford School in Prospect. Cabral was a mason for a construction firm. On Saturday evening 24th February 1973 Cabral met friends at the Rosebank Theatre. It was something Cabral and his friends did, standing around the car park of the theatre and talking.

At about 6pm that night Cabral got in his car at the Rosebank and told his friends he was going for a drive. He drove his Ford Escort car along Church Street West and then along Par-la-Ville Road as he wanted to turn into Front Street. He saw the Masters sign on his right and as he got level with the yard wall at the back of Masters he saw a black man jump off the top of the wall onto the sidewalk. A second man followed who was 'light-skinned'. (15)

Cabral noticed a green bag on the sidewalk beside them. One of the robbers approached Cabral's car and ordered him to stop. They jumped in the back of the cab and it was then Cabral noticed one of the men held a gun, 6 or 8 inches in total length and silver in colour. The robber pushed the gun into his left side between the two front seats. When the second man jumped into the cab Cabral noticed another gun lying on top of the green bag. One of the men, Cabral said, was wearing "two hats". The "lower one" was light green and "rolled up" to the top of "his forehead". There were two "eye holes" cut in the material.

Cabral was told by the robbers to drive along South Shore Road to a house in Devonshire called 'Gaytor'. He drove along Front Street towards Trimingham Hill then along to South Shore Road, passing the Botanical Gardens. As they passed a bakery in Crow Lane the gunmen ordered Cabral to stop so they could buy Marlboro cigarettes.

When they arrived at the house Cabral was ordered to join them as "they wanted to talk to him". Fearing for his safety, Cabral did as he was ordered. He said the "light-skinned guy", who he later identified as Larry Tacklyn, "moved by the bureau and was emptying the silver gun. I saw bullets falling into his hands". The gunmen told Cabral to write down his name and address then threatened him with death if he ever revealed what he had seen. Cabral gave them a false name. He said the gunmen kept referring to him as "brother". They also hugged him, shook his hand and asked them to "give me some skin". Before he was allowed to leave, Cabral overheard one of the gunmen say, "We have got a surprise for Bobby tonight." Cabral said he "would never forget their faces." (17)

On the 2nd March 1973 Dennis Bean was arrested and charged with the robbery which netted $6,989. He was also charged with possessing a revolver and "unlawfully depriving Mr Cabral of his personal liberty". Bean appeared in magistrate's Court and was remanded in custody until 30th March when he was granted bail. On the 28th May 1973 he pleaded guilty and was sentenced to a total of 12 ½ years in prison. He also admitted a robbery at Adderley's Store, St John's Road in Pembroke on 21st December 1972 when two masked men had entered the store around 9.15pm, pointed a gun at the owner, Stanley Adderley, and told him to place the contents of the till, $466, into a plastic bag. Bean told the judge the robbery was "…a racial act, as Adderley's was a white store in a black community". (18) Police were unable to link Tacklyn to the Adderleys' robbery. Nor did they have sufficient evidence to charge him with the Masters robbery.

*

On the 6th April 1973, less than a month following the Governor's assassination Larry Tacklyn and Buck Burrows targeted a supermarket store in Hamilton owned by business partners, Victor Rego and Mark Doe.

Victor Lima Rego was born in 1919 in the Azores. He came to Bermuda with his family in 1929 where he attended school. Rego spent most of his life as a grocer and in 1962 he became a partner with his brothers, Manuel and August, and they bought the Shopping Centre Supermarket, Victoria Street, Hamilton. 53 year old Rego was married with three children, Carole aged 26, Stephen aged 24 and Howard aged 22. Victor and his wife, Grace, lived in the family home 'Vasalia', on Point Finger Road in Paget. Former Bermudian police officer Territt Cabral was a relative and knew the family well. "Victor Rego was my Mother's cousin," Cabral said, "….We lived 100 yards away. Even though he was a cousin, we called him 'Uncle Victor' (19)

Mark Kenneth Doe was the junior partner in the business. He was a single man aged 21 years and was born in Bermuda on 9th March 1952. From the age of five he attended Mount Saint Agnes School where he stayed until graduating when he was 18. For approximately one year he was employed as an assistant in Boyle's Shoe shop then went to work for the Regos. He became a junior partner in the summer of 1972. Doe lived on South Shore Road. According to former police officer Territt Cabral, who knew Mark, "(He was) a young, bright, hard worker. (Mark) and Victor spent many long days and nights at the store and this proved to be their demise." (20)

On that day, around 9.30am, 65 year old Alpheus Lewis Stubbs was driving his car along Old Military Road, Devonshire towards Dock Hill. As Stubbs approached a derelict mortuary situated on the north side of the road he noticed two men, one standing by the north-east corner of the building and the other in the front doorway. Stubbs had a clear view of both men and saw that one of them, who he later identified as 'Buck' Burrows, was covering a hole in the earth by pushing into it with his foot. The other man, who he later identified as Larry Tacklyn, was holding a large brown paper bag into which he placed a length of blue coloured cord.

Later in the day Stubbs returned to the derelict mortuary and noticed an area of disturbed soil near the north-east corner of the building. He believed that something had been buried there and the men had been retrieving it. (21)

Harold Gaiton was employed as a general hand at the Piggly Wiggly Supermarket, Church Street, Hamilton and was also a member of the Bermuda Regiment. He had known Larry Tacklyn since he was a child and the petty criminal had visited his house in late March/ early April and borrowed Gaiton's Army jacket. He also asked Gaiton about guns and ammunition kept at Warwick Camp, the depot of the Bermuda Regiment.

A week before the Shopping Centre job Gaiton was on Court Street and met Tacklyn. Gaiton had worked with Tacklyn at the Piggly Wiggly some years before and he also knew Dennis Bean well. Tacklyn asked Gaiton to go to Greene's Grill with him and Gaiton agreed. When they entered the premises they were joined by Bobby Green who, Gaiton said, was then unknown to him. Dennis Bean joined the group and they discussed the takings on a Friday at the Piggly Wiggly, how and when it was counted and the general security of the store.

Gaiton told Greene and the others that he believed the manager and one other member of staff usually checked the money in an upstairs office after the store was closed. Tacklyn and the others then proposed to Gaiton that he leave the internal door of the drugs department unlocked whilst they could cut the protecting bars and force the side window of the drugs department. Their plan was to enter the premises when the shop was closed and all the customers and staff had left with the exception of the manager and whoever was with him checking the takings. It was proposed they could then "bump them off" and steal the cash. (22) Gaiton was given one week to gather the information about the Piggly Wiggly. However, Gaiton was alarmed by their criminal plans and did not return to the Court Street area.

When Rego and Doe's store was robbed Gaiton's first thought was of how the 'modus operandi' was identical to that discussed at Greene's Grill.

On the 6th April Renee Elouise McHardy and her sister Gladys Wainwright were the last members of staff to leave the store. Rego and Doe's duty that night was to place the day's takings into bags and then, on their way home, use the bank's night safe to deposit the money.

Judith Jo-Anne Spanswick, a 19 year old clerk who lived in Sayle Road, Smith's Parish, was riding pillion on her boyfriend's bike along Victoria Street at about 7.30pm that night. As they turned up Brunswick Street Judith heard the screech of car tyres behind her. When she looked back she saw three men in a car stop in the parking bay of Purvis Ltd. The men then walked across the street in the direction of the Shopping Center. Judith and her boyfriend, David Rose, a 20 year old clerk drove along Court Street to purchase some cannabis at a selling point near Greene's Grill. When they returned along the same route she saw the same car stop in front of them at the junction of Dundonald Street and Brunswick Street. As they were about to overtake the car it pulled off, turned slightly right and slowed down to enable two men to enter the vehicle. Spanswick later identified one of the men as Larry Tacklyn, who had run up Brunswick Street from the direction of the Shopping Centre. The car took off at high speed.

At approximately 9pm Victor's son Stephen called at the shop to find out why his father had not returned home at his usual time of 8pm. The steel shutters of the Shopping Centre were down and the street door was locked. When he obtained the keys Stephen, along with two friends William Mayo and Robert Feeley, entered and were confronted by a horrific and bloody scene. He discovered his father and Mark Doe lying on the floor near the check-out tills which were situated by the stairs leading to the offices. Rego had been shot twice through the chest and his hands and feet had been bound by blue cord. Doctors later determined that the cause of death was "…massive haemorrhage from tear of aorta…haemopericarium laceration of the right lung" (23) Mark Doe had been shot once through the chest, his hands were tied in front of him with blue cord and his feet were bound by a nylon jacket which had been taken from a nearby cashier's desk. Doctors determined that the cause of death was "a bullet wound through the heart."

(24)

Stephen immediately called the police and officers soon arrived. Detective Constable John Dunleavy was the first officer on the scene and immediately closed off the premises. An ambulance was called and Dr Michael Hall attended to Rego and Doe. He certified that Rego and Does' lives "were extinct". (25)

Police officers examined the scene of the murders and discovered the office had been ransacked. They later learned that $12,332 had been stolen. A side basement window had been forced from the outside and five glass slats had been removed from the louver window. A protecting iron had been sawn through and removed and the mesh screen had been pushed in. Outside the window police found a bundle of 100 $1 notes and $19 in cash.

An outside telephone wire had been cut which was reminiscent of the telephone wire that had been cut before George Duckett's murder. The telephone wire was later examined by Owen Facey of the Scotland Yard's Police Laboratory. He compared the cut wires with a wire cutter which was later found in the possession of 'Buck' Burrows. Facey said his examination of the cutting edges of the wire cutters and "…subsequent comparison with the cut ends of telephone wire revealed insufficient detail to allow a positive identification. However, the detail present was consistent and sufficient to indicate the wire cutters could have been those used to cut the telephone wires at the Shopping Centre Supermarket. No inconsistent detail was present to suggest to the contrary." (26)

On the inside of the store cartons of peas had been stacked parallel to the wall near the window and police believed the marks on the cartons indicated that someone had climbed up or down. Two bullets were found on the floor of the shop near the body of Mark Doe and a third on an ice cream freezer nearby. Microscopic comparison of these bullets with the one recovered from the body of Police Chief George Duckett showed them to have been fired from the same gun – a Schmidt .22 revolver.(27) However, they were not the type of bullets that were recovered from the bodies of Victor Rego and Mark Doe. Both men had been killed by an Ivor Johnson .32 handgun.

Police concluded that at least two guns had been used and therefore two persons were involved. They also concluded that the robbers may have concealed themselves in one of the back rooms or basement where they could have awaited the departure of the staff with the exception of Rego and Doe.

The evening following the murders Dennis Bean, who was on police bail for the Master's Store robbery, was working in Greene's Grill and was approached by Buck Burrows who asked him if he had got his share from "the job at the shopping centre" (28). Bean said he had not received any money. Burrows called over to Bobby Greene, "Didn't I tell you to give Dennis and these guys some of the money? You know what you should do."(29) Greene then handed Bean between $30 and $40. (30)

Bean later told police that on the day of the Shopping Centre murders he had been asked by Bobby Greene to drive Bobby's son, Colin Greene, to the shopping centre. Greene also asked Bean to "have a look around to sort of case it". The two men went inside the shop, looked around near the cash register and the steps to the office and "saw no problem". Bean later reported back to Greene about what he had observed. Bean also stated that he had intended "doing the job himself". (31)

John Henry Williams, a friend of Tacklyn's later asked him if he had been involved in the Shopping Centre murders. According to Williams, Tacklyn replied, "Yes, man. That Portuguese bastard hit me in the guts. That's the reason they both got shot." Tacklyn also told Williams he was "with a mate" but did not say who it was. Tacklyn said they had gotten into the "back of the premises" and the robbery had been a "pushover". (32)

Because police were now investigating five murders, one of which included the assassination of a colonial governor, the London Commissioner of the Metropolitan Police decided to send reinforcements. A team of detectives led by Commander John Morrison, Chief of the Murder Squad, together with Chief Superintendent Gordon Powell, a superintendent from Fingerprints Section, two teams of Scenes of Crime officers and four men from the Flying Squad, arrived in Bermuda April 13th. The team of detectives was the largest ever sent on a case overseas.

Scotland Yard officers soon became frustrated in their efforts to gather information about the murders from members of the public. They believed that the black community should have been more co-operative if Bermuda were to maintain its peaceful reputation.

The frustration detectives felt in gathering information was confirmed by ex-police officer Nick Bolton who said, "Bermuda will always skirt around the issues, it is too small and too closely interconnected, everyone knows everyone or is related to, married to or just had children with everyone else….The closeness in Bermuda prevented convictions in trials causing the formation of special juries. There were some people you could never convict such as Bobby Greene….I remember one trial (rape victim, white tourist) where they had print evidence, they still acquitted. A sad case as the (fingerprint) man shot himself shortly afterwards. Long time expatriates want to stay and they are not going to put themselves at risk making statements and opening cans of worms. I saw a work permit cancelled in my time over public statements someone made, stupid statements but to take his job?… Bermuda is a very close society, where they would rather keep their secrets rather than let the scandals loose, people of influence and money can still ruin a career or a life quite easily." (33)

*

In July 1973 Scotland Yard detectives had a breakthrough when they interviewed Bobby Greene who had been sent to Casemates Prison on an unrelated charge. Greene confessed to having knowledge of the murders of the Governor and Police Chief but tried at all times to avoid incriminating himself. According to a Scotland Yard Report, "On the 2nd July 1973 with the cooperation of the Prisons Department Greene was conveyed to Somerset Police Station where he was interviewed in the presence of Chief Inspector Sheehey and Detective Inspector Haddrell. Greene alleged that Tacklyn had shot the Governor and the dog and Burrows had shot Captain Sayers".

They had escaped via Marsh Folly and Bernard Park, he told the officers. However, in his eagerness to spill the beans Greene wrongly stated that Burrows had committed the Shopping Centre murders on his own and that (Dennis) Bean had shot the Commissioner of Police." (Greene) was unable to give any other detail as to how or why the crimes had been committed nor could he say where the murder weapons could be found", the report stated. (34)

Scotland Yard detectives returned to Casemates Prison on the 21st July 1973 and Commander Morrison, together with Bermudian police officers Chief Inspector Donald and Detective Inspector Swan re-interviewed Greene. Greene reiterated his previous information except he changed his story to say that either Bean *or* Burrows had murdered the police chief. (35)

The detectives concluded that Greene had financed the Black Berets as a way to distract police from his drug enterprises. However, the 'Godfather of Court Street' soon realized that the spate of murders and the subsequent heavy police surveillance was doing irreparable harm to his illegal enterprises. Although he had given Tacklyn and the 'third man' weapons to use to protect his drug business he claimed he had no knowledge they would use the guns to attack Bermuda's politicians.

SATELLITE PHOTO OF BERMUDA. The islands' wonderful climate and beauty attract thousands of visitors each year. It has been a second home over the years to prominent figures like Mark Twain, the Vanderbilt family, Mayor of New York Michael Bloomberg, Ross Perot (who has his own 'Perot Island') and Michael Douglas. (Photo: Wikipedia)

THE COAT OF ARMS OF BERMUDA depicts a red lion holding a shield and a wrecked ship. The red lion is a symbol of England. The wrecked ship is the Sea Venture the flag ship of theVirginia Company. *Quo Fata Ferunt*, means "Whither the Fates Carry (Us)" *(Photo: Wikipedia)*

RICHARD SHARPLES. In April 1972 the British Prime Minister, Ted Heath, a close friend of Sharples, announced he was to be the next Governor of Bermuda to succeed Lord Martonmere. *(Photo: Bermuda Police Magazine)*

GOVERNMENT HOUSE. The governor and his aide de camp Captain Hugh Sayers were shot as they approached the steps leading on to the gardens below the balustrades. *(Photo: Wikipedia)*

SIR RICHARD SHARPLES with his aide de camp Captain Hugh Sayers. Sayers' grandfather, Admiral Sir Ralph Leatham, had been Governor of Bermuda in the 1940s. *(Photo: Bermuda Police Magazine.)*

GOVERNOR SHARPLES AT THE ENTRANCE TO GOVERNMENT HOUSE, yards away from the place where he fell, the victim of assassins' bullets. *(Photo: Public Domain)*

POLICE COMMISSIONER GEORGE DUCKETT. *(Photo: Bermuda Police Magazine.)*

BUCK BURROWS. Burrows was a life long criminal who was manipulated by the Black Beret Cadre into participating in the assassinations of the Police chief and Governor. *(Photo: Public Domain)*

20 YEAR OLD LARRY TACKLYN was Burrows' accomplice in crime. The two men were long-time friends and former cellmates in Casemates Prison before the assassinations.

The funeral service and burial of Sir Richard Sharples and Captain Sayers took place at St Peter's Church. *(Photo: Wikipedia)*

SIR RICHARD SHARPLES' GRAVE
at St Peter's Church in St George's,
Bermuda. Captain Hugh Sayers is
buried alongside the Governor. *(Photo: Public Domain)*

COMMANDER JOHN MORRISON,
who took charge of the murder
investigations. *(Photo: Public Domain)*

**FRONT STREET HAM-
ILTON**, harbour area.
Court Street and the
Bassett Building were
behind Front Street. The
Bassett Building was the
center of operations for
the Black Beret Cadre.
(Photo: Wikipedia)

A ROYAL NAVY STATION, HMS Malabar is in the foreground. In the background stands the UK expatriate Prison Officers quarters situated half a mile from Casemates Prison. *(Photo: Public Domain)*

POLICE OFFICER TERRY CABRAL. Terry Cabral was a serving police officer at the time of the assassinations of the Police Chief and Governor. He provided the author with background material about the criminal fraternity in Bermuda. *(Photo: Terry Cabral)*

CASEMATES PRISON where the Governor's assassins were executed. Both men were buried in the grounds of the prison. *(Photo: Mel Ayton)*

ARREST AND IMPRISONMENT

"I was lying prostrate across (Burrows) – we were both wrestling for this handgun….a guy from Scotland Yard cocked his gun at (Burrows), ready to fire…"
Police Officer Larry Smith

"There is a special section in Casemates for Burrows and Tacklyn…. Buck smashed up (his cell) the other night, he says he is going to 'kill or be killed'……..Tacklyn blew his top….. He kicked Charlie Brown in the chest and punched me in the face. Charlie put the stick on him and I punched his face until I put my thumb out. There was blood everywhere…."
Prison Officer Roy Carden

O N THE 6TH April 1973 a group of young black Bermudians were detained by Bermuda Police and questioned about the murders of Mark Doe and Victor Rego. They were eventually released and on the 9th April 1973 six of them, including Larry Tacklyn, appeared on Bermuda's ZFB television and complained of harassment by the police. The men were standing in a line as they were interviewed as though they were in a police line-up. (1)

On the 13th May Barbara Francis, who had observed two men running away from the direction of Government House on the evening of the Governor's assassination, was taken by police to the ZFB studios to view a video tape of the interview. She identified Larry Tacklyn as one of the men she had seen running away from the direction of the Governor's mansion.(2)

Tacklyn fled the islands by air that same day accompanied by two friends. On arrival at Toronto airport all three men were detained by immigration officers. At the request of the Bermuda Police Force Tacklyn was put on a plane for Bermuda. For some unknown reason, which will be discussed in a later chapter, the two men, both Black Berets, were allowed to remain in Canada. (3)

On the 16th May at Bermuda's Civil Air Terminal after Tacklyn had been returned to the island he was identified by Judith Spanswick and Albert Cabral as he intermingled with passengers and others. (4) Tacklyn was arrested and taken to St George's Police Station where he was interviewed but denied all knowledge of the murders and refused to answer any questions. His behaviour was characterized by arresting officers as akin to a "wild animal" and he repeatedly shouted racial insults to police officers, forecasting their fate when the island eventually embraced "Black Supremacy".

Although their investigation would take longer than expected with regard to Tacklyn's role in the Governor's murder and the murders of Rego and Doe they had by now gathered enough evidence to charge him with the Masters robbery. He appeared in Magistrates Court on 22nd May 1973, was remanded in custody and sent to Casemates Prison. However, he was out on bail between the 5th and the 9th July. On the 22nd July Tacklyn was arraigned before Judge Hector Barcilon at the Supreme Court where he pleaded 'Not Guilty' to participating in the Masters Store robbery. However, a jury found him guilty and sentenced him to a total of 15 and half years in prison, later reduced to 15 years. Dennis Bean had already received his prison sentence for the robbery the previous May.

*

Burrows had become aware of police interest in him when he was questioned and his quarters searched after an incident at police headquarters which occurred some 12 hours after the arrival in Bermuda of the new Governor and Commander-in-Chief, Sir Edwin Leather.

The incident occurred around 2am on the 23rd May 1973 when five shots were fired from a .38 revolver at police headquarters buildings. The headquarters was spread over a large area and a road used by the public ran through the middle. The assailant, riding pillion on the back of a motorbike, fired two bullets which hit an outside wall of the police training school.

It was no coincidence the training school was at the time being used as a 'Murder Incident Room'. Other bullets hit the wall of the Officer's Mess, another passed through a window and the last bullet smashed through a window of an unoccupied room of the single men's quarters. No one was injured. Five badly damaged bullets were recovered and sent to the Forensic Laboratory at Scotland Yard. (5)

On 6th July 1973 Burrows was granted 12 days holiday but when this expired and he failed to return to his job at Police Headquarters he was dismissed for absenteeism. Around this time he stayed with a friend, Dice Wade. He never told Wade what he was fired for. He just told him he did not work at Police Headquarters anymore and he wanted a place to stay. Wade told Burrows he could stay at his house as he was spending more time at his girlfriend's house in Pembroke. Wade called to see Burrows every now and again, " …mainly on Sundays when all the guys were off from work and we used to meet at Noel Brown's place, which is right next door to mine". Burrows was not always there when Wade called, "but if he was we used to talk about gambling, the movies and a lot of stupid things – but never about (criminal) jobs he had done or intended to do". One Sunday Wade arrived at Brown's house and found Burrows cooking cod fish and potatoes, "as (we) did every Sunday". After eating, Wade said Burrows, "… gripped up an airline bag and pulled out a dark coloured handgun . . . I was really surprised because it was the first time I had seen a gun. He gave it to me and said, 'Look what I am got'. I gripped hold of it, played with it a bit and gave it back. He had the barrel open but I did not see any bullets inside so I know it was not loaded."(6)

On the 15th July 1973 at about 2.15am three shots were fired from a shotgun and a revolver at a Police Headquarters rooming block. The bullet went through the window of a room occupied by a resident, police officer PC Garville Murrell, who dropped to the floor and stayed there until the barrage of gunfire subsided. When he got up he discovered holes in his window screen and two bullet fragments on the floor. Murrell was uninjured.

.At 2.15am on 1st August 1973 Burrows and an accomplice wearing dark clothing and capes wrapped around their faces robbed a taxi driver, Ernest Donvell Burgess, at Fort Langton, Devonshire. One of the men shot out the windscreen of the car when Burgess asked what they were doing. The assailants then fired at Burgess hitting him twice, once in the stomach and once in the right leg. One spent bullet was retrieved from the scene of the crime and examined by ballistics experts. It proved to have been fired from the same gun responsible for the murders of Governor Sharples and Captain Sayers.(7)

Police reasoned that as Larry Tacklyn had been sentenced to a long term in prison in July 1973 for the Masters robbery , "…it may be considered safe to assume he left Burrows in possession of the weapon and that the latter person was responsible for placing it in (Wayne Michael) Jackson's apartment".(8)

On the 1st September 1973 at 9.10pm two rounds from a shotgun were fired through a plate glass door of the Piggly Wiggly Plaza supermarket in Shelley Bay before two men entered and robbed the store. Buck Burrows was identified as a suspect. Burrows was accompanied by a man Scotland Yard detectives identified as Wayne Jackson. It was believed the robbers made off with $2,100. When the supermarket was examined by forensics officers a spent shotgun cartridge case was found. Police also discovered that six telephone cables leading to the store had been cut. The cables were later matched to Burrows' wire cutters which were discovered by police when Burrows went missing from his room at Police Headquarters in July. According to a police report, "Wire cutters found in a room formerly occupied by Burrows were identified by Owen Facey of the Metropolitan Police Laboratory as the tool used to sever the telephone wires in the course of an attempted robbery at the Piggly Wiggly Plaza." (9)

On 9th September 1973, the first anniversary of Police Chief George Duckett's death, five shots were fired from a shotgun at 'Bleak House' (now renamed Tyne Bay House). The house was occupied by a teacher, Alan Davies, who remained   unharmed. Police searched the area around the house and discovered slight damage to the exterior of the property and three spent shotgun cartridge shells nearby. The shells were later matched to Burrows' shotgun, a single-barrel, automatic pump action repeater capable of holding six shells. The gun was capable of being fired rapidly, weighed about five or six pounds and was between 30 inches and three feet long.

The shells used were the number 8 type containing numerous small pellets which spray out rapidly to cover a large area. (10)

On 23rd September 1973 at 1.15 in the morning a shotgun was fired at four houses on Fourth Avenue, Cavendish Heights, Devonshire causing damage to property but no one was injured. Later police matched the four cartridge shells found in the area to Burrows' shotgun. (11)

At approximately 2pm on the 25th September Burrows, dressed in a dark three-quarter length rain coat, a black woollen covering his face, robbed the Church Street, Hamilton Branch of the Bank of Bermuda. He was armed with a sawn-off shotgun strapped over his shoulder and a .32 pistol. After the entered the bank he pointed the shotgun at the bank clerks, quickly moving to four different cash draws to take several thousands of dollars from each one. No shots were fired and the hold-up lasted less than two minutes. As Burrows escaped a bank clerk activated the alarm. The first police car arrived within three minutes after the alarm was raised but by then Burrows had ran east along Church Street and took off on a stolen black 50cc motorcycle. The police manhunt was extremely difficult as that afternoon a heavy rainfall spread over the island.

Burrows had gotten away with more than $20,000. However, he was seen and identified and this was the break police had been waiting for. The evidence had been piling up. Detectives found that telephone wires had been cut at the bank. When Chief Superintendent Wright and Inspector Haddrell searched Burrows' room they found a pair of wire cutters which were sent to the Scotland Yard laboratory. There the forensics experts found the cutting blades of the wire cutters compared exactly with the striation marks on the cut ends of the telephone wires at Bleak House, the scene of the police chief's murder and the telephone wires at the Shopping Centre supermarket. (12)

On 28th September 1973 at about 2.00am Burrows struck again. The targets were two houses near Fort Hamilton and a parked car. At 'Sunslope', the home of Graham Lobb and his wife Carol and their two daughters aged 11 and 13, pellets from the shotgun tore through a closed wooden shutter on the living room window. The shots shattered two panes of glass and hit the wall 15 feet away on the far side of the room. Carol was in bed and had been awoken by a loud 'crash' and she walked to the kitchen. Her daughters slept through the incident. The Lobb's Ford Cortina Estate car was also hit and its windscreen was shattered. A further shot was fired at nearby 'Fort House', the home of Raymond Daly. The house was in the same cul-de-sac. It was thought Burrows was trying to shoot a police officer whose residence was nearby. A nearby police patrol heard the shotgun blasts but were unable to make an arrest. It was believed Burrows escaped on foot. (13)

When intelligence reports convinced police of Burrows' whereabouts discussions were held as to the method of capturing the fugitive. One plan involved having a police marksman shoot Burrows out of the tree where he was living.

What the police characterized as 'long and painstaking detective work' finally resulted in pinning Burrows down in one of the few deserted areas of Bermuda. Having information from informants that he was "armed and alert like a wild animal", Police Chief Nobby Clark was anxious to capture Burrows alive and without the use of weapons. However, "some individuals from Government House and the Bermuda Police leadership" were sceptical that Burrows could be arrested without bloodshed. One officer said it was "a dangerously long chance". More drastic measures "were considered" but Clark won the day and his plan was put into effect. (14)

Bermuda police officers, Clive Donald and Larry Smith, were assigned to capture Burrows. Detectives spent three days staking out the fugitive after police intelligence determined his whereabouts, a house in Parson's Road, Pembroke, which was in a black neighborhood. Larry Smith said, "It was decided let's see if we can take this guy by surprise as he was walking or riding out of the driveway." According to Smith there were discussions as to which officers would be in the front line. They agreed Smith would be the arresting officer, possibly because he had an Afro haircut and would blend in well with the locals. Smith had reservations about his role. He later said, "I pondered it for a while because I thought 'I'm going into something with a guy who is armed, and I'm not going to be armed.' (15)

On the night of October 17th 1973 a Police Team consisting of Chief Inspector Clive Donald, Scotland Yard's Basil Haddrell, Detective Sergeants Larry Smith and Neville Darrell and Detective Constable Norrell Hull staked out the vicinity of Parson's Road. When Burrows came into sight the officers believed he was carrying weapons under his coat. Burrows acted 'nervous' and walked a short distance on one side of the road. However, this first attempt to capture Burrows failed when the van that held the policemen was lit up. Senior officers decided to cancel. According to Larry Smith, "Burrows showed up on a cycle (moped), which threw us a bit. As fate would have it, as we were coming in (the driveway) and Burrows was driving out, another car lit us up. Donald slid down an embankment but got up just in time."(16) Police decided to resume their surveillance the next day.

On the evening of October 18th Chief Inspector Donald, together with police officers Haddrell, Smith, Ganson, Jent and Hull again positioned themselves on Parson's Road. Burrows was observed talking to a man on Tribe Road who, unknown to the fugitive, was a police informant As the group of police officers waited they heard the staccato stutter of what sounded like a Thompson machine gun and wondered if Burrows had recruited some armed colleagues to assist him. In fact, it was the noise of the Fire Brigade's transmitter valves exploding. As the explosions ceased, Burrows came into view.

As the fugitive came towards the group of officers hidden by the side of the road Chief Inspector John Donald lunged towards Burrows knocking him off the bike. As both men fell to the ground Officer Smith dived in, spotted the handgun and kicked it out of Burrows' reach. During the struggle the remaining officers struggled to grasp Burrows' weapons. Smith grabbed the .32 calibre pistol. As he reached out he felt something stick in his chest. It was Burrows' pump-action shotgun.

Smith said he had been , "… lying prostrate across him – we were both wrestling for this handgun….a guy from Scotland Yard cocked his gun at (Burrows), ready to fire…I shouted 'no, that's my hand' (and) as I lay across Burrows, I felt an obstruction, or a lump, in the stomach area. It wasn't until we got off him that we realized he had a sawn-off shotgun under his shirt. If it had gone off, he would have blown me (away)." Reacting immediately, Ganson and Haddrell eventually managed to take the fully loaded shotgun from Burrows. The officers eventually overpowered Burrows and he was handcuffed. Smith said Burrows had enough ammunition on him, "probably to go to war". (17)

Later Smith asked Burrows if he would have shot him. Burrows made no reply. "From that question to the time of his sentence", Smith said, "he always had a vacant stare." (18) A retired senior detective in Bermuda who was involved in the murder investigations and who wished to remain anonymous, told the Bermuda Sun, "It is a known fact that when Burrows was arrested he put up a tremendous fight and if he had been able to get to his pistol or sawn-off shotgun which he was carrying, he would have undoubtedly killed both arresting officers." The former Police officer added, "Burrows was charged....with five murders and if he had not been arrested would have undoubtedly committed further serious offences.... (19)

When he was searched Burrows had 13 live shotgun shells in his bag. The shotgun had been used in the Cavendish Heights attack, the Fort Hamilton shootings, the Piggly Wiggly supermarket robbery and the shooting at 'Bleak House' on the first anniversary of the Duckett murder.

Burrows was taken to the police station. He was found to have on his person $2,410 in cash, a packet of marijuana, several marijuana cigarettes, 18 copies of letters, a cartridge pouch and a pistol holster. When Burrows was interviewed by Scotland Yard Chief Superintendent Wright and Bermudian Officers Sheehy and Donald, he confessed to the armed robberies, the residential shooting sprees and possession of firearms.

Police later discovered evidence which revealed that plans had been made 'by others' to get Burrows off the island. According to Burrows' friend Lance Furbert, "Buck was friend of mine...He stayed with me when the police first started to look for him." Furbert received a "call from a mutual friend" one night in 1973, telling him someone was going to be staying in his Southampton house for a couple of nights. Furbert said, "Plans had been made for Buck to get off the island. One of the first arrangements we made is that we would not talk about anything that had to do with the murders or any of his criminal activity. I didn't know and didn't ask and he didn't tell me." (20)

Bermuda's new Governor Sir Edwin Leather described Burrows' arrest as, "a superb piece of police work" which had required "the highest team work, intelligence and quite outstanding courage". Sir Edwin immediately requested that the British government give him permission to award

Detective Chief Inspector Clive Donald and Detective Sergeant Smith the Colonial Police Medal for "conspicuous gallantry".

Prior to Burrows' arrest Bermuda Police received information from an informant that Burrows would make an attempt to kidnap the Premier, Sir Edwin Richards, and "a white child" and hold them as hostages for the release of Dennis Bean and Larry Tacklyn. As a fugitive, Burrows had not only used a tree house to hide out but also a cave on an unpopulated part of the island. When police later searched the cave after his arrest they found two letters in a plastic bottle outlining the terms for the release of the hostages and two Molotov cocktails and a plastic bottle of gasoline The terms stipulated in the letter included the sum of $150,000 and an aircraft to take him to Algeria with his hostages accompanying him. The note was written by 'the hand of COBA'. COBA was one of the aliases used by Burrows. Burrows also described himself as a 'guerrilla'. It is notable that during this period the Black Panther leader Eldridge Cleaver had established a 'government-in-exile' in Algiers. Cleaver's group was supported by North Vietnam. His presence in Algeria had attracted a number of former criminals/revolutionaries, some of whom hijacked airplanes. These hijackings had inspired Burrows. Later, Burrows admitted the Molotov cocktails were to be used for a planned aircraft hijacking. (21)

Burrows was interrogated over the weekend and by Monday October 22nd 1973 he had admitted robbing the Bank of Bermuda's Church Street Branch on September 25th of more than $20,000 and the robbery of the Piggly Wiggly supermarket at Shelley Bay on September 29th. He also confessed to the shotgun shooting incident at Cavendish Heights on September 23rd and the shooting at Fort Hamilton on September 28th. Police believed that with Burrows' prison record, the firearms charges alone were sufficient to put him away for 15 years.

Burrows was remanded to Casemates Prison at the tip of the Western end of the island. He was not unfamiliar with the fortress-like structure which was situated near the Dockyards on Ireland Island. Burrows had spent most of his life in and out of Casemates for petty crimes like handbag snatching and house burglaries.

The Old Royal Marine Barracks became the maximum security

Casemates Prison in 1960. It's positioning commanded wonderful ocean vistas, probably only next to those of Gibb's Hill Lighthouse. HMS Malibu, the permanent British navy base, and the Bermuda Prison Officers' single men's quarters were situated down the road from the prison. Casemates was an imposing and sinister-looking maximum security fortress but the regime inside the prison bore no resemblance to the descriptions the Berets gave their supporters in which they described the regime as 'brutal'. Housing, food and recreation were of a decent standard and educational facilities were provided for prisoners.

The central housing unit of Casemates Prison was divided into two floors and four prison wings. Each wing had approximately 10 cells, some housing between two and four prisoners. The cells were designed along the English system, each cell having 'sprung locks'. The cells were spacious and clean and many inmates were provided with medical care and the opportunity to work, either within the prison or on outside work parties. There were no communal eating arrangements; each prisoner's meal was delivered to his cell. During the evening recreation period the prisoners would meet in the communal areas between the wings.

The regime was far from 'brutal' as Black Berets characterized it. Prisoners were given plenty of opportunity to pursue leisure activities, there were no indiscriminate beatings, no harsh punishments for offences against prison rules and prisoners had every opportunity to make contact with their lawyers and families. A large recreation yard at the rear of the prison was used for basketball and 'association'. The prisoners were allowed exercise each day in a basketball court, showers were provided and the prison had an education programme for prisoners. As the weather was near perfect all year round it was a comfortable environment.

Some inmates were allowed to work outside the prison, tending the houses of prison staff and prison and police administration buildings. During his sentences at Casemates, and before the spate of robberies and murders, Buck Burrows was put on one of these details and worked at police headquarters. Usually the prison party was made up of prisoners classed as non-violent or prisoners who were approaching the end of their sentences. Each day a truck, usually driven by English prison officer Vic Pegly would take prisoners on cleaning duties to police stations around Bermuda and the Prison Officers Mess on Ireland Island.

*

Despite efforts by the government to hire qualified Bermudian officers, the department still needed experienced and professional staff from abroad. The Warden of Prisons, John Bull, and his Deputy were English but the senior officers were mostly black Bermudians, including Divisional Officers S. Butterfield, A. Simons, A. Dixon, A. Dean, I. Dean and D. Bean. As a response, a contingent of 12 UK officers had been recruited for the Bermudian Prison Department in late 1971.

The new group of officers were interviewed at the Bermuda Tourist offices in London and there were a great number of applicants. Most of them had worked in British prisons or the British armed forces. The officers were chosen, in part, because they had no racial prejudice. Later, in 1972 a contingent of approximately four prison officers was recruited from Barbados to afford 'racial balance' to the expatriate force.

The newly recruited British officers flew to Bermuda together aboard a BOAC flight from Heathrow and had great expectations about their roles in Bermuda. When they arrived they were given a debriefing and spent the first week in the officer's training school. They were also briefed about the 'new Bermuda' which was swiftly moving towards full integration. The majority were detailed to work in the maximum security Casemates Prison. A number of officers worked in the Prison Department headquarters in the capital, Hamilton.

The 12 officers from Britain came to be known as the 'Dirty Dozen' after a popular Clint Eastwood movie of the time. The group included two Scotsmen, John Boyle and Robbie Robertson and English officers Roy Carden, Bill Jordan, John Huckstep, Terry Jamieson, Robbie Aldred, Pete Sayer and James Taggart. Each division of prison officers, who controlled the prison at any one time and worked shifts around the clock, was racially integrated.

The 'Dirty Dozen' had a vast amount of experience between them working in British prisons but they were soon disabused of the expectations of an easy life that working in a paradise island would suggest. When the Dirty Dozen started work in the prison, prisoners taunted them with racist remarks and challenged their authority. The verbal abuse from many prisoners, who were obviously mentally unstable, was commonplace.

The Dirty Dozen recalled the time Burrows and Tacklyn spent at Casemates. When Tacklyn first arrived he was frequently questioned by police officers about his alleged involvement in the murders. During one interview he became '...irrational, violent and shouted racial abuse... (he was) uncontrollable and impossible to converse with.' (22) The two assassins had their violent moments as soon as they arrived and one officer remembered how many of the prisoners were sympathetic towards them. Many of the prisoners, if not actually Black Beret members, were certainly supportive of the organization. This tense atmosphere led to violent incidents on many occasions. A typical discipline report from the expatriate officers would include verbal abuse from the more militant prisoners towards the British officers and sometimes incidents of assault.

Although the British officers were professional in their duties they discovered that some black Bermudian officers had been put in a difficult situation when they joined the department. They were frequently asked to guard a member of their extended family. Often inmates would call Bermudian officers by their Christian names or their surnames. Their attitude and relationships towards some of the inmates were therefore judged by British officers as being "too familiar". The English officers, on the other hand, carried out their duties in a fair and friendly manner but did not become too familiar with the inmates. (23)

In 1972 most of the expatriate officers at Casemates were assigned to 'death watch' duties during the period of time Paul Augustus Belvin was placed on death row. In reality, death row was the segregation unit situated near the exercise yard. During the few months Belvin remained there, before the commutation of his death sentence, he was guarded around the clock by two officers and the expatriate officers were the ones usually chosen.

Following their arrests, Tacklyn and Burrows had been placed in the main body of the prison and no efforts had been made to completely isolate them from the other prisoners. Although Tacklyn had been put in a cell on the second floor of the prison and Burrows was given a cell on the ground floor in an effort to separate the two, there was no real effort by prison authorities to make sure they never came into contact with each other. There were many occasions when they had the opportunity to communicate. In this pre-trial period expatriate officers said the two killers made contact with Black Beret members inside the prison on numerous occasions.

From the time he entered Casemates until his trials Burrows remained partially mute, rarely speaking to prison staff or the Scotland Yard detectives who frequently came to the prison to interview him. A black Bermudian senior officer, Ed Dyer, who was 'professional and experienced' and well-liked by the British prison officers, met with the assassins on numerous occasions in the course of his duties and regularly spoke to them. He described Burrows as a "difficult prisoner" who frequently protested in "strange ways". Burrows told Dyer he acted mute as a form of "passive protest". Dyer said he found Burrows to be a man of few words but, "never found him incapable of replying or understanding although there were times he would not speak with me, this was a result of decisions I made against his favour". Dyer discussed the murders with Burrows on one occasion, "immediately after the Duckett Inquest". Burrows said, "…something to the fact that his life was in the hands of the 'Father' and he did not wish any assistance." (24)

Shortly after his arrival at Casemates, Burrows was interviewed by a psychiatrist. Burrows had been referred by the Chief Prison Officer at Casemates Prison because he was protesting violently and disturbing the whole prison population.

Consultant Psychiatrist P.G. Eames reported that Burrows' use of English "would not be out of place in an Institute of Higher Education". The psychiatrist concluded from his conversations with the assassin that he did not have "delusions" nor was there any evidence of, "disorder in the form of thought although his speaking in a normal way, his careful thought out use of language leads to a somewhat pedantic flavour. Except on the most ordinary and nocuous of subjects and sometimes even on such subjects the overwhelming majority of his responses to any discussion are of a part religious type consisting almost exclusively of apparently well-rehearsed assertions of his spirituality….I am therefore most positive of the opinion that his mute state is elective, in other words he is a mute by choice."(25)

British prison officers knew that the security arrangements for Dennis

Bean, Larry Tacklyn and Buck Burrows were inadequate and made their fears known to higher authorities. However, these representations were ignored by senior officers.

In time the prison authorities made arrangements to segregate Burrows and Tacklyn form the main prison population. One of the 'Dirty Dozen', Roy Carden, remembered the time when Burrows and Tacklyn were sent to a special section of the prison which was constructed especially for them. Carden said that on one occasion in the special section, ".... .....Buck smashed up (his cell), he says he is going to 'kill or be killed'."(26)

The authorities were afraid that associates of Burrows and Tacklyn would help them to escape so the prison authorities built two observation towers on the roof of the prison which housed outside patrol officers during the night shift. At certain periods of unrest the prison officers were joined by armed police officers from Somerset Police Station. (27)

Although British expatriate prison officers were subject to racist taunts and violent assaults there was never any kind of retribution. However, officers had to defend themselves, sometimes in brutal ways. When prisoners became violent towards prison staff or other inmates they were restrained physically and taken to the 'punishment cells' or 'segregation unit' which had all the facilities of the normal cell blocks. When a prisoner was taken to this unit he was not subjected to beatings, despite the claims made by former Berets in the Bermudian press.

At first Larry Tacklyn was a difficult prisoner and would verbally abuse prison staff. On more than one occasion during this period he would lash out and strike officers. As time passed, Tacklyn mellowed, according to Carden. "(Tacklyn) is all 'yes sir''no sir', he's no trouble at all." (28) However, Tacklyn soon returned to his old ways. In June 1975 Carden said, "Tacklyn blew his top ..... He kicked (Officer) Charlie Brown in the chest and punched me in the face. Charlie put the stick on him and I punched his face until I put my thumb out. There was blood everywhere...." Carden also noticed that Bean, "...has got religion and is fast going around the bend, or is perhaps trying to work his ticket! *(author's note – feign insanity)*"(29)

This level of violence within the prison was corroborated 30 years later by former Casemates 'Food Officer' Edward Robinson who spoke to the

Bermuda Sun. "Locked away at Casemates for any portion of the day was quite something" he remembered, "It was a different environment; a very close community. The officers had more control over the prisoners than they do at Westgate (the new maximum security prison built in the 1980s) because of the layout of the physical plant – it was much more contained". Robinson said that violence happened and people should not be too surprised. He said that the violence was usually "orchestrated" and the prisoners would set up a slight diversion so they could "perpetrate the crime".... For example, it might be a case of 'You were supposed to do something for me. It didn't go down the way it was supposed to, so you have to be dealt with' – so they deal with you. If the individual makes up their mind to get someone, given the opportunity, they're going to do it." Robinson confirmed that Casemates held "hard-core" criminals who ruled by "fear". "I've been whooped. I got beat up one time." He said, "A fella snatched my truncheon and smacked me on the head and split my ear."(30)

Like prisons everywhere Casemates suffered from the scourge of smuggled drugs, especially marijuana and the authorities had difficulties in stemming the tide. Prison officers on outside patrol would frequently smell the pungent aroma of marijuana cigarettes wafting from the open cell windows but searches rarely produced any contraband. "(Drugs are) a universal problem", Edward Robinson said, "What the prison authorities do is try to minimize or eradicate it and that only comes through proper training for detection. But as long as you have prisons, you will have people trying to get things in and out. They tell me it is quite easy but I have never experienced it personally. Although officers have been labelled over the years – and they have been subjected to random drug searches – no one has been caught. I don't believe for one minute that a colleague of mine would purposefully smuggle drugs in when they know what the consequences will be. It's very difficult to control individuals under any type of substance – their behaviour becomes too erratic. A colleague would not endanger staff in that regard – at least that's what I want to think." (31)

Following the assassinations and the eventual executions of the murderers, most of the expatriate prison officers at Casemates Prison and the police officers stationed at the local Somerset Police Station became disillusioned with their jobs. The process of 'Bermudianization' was having its full effects on the officers and many saw the writing on the wall. In 1974 Police Officer Ken Wright said, "I've been considering leaving Bermuda at the end of this year (1974) as there's no future here for us 'foreigners' in the long run." (32) In 1975 Prison Officer Roy Carden said, "The feelings against ex-pats are even worse now...." (33) By 1979 Carden was completely disillusioned with the prison system; "...time is running out here. I only have two more weeks to do. We leave here 1ˢᵗ October (1979). The prison service is in a hell of a mess now, it is 'Bermudianized'...there are only two (white officers) at Casemates...they are determined to get rid of us....Bermuda is going down hill fast. Every day gangs of kids are attacking police cars etc. It gets more like New York each day."(34)

Most of the 'Dirty Dozen' tried to make sense of the violence that erupted on the island only a few months after they arrived and of how that violence was allowed to escalate. The authorities knew the Black Berets were a credible threat to Bermudian society but they acted too little and too late. There was also a concern amongst the Dirty Dozen that the authorities had never allowed the prison staff to know which prisoners were members of the Black Berets. Had they known, they may have been able to do more in keeping a closer eye when the Berets plotted to murder the island's leading politicians.

After all that went on following the Police Chief's murder the authorities simply refused to recognise that the race issue was the cornerstone of the Duckett murder investigation. Questions remained with the expatriate officers about why the authorities dithered when it came to stemming the power of the Berets and why they didn't have the organization's more militant members kept under 24 hour surveillance. Furthermore, during the Cold War Bermuda was a vital strategic point in the Atlantic Ocean especially when it came to tracking Soviet nuclear submarines. Considering the situation in Bermuda at the time and the definite possibility the island could have been taken over by pro-Castro political groups it seems reasonable to ask why American and British intelligence agencies were not more pro-active.

CONSPIRATORS ON TRIAL

"Movie trials produce truth and so always does Perry Mason, but most adversary proceedings have a way of inhibiting the free flow of information to the jury and to the public it supposedly serves."
Robert Blair Kaiser

"I, Erskine Durrant Burrows, being of sound mind and body, wish to make known the following truths. First of all I wish to make known the truth that I, Erskine Durrant Burrows was the person who shot and killed Mr George Duckett…"

"I Erskine Durrant Burrows, as former commander-in-chief of all anti-colonialist forces in the Island of Bermuda, wish to willingly reveal the part I played in the assassination and murder of the former Governor of Bermuda Mr Richard Sharples and his A.D.C. Captain Hugh Sayers."

THE MURDER WEAPONS
Police determined that Police Commissioner George Duckett had been shot with a .22 revolver, Sir Richard Sharples and Captain Sayers with a .38 revolver and Rego and Doe with a .32 handgun. They set to work looking for the guns and the provenance of each weapon.

The Shopping Centre Murder Weapon

On the 22nd May 1975 Police Constable 470 Trott visited his cousin, Pamela Vernelle Hardtman at her ground floor apartment, Al Roca, North Shore Road, Pembroke. According to Terry Cabral, "…everyone knew the Hardtman family. (They were all) career criminals…Fitzgerald Hardtman was the worst…Pamela Hardtman (was)…very anti police …basically because of the amount of times police searched their residence on…Princess Street." (1)

Pamela Hardtman asked her cousin if he would assist her in removing a tree stump from her garden. She said she had been thinking of using it as an ornament. When PC Trott began to dig a hole he noticed a package wrapped in cellophane. When he felt it he realised he was holding a revolver. He replaced the package in the hole and informed his superior police officer Detective Chief Inspector Donald. Donald collected the package and took it to Police Headquarters in Hamilton. When Donald examined the package he found it contained an Ivor-Johnson .32 five-shot revolver, serial no: 8445 loaded with five rounds of .32 bullets. The package also contained two pages of the *Royal Gazette* dated 16th August 1973. It was clear to police that the weapon's corroded condition meant it had been buried for some considerable time, probably since the date of the newspaper.

When questioned by police Pamela Hardtman denied all knowledge of the gun but she later admitted her husband, 35 year old William Green Hardtman brought the gun to her home in the summer of 1973. She remembered that on the day he brought it home he arrived with one of his friends, 'Porkchop' Mills. Pamela Hardtman told her husband she did not want the gun in her house and asked him to get rid of it. Later her husband told her he had buried it in the garden.

When questioned by police at Somerset Police Station William Hardtman said he had obtained the gun from a friend, Randolph Eugene Mills, who had asked him to 'look after it'. Mills, in turn, told police he had been given the gun by a man he knew as 'Dewey' Durrant who he had met in Court Street about 3 or 4 months after the Shopping Centre murders.

Mills had given the gun to Hardtman because three or four days after purchasing it, he was told by Michael Hollis that the gun had likely been used by 'Buck' Burrows during the Shopping Centre murders.

Police officers interviewed 35 year old Winslow Vancourt Durrant, an inmate at Fox Hill Prison, Nassau, Bahamas. He had been convicted for drug dealing. Durrant told police that in August 1973 he had been asked by Michael Stanley Hollis to sell firearms. Hollis had handed him three handguns one of which was a .32 revolver. Durrant positively identified the

.32 revolver shown to him as the weapon he sold to Randolph Mills.

When police interviewed Michael Hollis they learned how Hollis had been approached by 'Buck' Burrows to sell 4 handguns on his behalf. Three guns, the .38, .32 and .45, passed into the hands of Winslow Durrant.

According to the Scotland Yard Report, "…The two bullets recovered from the body of Mr Rego and the single bullet recovered from the body of Mark Doe were .32 calibre and had been fired from the same weapon, that being a revolver with five right-hand twist rifling, having chambers not accurately aligned with the bore….The remaining three bullets recovered at the scene of the murders were identified as being a .22 long rifle calibre, all having been fired from the same weapon, that being a revolver with 8 right-hand twist rifling." Scotland Yard experts also examined the Schmidt .22 revolver traced to the possession of 'Buck' Burrows and concluded it was the same gun used during the Shopping Centre robbery.

On the 28th May 1975 the Ivor-Johnson .32 revolver was examined by ballistics expert Brian Arnold at the Metropolitan Police Laboratory in London. Arnold tested the gun and concluded the test bullets matched those recovered from the bodies of Victor Rego and Mark Doe, having the same rifling marks and the same degree of misalignment. He concluded the gun was 'in probability' the same gun used to kill Rego and Doe.

In 1975 Wayne Michael Jackson was shown the Ivor-Johnson .32 handgun and told police it was the gun he saw handed to Larry Tacklyn and Ottiwell Simmons Jr by Bobby Greene on Court Street in late 1972 or early 1973. Police concluded that as Tacklyn was out of the colony in late 1972, '…the latter date suggested by Jackson is more likely to be accurate.' Jackson also told police that he went with Tacklyn and Simmons to Fort Hamilton where they all fired the weapon. Jackson recalled how the weapon frequently misfired. His recollections were supported by ballistics evidence which indicated a misalignment between the chamber and the bore of the Ivor Johnson .32 which was recovered by PC Trott.

The Sharples and Sayers Murder Weapon.

Police asked Winslow Durrant about the .38 revolver that came into his possession in August 1973, along with the Ivor Johnson .32 that had been used in the Shopping Centre murders. Durrant said Michael Hollis had asked him to sell the weapon. The day after Hollis had handed over the .38 gun Durrant sold it to one of his friends, 36 year old Frederick Robinson, who lived at Spanish Point. Robinson paid $100 for the weapon and Durrant received a commission from Hollis of $25.

However, a week later Hollis was told by 'Buck' Burrows that the .38 was 'hot' and demanded it be returned to him. Hollis agreed and asked Durrant to return the .38 because it was 'hot' and had been used in a murder. When Durrant asked Robinson to return the gun Robinson refused. Durrant informed Hollis of Robinson's refusal and Hollis decided to take matters into his own hands. Hollis, together with a friend, George Atkins, called at Robinson's home and demanded the return of the gun. Durrant was present and recalled that Hollis and Atkins conferred with Robinson in the bedroom. When they returned to the lounge Hollis was carrying the murder weapon. Robinson had eventually agreed to hand the weapon over for $225. Hollis then handed the gun over to Atkins who returned it to 'Buck' Burrows.

Burrows used the Sharples murder weapon in the commission of a robbery after he had retrieved it from Hollis. At 2.15am on 1st August 1973 Burrows robbed a taxi driver, Ernest Donvell Burgess at Fort Langton, Devonshire. Burgess was shot twice by the .38 handgun. One spent bullet was retrieved from the scene of the crime and was examined by ballistics experts. It proved to have been fired from the same gun responsible for the murders of Governor Sharples and Captain Sayers.

Police reasoned that as Larry Tacklyn had been sentenced to a long term in prison in July 1973 for the Masters robbery , "…it may be considered safe to assume he left Burrows in possession of the weapon and that the latter person was responsible for placing it in (Wayne Michael) Jackson's apartment'.

Scotland Yard detectives did not discover what had happened to the gun that shot Sharples and Sayers until they interviewed Wayne Michael Jackson in 1975. Jackson told police he had a 'keen interest and sound knowledge of firearms' and when he discovered the .38 revolver in the basement apartment at Harris Bay recognised it as the weapon shown to him by Larry Tacklyn on the night of the Governor's murder.

Concerned at being implicated should the weapon be found by police,

Jackson borrowed a boat and dropped the .38 gun, a .22 revolver (not Burrows' 'personal weapon') and some ammunition into the sea at a point south of Castle Point. A search of the area by Police and US Navy divers failed to find the weapons. Investigators discovered that the point where Jackson dropped the guns into the sea was an undulating sea-bed, of a depth of between 80 feet and 240 feet, making the likelihood of locating any small object extremely difficult if not impossible. Police later stated in a report that, "…there can be little doubt (the .38 revolver) was the same revolver dropped into the sea by Wayne Jackson.….Similarly, there can be little doubt this weapon was used to assassinate Sir Richard Sharples and Captain Hugh Sayers. Jackson's description of the right-hand twist rifling in the barrel of the revolver held by Tacklyn on 10th March 1973 is corroborated by ballistic evidence indicating the murder weapon had a rifling consisting of six right-hand twists.…. Support from this assumption may be found in the comment of Burrows to Hollis, when the former indicated the weapon was 'hot' and had been used in murder and by his determination to retrieve same."

The Duckett Murder Weapon

Between 1st June and the 25th September George Atkins accompanied Michael Hollis to Smith's Hill to meet Erskine 'Buck' Burrows. Burrows handed Hollis a .22 Schmidt revolver for Hollis to sell it for him. Burrows made clear that Hollis should return later that evening with the required amount of money.

Atkins told police he went with Hollis to the home of Edgar 'Biscuits' Burrows, a relative of 'Buck' Burrows. Edgar Burrows bought the handgun for $100 and on completion of the sale Atkins and Hollis returned to Smith's Hill where they handed the cash over to Buck Burrows.

Wayne Michael Jackson was shown the Schmidt .22 revolver on 16th July 1975 and immediately identified it as the one in the possession of Burrows on the day of the Governor's assassination. By this identification Burrows was proven to have been in possession of the Duckett murder weapon some three months before he handed it to Michael Hollis and George Atkins to sell on his behalf.

Metropolitan Police ballistics expert Brian Arnold examined the Schmidt

.22 revolver traced to Burrows and recovered by Detective Chief Inspector Clive Donald when he searched a car belonging to Sidney Carl Pitt, a criminal associate of Densworth Darrell and George Atkins. Darrell had asked Atkins to borrow the gun from 'Biscuits' Burrows to use in a robbery.

Arnold's report stated that, "....a ballistic comparison of test bullets fired from (the Schmidt .22 revolver, Burrows' 'personal weapon') with the three .22 bullets recovered from the Shopping Centre Supermarket, revealed all had been fired from the same weapon as being used in the course of the Shopping Centre murders....it will be recalled that the same Schmidt .22 revolver was identified as the murder weapon used to murder Mr George Duckett on 9 September 1972. (2)

*

In 1975 the inquests into the murders were all held under the senior coroner, James R. Astwood. The racially mixed juries quickly came to their verdicts and found that Burrows had murdered Duckett; Burrows, Tacklyn and others had assassinated the Governor and Rego and Doe had been murdered by 'a person or persons unknown', but that Burrows and Tacklyn were accessories after the fact.

Following the results of the Coroner's Inquests Gerald Collett, Attorney General for Bermuda, made application to the Chief Justice Sir John Summerfield requesting that the evidence of witnesses called in the Inquest proceedings be accepted. He also requested that Buck Burrows stand trial on five counts of murder (Duckett, Sharples, Sayers, Rego and Doe) and Larry Tacklyn on four counts of murder (Sharples, Sayers, Rego and Doe) The application for Burrows and Tacklyn to stand trial for 'conspiracy to murder' was initially refused on technical grounds but after an amended application was later submitted, it was accepted.

*

Burrows and Tacklyn were arraigned before Chief Justice Seaton on 4th April 1976 at the Supreme Court in Hamilton on the following indictments:

1. Erskine Durrant Burrows, Larry Winfield Tacklyn and others not before this court, between the 1st day of January 1970 and the 9th July 1973 in Pembroke

Parish and elsewhere within and without these islands conspired together to murder high officials of Her Majesty's Government for Bermuda.

2. Erskine Durrant Burrows on 9th September 1972, in Devonshire Parish murdered George Duckett.

3. Erskine Durrant Burrows, Larry Winfield Tacklyn and others not before the court on 10th day of March, 1973, in Pembroke Parish, murdered Sir Richard Sharples.

4. Erskine Durrant Burrows, Larry Winfield Tacklyn and others not before this court, on 10th day of March 1973, in Pembroke Parish, murdered Captain Hugh Sayers.

5. Erskine Durrant Burrows, Larry Winfield Tacklyn and others not before the court, on 6th day of April 1973, in Pembroke Parish, murdered Victor Rego.

6. Erskine Durrant Burrows, Larry Winfield Tacklyn and others not before the court, on 6th day of April 1973, in Pembroke Parish, murdered Mark Doe.

7. Erskine Durrant Burrows, Larry Winfield Tacklyn and others not before the court, on 6th day of April 1973, in Pembroke Parish, being armed with offensive weapons, namely handguns, robbed Victor Rego and Mark Doe of $12,332 in money.

John Marriage QC was appointed prosecutor, assisted by Alistair Gunning. Burrows declined all offers of legal representation and remained mute. Because he refused to answer the charge a special jury was selected to determine if he was mute by malice or because he was mentally unfit to stand trial. The Court appointed Bermudian barrister Peter Smith as Amicus Curae (friend of the court). After deliberating for two hours the jury decided Burrows was mute by malice. Later during his trial and at Burrows' request, the judge dismissed Smith.

The trials were held during an election year in Bermuda. Although the UBP won there was some belief that the trials impacted on the election process. Barbara Harries Hunter wrote, "One …factor in the decline in popularity of (UBP leader, Jack) Sharpe and the UBP may have been the arrest and start of proceedings against Burrows and Tacklyn. The horror of the crime had worn off, especially for some of the black youth, and we now had two young black men facing trial before a white prosecution for the murders of white men." (3)

The trials finally began in June 1976. Burrows was charged with the murders of Sharples, Sayers and Duckett and Tacklyn was charged with the murders of Sharples and Sayers. Burrows' trial for the murder of the Police Commissioner was heard first. Throughout the trial Burrows remained an elective mute. Sitting quietly, clutching a Bible, he responded to questions with a straightforward denial or simply grinned. During the trial Burrows sent a letter to Marriage who had arrived from the UK especially for the trials. In the letter Burrows confessed to the murder of George Duckett and stated he committed the murder alone.

Burrows had written the letter in Casemates Prison. According to the Scotland Yard files, Officer Eric McLean Davis had told police, "During my normal rounds as officer in charge of Casemates Prison I spoke to Erskine Durrant Burrows at about 10.30am on Sunday 13th June 1976. Burrows told me that he had a letter written to Mr Marriage and I saw that he had something written on rough pieces of paper. I then suggested to him that if he was going to send a letter to Mr Marriage he should write it on official inmate stationary. He readily agreed with my suggestion and thereupon I issued him stationary for this purpose." (4) The letter stated:

"This is for Mr Marriage who is the Crown prosecutor. Sir, I, Erskine Durrant Burrows, being of sound mind and body, wish to make known the following truths. First of all I wish to make known the truth that I, Erskine Durrant Burrows was the person who shot and killed Mr George Duckett at his home at Bleak House on the night as stated by the prosecution. I shot him in the back. I am also the person who fired the other bullets through the kitchen window, one of which wounded his daughter, Marcia Duckett. I wish to state again that what I have written and revealed is all true.

I wish to reveal also that I cut the telephone wires beforehand. I also cut the wire to Mr Duckett's car radio beforehand. I came on foot and left on foot. I was alone, no one else was with me.

I wish to reveal also that I was the person who fired the shotgun pellets at Bleak House a year after the murder had taken place. Finally I wish to state that I have made all these revelations of my own free will. No one has forced or persuaded me into doing so. I also add my signature willingly and of my own free will. Signed, Erskine Durrant Burrows."(5)

Later, during his trial, Burrows sent another letter to Marriage confessing to the murders of Sir Richard Sharples and Captain Hugh Sayers. The letter was also written in Casemates Prison:

Sir,

I Erskine Durrant Burrows, as former commander-in-chief of all anti-colonialist forces in the Island of Bermuda, wish to willingly reveal the part I played in the assassination and murder of the former Governor of Bermuda Mr Richard Sharples and his A.D.C. Captain Hugh Sayers.

I wish to state, not forgetting that killing is wrong and sinful, that it was upon my direct orders and inspired efforts and determination, that what was done was done, performed with a Magnum .357 six-shot handgun.

I was not alone when I went up to Government House to kill the Governor, but I shall never reveal who or how many others were with me.

Now, one week before the Governor and his A.D.C. were killed, I went up to Government House and as I hid in the bushes which were to the right of the front doorway facing north I saw the Governor and his A.D.C and his dog Horsa come out of Government House, walk across the terrace and go down the steps. I was glad to see this because it revealed that the enemy was to be delivered right into my hands.

The following week I again went to Government House, with my chief goal and motive being to kill the Governor, not forgetting the truth that it is wrong and sinful to kill anyone.

Again I reveal that I was not alone. I was dressed in dark clothing. I had two guns on me myself. One was to shoot at the Governor with and the other was to be used on anyone who might have tried to stop me from getting away.

We arrived at Government House at about 10.15 at night and waited just to the right of the steps leading down into the grounds of Government House.

After we had been waiting for some time we saw some people come out of Government House and begin to leave in cars that were parked outside. After they were gone it was suggested to me that maybe the Governor wasn't going to come out and that we should leave. But I insisted that we continue to wait a bit longer.

Now, soon after this short conversation we heard some noise coming from the front of the house. I looked through the opening in the balcony and saw someone walking towards the steps in our direction. Before he reached the steps someone else came out of Government House and hurried to catch up with the first person.

When they both reached the top of the steps they stopped and I heard them quietly conversing together. Now, right about this time the dog came down the steps and came right around to where we were. I was minded to shoot him then although I was not the one who eventually killed the dog, for I realised that to have done so then would have given undue warning to our victims. So I ignored the dog, cocked the gun I had in my right hand, aimed, and began to fire at the two persons who were standing at the top of the steps.

They both fell to the ground right away. One of them didn't make any sound at all but I heard a groaning sound coming from the other person. I commenced shooting at them from between the openings that were between the wall that was on the right hand side of the steps facing north.

The dog was shot immediately after this as it was blocking our path of escape.

It is sufficient for me to say that we came on foot and left on foot.

But the falling thunder brought great fear and tears to the eyes of many of the people. Thus it shall forever be for all those who do not heed the warning.

The motive for killing the Governor (his A.D.C was not our objective, he was shot only because he happened to be with the Governor at the time) was to seek to make the people, black people in particular, become aware of the evilness and wickedness of the colonialist system in this island of Bermuda. One of the major evil strategies being to seek and encourage the black people to hate and fight each other, while those who are putting this evil strategy into effect laugh and pat themselves on their backs saying, yeah look, we have got them, we have got them conquered.

This ought not to be but it clearly can be seen that there is no strong backbone in the people so that they may stand strong and united against this evil way.

Secondly the motive was to show that these colonialists were just ordinary people like ourselves who eat, sleep and die just like anybody else and that we need not stand in fear and awe of them.

Finally the motive was to reveal black people to themselves. This refers to the revealed reactions of many black people during the Governor's funeral, when black people were seen to be standing with tears in their eyes crying for a man who when he was alive didn't care if they lived or died and here they were crying for a white Governor and yet when many of their own people pass away there is sometimes hardly a tear shed for them. This shows clearly the evil effects that the colonialist propaganda has had over the long years they have ruled over this little island.

And my beloved brothers and sisters this ought not to be because there is a supreme authority we can all appeal to and pray to free us from suppression, sin and any evil domination we might be under.

I give thanks that I have been given eternal freedom from sin and death through the love and mercy and forgiveness of Jesus Christ my Lord and master and Saviour forever. I can even proclaim with humbleness and sincereness and in truth that what Jesus Christ has done for me he stands ready and anxious to do for you.

Jesus Christ stands prepared to forgive any of you of all your sins if you would only repent to him of all your sins and believe in him and accept him as your own personal saviour. Amen. (6)

Both of these letters were eventually admitted as evidence. The revelations led to Burrows and Tacklyn being tried separately.

Former Bermudian police officer, Neville Darrell, in his book *Acel d'Ama*, poured scorn on the letters and intimated that they may have been written under duress. Darrell described them as "the so-called letters of confession" and wondered if the well-articulated documents were in fact not written by Burrows at all. "With Buck's mentality" Darrell wrote, "what would his personal motive have been to murder the Governor and Police Commissioner?"(7) However, three black Bermudian prison officers, Principal Officer Dennis Bernard Bean, Divisional Officer Crockwell and Chief Officer Pringle witnessed Burrows writing the letters and their integrity has never been questioned.

Principal Officer Bean, in a sworn statement, said he had been acting as officer in charge of Casemates Prison on Sunday 27th June 1976, when Divisional Officer Crockwell informed him that Burrows had requested an envelope. Bean, accompanied by Crockwell, asked Burrows if he would like writing paper and an envelope and Burrows said he would take the envelope but turned down the offer of writing paper. Bean and Crockwell returned later with Chief Officer Pringle and as they approached his cell they saw him praying. After waiting until Burrows finished his prayers the officers the envelope and Burrows placed his letter inside and sealed it, placing his signature on the back of the envelope.(8).

In his confession to the murders of Governor Sharples and Captain Sayers

Burrows said both men and the dog were shot by a .357 magnum. However, the weapon believed to have been used in the murders was described as a .38 revolver. The discrepancy was cleared up by Scotland Yard Senior Scientific Officer Brian Arnold, who said the .38 and .357 revolvers were virtually identical and each could fire .38 ammunition. However, a .38 revolver could not fire .357 ammunition and as the spent rounds recovered from Captain Sayers and Government House grounds were of .38 special ammunition, it became clear that Burrows and the witnesses were referring to the same weapon.

Burrows declined to give evidence or to call witnesses. However, he did reveal his political ideology by making disparaging remarks about the British Royal Family and by raising a Black Power clenched-fist salute. At the conclusion of the trial on 6th July 1976 the jury returned a majority verdict of 9 to 3, after only three hours deliberation. Burrows was found guilty of the murders of George Duckett, Governor Sharples and Captain Sayers and the judge sentenced him to death. Burrows did not appeal which left the courts free to try Tacklyn for the murders of Sir Richard Sharples and Captain Hugh Sayers. As he was sentenced Burrows shouted slogans supporting the Black Beret Cadre and, in broken Spanish, revolutionary Cuba.

On the 7th July 1976 Tacklyn was brought from Casemates Prison where he was serving a 15 year sentence for the Masters robbery, and arraigned before Mr Justice Barcilon, a former Bermuda Solicitor General, for the murders of the Governor and Captain Sayers. The trial commenced on 12th July. Tacklyn was represented by black Jamaican lawyer, Ian Ramsay, assisted by PLP leader Lois Browne-Evans. Tacklyn declined to give evidence on his own behalf or to call witnesses. Whenever he appeared in court, Tacklyn carried a copy of the Koran.

Bermuda police officer Deallie, who was on duty at Government House on the night of the murders, was the first to be called and he related the circumstances surrounding the shooting. The Governor had been shot twice, he said, and Captain Sayers once, both victims of .38 bullets.

There were two principal prosecution witnesses at Tacklyn's trial. The first 'star' witness was Tacklyn's friend, Wayne Michael Jackson. He was described as Tacklyn's 'landlord' and a notorious professional criminal. The second was

John Henry Williams, a man whom Scotland Yard detectives described as "a man of dreadful character". (9) The court was told that both Jackson and Williams had strong ties to Bermuda's criminal fraternity.

Jackson testified he had heard Burrows and Tacklyn planning the Governor's murder. He said Tacklyn had told him how he had "taken care of" the Governor and his ADC and that he was the person who fired the shots that killed them. Jackson said Burrows had shot the dog. During his testimony he also confessed to offering to destroy Tacklyn's handgun and clothing and stated he had given police a bullet which he said came from Tacklyn's room. Jackson also admitted disposing of the gun by taking a boat out to sea and throwing it overboard.

The second principal witness against Tacklyn, John Henry Williams, was described as a single man, physically strong who was held in fear by the island's criminal underworld. Scotland Yard detectives said the information he supplied them as, "…(information) which could only have been known to one of the assassins or investigators…." (10) They said, "Whilst (Williams) may be considered to be somewhat of a 'mercenary' and a person not to be trusted, his information in relation to a conversation with Tacklyn was capable of corroboration from known facts and played a major role in the prosecution cases in the Government House and Shopping Center murders".

Williams told the court that Tacklyn had admitted to him that he had killed Governor Sharples and Captain Sayers and that Tacklyn also told him the escape route from Government House was via the railway track, across Marsh Folly Road to his home in Deepdale. This was the same route taken by the two men seen by Barbara Francis immediately after the murders. The method described by Williams to police was practically identical to what police had known about the circumstances of the murders. As these details were never disclosed to the press the jury was asked to accept Williams' account as "truthful". (11)

During the trial's proceedings several witnesses had been given immunity from prosecution for firearms offences and no defense witness was called to rebut the testimony of the prosecution witnesses. The only witness the defense called was Tacklyn who appeared in the dock and said, "My name is Larry Tacklyn. I am a Bermudian. Jackson and Williams are telling lies against me.

I never had such conversations with them. I am innocent of these charges, sir."(12)

During the course of Tacklyn's trial it became evident that Burrows' confession and the testimonies of Jackson and Williams were contradictory. Was Burrows trying to save Tacklyn's life? Was Tacklyn's confession to Jackson and Williams mere boasting? The Judge tried to place some rational explanation for the contradictions when he said, "…there is little to be said in (the two witnesses') favour. Certainly Williams has a record as long as your arm. As far as Jackson is concerned, you might put him in the lower class of criminal. But his record also includes dishonesty. You want to look at their evidence very much more closely than you would that of a bishop." The Judge described Williams as an "unsavoury character" who had convictions for "dishonesty, violence and drug offences".(13)

The Judge instructed the jury that they must be satisfied that Tacklyn had been present at Government House "aiding and abetting" no matter who pulled the trigger. After reading the full transcript of Jackson's testimony he told the jury, "It must be apparent to you there were a large number of discrepancies. As I told you earlier, it will be for you to analyse them, and decide whether they give his story the stamp of a lie, or whether they could be accounted for on the grounds of an honest mistake. There is no doubt he is a bad hat. But it is wrong to say that just because he has committed crimes he should not be believed for the rest of his life."(14)

The jury were also asked to consider what sort of person Tacklyn would associate with. They were also asked to consider what motive Jackson had in implicating Tacklyn. The judge asked the jury to consider that Jackson was an "accessory after the fact" and thus had a motive in giving police this evidence. Jackson may have thought that in exchange for his evidence the firearms charges against him would be dropped. The Judge also told the jury that there was no evidence that Williams was a "professional witness" meaning Williams had no real motive in implicating Tacklyn.

The jury deliberated for three and a half hours and found Tacklyn "not guilty" of the murders of Sir Richard Sharples and Captain Hugh Sayers. The courtroom burst into applause. Tacklyn raised his clenched fist and said, "Thank you Allah…thank you, people of Bermuda, for helping me."(15)

Writer Barbara Harries Hunter believes it was "hardly surprising" the jury gave majority verdicts of 'not guilty' on both murders. "One of the jurors", she wrote, "a black woman, has told me that most of the panel felt that Tacklyn was involved, but the majority did not feel that the evidence was strong enough".(16)

Tacklyn had little opportunity to rejoice. The Attorney General now started proceedings to try Tacklyn for the Shopping Center murders. It was decided that the conspiracy to murder indictment would not be acted upon until the conclusion of the Shopping Center trial. Tacklyn was returned to Casemates Prison to serve the remaining part of his 15 year sentence for the Masters robbery.

On 5th October 1976 a special jury was empanelled at the Supreme Court before the Chief Justice, Sir John Summerfield. It was felt that a jury selected in the usual manner would be too prejudiced in favour of the defendants. The ethnic composition of the jury was nine blacks and three whites, 11 men and 1 woman. The prosecutor was Brian Leary, Senior Treasury Counsel and he was assisted by Alistair Gunning. Tacklyn was represented by Lois Browne-Evans assisted by Shirley Simmons. Burrows again declined all offers of legal representation and remained mute throughout the Shopping Center Murder trial.

On the advice of his lawyers Tacklyn refused to plead to the indictment and, as Burrows remained mute, the Chief Justice entered pleas of 'not guilty' on their behalf. During the trial Burrows confession in respect of the murder of George Duckett was admitted into evidence. Tacklyn had not been charged with the murder of Duckett as police knew he had not been in Bermuda when the crime was committed.

The relevance of Burrows' confession was summarized during the trial:

*As the murder weapon used to murder George Duckett, a Schmidt .22, was identified as the same used in the Shopping Center murders, Burrows was proved to be in possession of the weapon several months before the murders of Rego and Doe and some two months after their deaths.

*The wire cutters traced to Burrows were identified as those used to cut the telephone wires at the Piggly Wiggly Plaza, Shelley Bay on 1st September 1973 during an attempted robbery. The shotgun used in that offence was identified as belonging to Burrows when he was arrested in October 1973.

*As the shotgun was also used at Bleak House on the anniversary of George Duckett's murder there was a probability of the same wire cutters being used in both the Duckett murder and the Shopping Center murders.(17)

*

Victor Rego's brother was called as a witness and identified Burrows as a regular customer of the store. Judith Spanswick identified Tacklyn as one of the men she saw leaving the supermarket on the evening of the murders. She also said a third man was driving them. Her testimony was judged to be of the utmost importance. Albert Cabral was also called to give testimony. He recounted how he had been stopped at gunpoint on the day of the Masters robbery. The gun was identified as resembling the one used in the Shopping Centre murders. Cabral identified Tacklyn as one of the men. Jackson and Williams also testified at this trial. Jackson said he had visited Fort Hamilton and Harris Bay with Tacklyn "and others" when one of the guns used in the Shopping Centre murders was fired. Williams said Tacklyn told him he would not have shot Rego and Doe if, "...the lousy Portuguese bastard hadn't hit him in the guts.'(18)

Another witness was 65 year old Alpheus Lewis Stubbs. He testified that Burrows and Tacklyn handled rope similar to that used in the murders of Rego and Doe on the morning before the robbery. Stubbs had been unable to relate his story to police at the time of the murders because of a miscommunication and his information was not brought to light for three years.

The court heard how, the day after the Shopping Centre murders, Stubbs endeavoured to inform police of what he had seen when he drove his car along Old Military Road on the morning of the murders. Stubbs had noticed two men in a derelict mortuary who had been covering a hole in the ground and the other placing a length of blue cord into a large brown paper bag. Stubbs telephoned police headquarters and requested to speak to the Police Commissioner but was told he was not available. Stubbs declined to give his name to the officer he spoke to.

Through an article in the *Royal Gazette*, dated 16th April 1973, police had attempted to secure the public's assistance in identifying the blue cord rope. Stubbs read the article and again telephoned police this time requesting to speak to the officers in charge of the investigation. When Stubbs was told that the officers were engaged elsewhere he said police should place a message in the advertisement column of the *Royal Gazette* if they wished to speak to him. Stubbs did not relate why he wished to speak with the officers. Unfortunately, the murder squad officers were not told of Stubbs' phone call and the willing witness gave up hope that his story would be heard.

However, Stubbs decided to attend the trials as a spectator. In court he recognised Larry Tacklyn as the man he saw placing the blue rope in a paper bag on the morning of the murder. He had previously recognised Burrows from a newspaper photograph published in September of 1973 as the other person he saw that day. Stubbs decided to approach Detective Chief Inspector Clive Donald and complained about how he had been ignored by police at the time of the murders. Stubbs also informed Donald about what he had observed on the morning of the murders and gave a statement to that effect. Stubbs was then enlisted as a witness in the trial. His story was corroborated by Burrows who admitted using the derelict mortuary on Old Military Road to bury the proceeds of the robbery. Burrows identified as his property a Pan American airlines bag containing a garden trowel found there by police.(19)

The Scotland Yard files described Stubbs as a "man of good character and a most credible witness". The report went on to say that Stubbs' evidence "…at the eleventh hour played an important part in bringing the investigations into the Shopping Center murders to a successful conclusion."(20)

The trials concluded on the 18th November 1976 when the jury, after deliberating for 6 hours and 39 minutes, returned majority verdicts of 'guilty' on all counts against both Burrows and Tacklyn. The Chief Justice sentenced them to death. When asked by Chief Justice Sir John Summerfield whether they had anything to say, Tacklyn replied, "God knows the truth. The jury has made a mistake." Burrows remained silent.

As Barbara Harries Hunter wrote, "If political motives can be a reason for murder there was no such excuse here…..The Shopping Center murders were not an isolated incident, linked only to the political murders. They had in fact been preceded by a series of six armed robberies including those at the Piggly

Wiggly and Masters, in three of which shots had actually been fired. I recall the feeling of unease in Bermuda at these revelations of a much more vicious underworld than most of us had supposed existed. But, as many of us did not realize it at the time, Bermuda was fast moving into the years of the drug trade, with all its evils and with the 'get rich quick' opportunities it presented to those young people who felt left out of the tremendous prosperity they saw all around."(21)

During the course of the trials members and supporters of the Black Beret Cadre attempted to intimidate prosecution witnesses, with the exception of John Henry Williams, a man who was held in fear by the criminal underworld.

The 'star' witness at the Shopping Center trial was Judy Spanswick who was later commended by the judge for her courage. On 25th October 1976, during a lunch break in the course of the trial, and following her initial testimony, Spanswick had been verbally abused by Beret associate Malcolm Marsden Dears, a 26 year old man who appeared at the trial to give his support to the defendants. He was seated in the public gallery and, as Spanswick walked from the witness box and passed him, Dears said, "You fucking witch!" Spanswick was visibly shaken and told officials of the court. After hearing evidence in respect of the incident the Chief Justice found Dears in contempt of the court and sentenced him to two month's imprisonment.(22)

Spanswick was the first member of the public to offer relevant information to the Bermuda Police and Scotland Yard detectives. The incident during the trial was not the only time Spanswick had been subjected to intimidation and threats by Black Beret supporters. There had been constant abuse and her baby was even threatened by criminal associates of Tacklyn and Burrows. The abuse had a terrible psychological effect on Spanswick. She had endured 18 months of fear and eventually suffered a nervous breakdown and was admitted into hospital. (23)

Spanswick was not the only important witness to suffer for their testimonies. Police officer Sylvan Musson was a former Black Beret who had told police officers of four 'reconnoitres' of Government House. On each occasion, Musson said, he had been under the instruction of a senior Beret (the third man'). He said plans had been drawn of the buildings and notes made of important points and weaknesses of the properties. On the

1st June 1976, the day after his statement was handed to the defence lawyers in the trials of Burrows and Tacklyn, he was threatened in the street by a senior Beret, Jerome Edward Delano Perinchief. Perinchief was later charged with attempting to obstruct the course of justice. However, after a meeting between the Attorney General and the Solicitor General the charges were dropped. (24)

On the 10th July 1976, a day before he was due to be called to give evidence in Tacklyn's trial for the murder of the Governor and Captain Sayers, Wayne Jackson was subjected to an abortive drugs importation 'frame-up' by supporters of Burrows, Tacklyn and the Black Berets. On the 9th July 1976 30 year old Neville Spencer had attempted to collect a package at the Civil Air Terminal which had arrived on a British Airways flight from Jamaica. The package was addressed to 'Mr Earl Spencer' and was held by HM Customs awaiting collection. A Customs Officer recognised Spencer, and as the names differed, he was told he could not collect it.

Spencer asked Jackson to collect the package on his behalf. Jackson agreed after having been assured by Spencer that it did not contain anything illegal. At the Civil Air Terminal Jackson handed the collection document to Customs and Police officers and said he knew nothing about the package's contents; he was simply collecting it on behalf of a friend. The carton was opened in his presence and was found to be holding two and a half pounds of cannabis.

When police interviewed Spencer he denied any knowledge of the package or ever asking Jackson to collect it on his behalf. Spencer was found to be lying when customs officers told police that Spencer had tried to collect the carton the previous day. The evidence was examined by the Attorney General who decided that Jackson should not stand trial but instead appear as a witness against Spencer. Spencer was charged with the "importation of dangerous drugs". According to the Scotland Yard files, "despite the lack of proof the aforementioned incident would appear to have been a deliberate attempt…to discredit Jackson, a vital witness, prior to his testimony against Tacklyn."(25)

The Black Berets and their supporters made further attempts to "interfere with the course of justice" when they persuaded 17 year old Sharon Laverne Beach, an inmate at the women's prison, to "confess" that she and five other youths were responsible for the Shopping Center murders. On June 30th 1976 she made her 'confession'. Following an investigation of Beach's claims the 'confession' was found to be bogus. On the 7th July 1976 Beach admitted making a false statement during her second interview.(26)

Beach's 'confession' was made during the course of the trials and police believed it was not coincidental. Police believed she had been "open to considerable influence from members of the criminal fraternity". Many of the details of the Shopping Center murders she had related in her statement had been, "accurate and it is possible she had been instructed by persons unknown to make this false allegation. It appears too coincidental that her allegation should be made during the course of the trials around the same time as other attempts were made to interfere with the course of justice."(27)

The judge commended Wayne Michael Jackson for his "considerable courage" in giving evidence against Tacklyn and Burrows on five occasions over a period of 18 months. During this time Jackson and his family were subjected to continual fear, abuse, threats and intimidation.(28) He also commended Judith Spanswick for her 'courage and public spirit'.(29)

It was noted by the court that many of the prosecution witnesses incriminated themselves when admitting illegal possession of firearms but, "in the interests of justice", the Attorney General decided not to charge any of these individuals. (30) Count one of the indictments – conspiracy to murder - was held in abeyance but the count would, "remain in the court files to be resurrected should any other person prove to be concerned in the conspiracy come to light or return to Bermuda".(31)

The 'conspiracy to murder' count remained open because the police were convinced that others had participated in "the conspiracy". The decision to leave count one open was, "in the best interest of justice particularly in view of the statement of Police Constable Sylvan Musson, a former member of the Black Beret Cadre." The report then noted that a leading member of the Berets, the 'third man' who Scotland Yard detectives were convinced had not only accompanied Musson on reconnaissance missions to Government House but also participated in the Governor's assassination, "left Bermuda on 7th August 1973 and has not since returned. He is currently believed to be residing in Canada or the USA."(32)

WHAT REALLY HAPPENED?

"Truth will come to light; murder cannot be hid long."
William Shakespeare.

"Catholics and Communists have committed great crimes, but at least they have not stood aside, like an established society, and been indifferent. I would rather have blood on my hands than water like Pilate."
Graham Greene 'The Comedians'.

"What I am convinced happened is that, at that moment of time, and probably quite accidentally, the small ring of Black Beret Cadre leaders still meeting together.…suddenly realised that fate had put a new weapon in their hands in the form of these easily impressed and not very bright young criminals. They played on them, influenced them, almost certainly inspired some of the violent acts that followed and very probably planned them." **Acting Governor Ian Kinnear**

THE WHOLE TRUTH about the Bermuda murders remained elusive during the trials. Burrows elected to remain mute except to say he was not alone when he murdered the Governor and that he was assisted by, "others I will never name." Tacklyn pleaded "not guilty" to all the murders therefore his every effort centered on the premise he knew nothing about the murders.

Trials are never designed to deliver justice - and truth is not the main concern of the judicial process. Right and wrong is not under the purview of the law – only legal and illegal. Frequently, truth is lost in the gladiatorial excesses of the system. Furthermore, trials are based on the principal that it is better to see a hundred guilty men go free than one innocent man be convicted. Trials can also ignore relevant truths if the evidence appears to be 'tainted' or characterized by the defense or prosecution as 'hearsay'. The law of search and seizure, for example, is ambiguous, incoherent, and inconsistent. And the exclusionary rule is an issue that calls into question the basic tenets of the judicial process and the capacity of the legal process to deal with crime. There are also questions about one of the underlying assumptions of the process - that most jury verdicts reflect the facts and the truth. Critics of the jury system point to the fact-finding ability of the jury. They note that jurors have the power of nullification and are asked to decide cases based primarily on their own common sense notions of plausibility and credibility, on their own 'hunches' and 'feelings' about what exactly happened. This is not fact-finding, critics assert; it is virtual justice.(1)

The truth about the assassinations remained hidden for thirty years because there was a collision between two methods of discovering the truth. First there is the advocacy method, used in trials. The advocacy method, or legal system, chooses one side of an issue and builds a case by presenting those facts which support that issue alone. The prosecuting lawyers 'prove' that the suspect committed the murder, and the defense lawyer 'proves' that doubts about guilt are so strong a guilty verdict is unsafe. Each side does not want anything to interfere with their position. In fact, they may work to prevent any further evidence from disrupting their carefully built case. The second method is an investigative enquiry which is used in Government–initiated 'Commissions of Enquiry' if criminal acts are deemed to be of regional or national importance. Had the latter system been employed it is unlikely the truths about the assassinations would have been hidden for so long.

A trial should be about truth but too often it is about playing and winning. (The arguments for the exclusion of evidence, for example, are extremely weak). The prevailing theory is that with both sides arguing their points the truth will eventually emerge. However, as government prosecutors were unable or unwilling to charge others in the conspiracy to assassinate the Governor, the whole truth never emerged. The Bermudian Government were unwilling to take measures to secure a deal with Tacklyn who could have given up the names of others in the conspiracy. It was unlikely from the start that Burrows would ever talk. He had made that commitment from the beginning, vowing to withhold the names of the other conspirators. However, no effort had been made to offer them a way out of the death sentences that were eventually handed down.

The 'Commission of Enquiry' method is designed to avoid the traps inherent in the advocacy system and can reach "truths" by laying out all the bits of relevant evidence and debate them in a collegial rather than adversarial manner. The aim of a Commission is to remain neutral thereby ensuring the investigation identifies the one interpretation that best fits the evidence and thus the whole truth emerges.

Information about crimes can also remain hidden if pertinent facts are judged to be outside the limits of evidence and testimony set by the court. James Earl Ray, for example, was convicted of the assassination of Dr Martin Luther King Jr yet the true circumstances surrounding the assassin's motives and possible assistance in committing the crime were not revealed at the time of his trial. Trials, therefore, can only provide 'partial truth'. Furthermore, trials alone cannot provide researchers with the complete facts which are prerequisites in establishing historical truths.

*

Based on the Scotland Yard and Foreign Office files a compelling and convincing chronicle of events can be established, although not with absolute precision. What follows is a *presumed* train of events, based on the Bermuda Police and Scotland Yard files, that led to the assassinations of Police Commissioner George Duckett, Bermuda's Governor Sir Richard Sharples and his aide de camp Captain Hugh Sayers, and the murders of the two supermarket owners, Victor Rego and Mark Doe.

The report of the Commission of Enquiry into the 1968 riots, headed by Sir Hugh Wooding, former Chief Justice of Trinidad, stressed the urgent need for speedy racial integration if disorder was to be averted. Progressive legislation had been implemented but for some black Bermudians the pace had been far too slow. The heart of the problem was that the island's 30,000 blacks were in the process of challenging the established leaders of the white minority. In other Caribbean nations and colonies the confrontation had been sharper and the pace of reform quicker. The Bahamas, the next Caribbean island to Bermuda lying in the south-west Atlantic, had already voted for independence and taken steps towards sovereignty without the discord seen in Bermuda. In Bermuda prosperity and enlightened conservatism served to blunt the emerging Black Nationalism. The frustration in the slow gains made by the PLP created a vacuum in which Bermuda's black militants took advantage.

For the half-million tourists who went to Bermuda in the early seventies the island was an expensive paradise of narrow winding roads and beautiful stretches of unspoilt beaches. With its old- fashioned charm and cosy suburban British appeal Bermuda appeared to have been transplanted in time and place – a tranquil English village in the middle of the Atlantic Ocean. However, the atmosphere was deceptive and hid the underlying tensions on the island which were quite obvious to the expatriate police and prison officers who saw Bermuda's 'dark side'.

However, there were some enlightened voices in government who knew the precarious situation the island was in but they also believed they had a responsibility to promote the impression that Bermuda was a civilized and stable country; the island was in danger of facing economic disaster because of the growing political violence and the effects on tourism were considerations that could not be ignored.

From the beginning Acting Governor Kinnear knew that black militants were behind the murders of the Police Chief and the Governor. He believed that the Black Beret Cadre, although overtly participating in the political process, wanted to secretly overthrow the 'system' and destroy the colonial government which stood in its way. Kinnear also believed that the Berets acted out of a sense of frustration at its failures to achieve change and its lack of support amongst the majority of black Bermudians. He knew that the Berets could only achieve their objectives by working outside the system and that their only method in accomplishing those objectives was through violent methods.

The Berets had fallen into a kind of apathetic state by late 1972 but a small group within the organization was still fanatical in its approach to ridding the island of colonial rule. A leading member of the Black Berets (the 'third man') yearned to re-invigorate and lead the organisation. If he succeeded in organizing some kind of shocking event as a prelude to the 'revolution' this would have indeed made him the 'top dog'. According to a Bermuda Intelligence Committee Report, "(he) has been restless recently, has changed his job a number of times and has caused his father a good deal of worry. His interest in re-establishing the Cadre may be an outlet for his leadership ambitions in the absence of (Beret leader) Bassett from the island."(2)

In 1972 the zealots within the Black Berets began to compile a 'hit-list' of the Bermuda 'pigs' they intended to 'execute'. The list bore the names of nine senior government officials to be removed, including the Commissioner of Police and the Governor and Commander-in-Chief. Whilst Rego and Doe were not included on the "Death List" they were murdered in the course of a "Fund Raising Mission" for the Black Beret Cadre. The object of the mission was to take money from members of the white population for use in the purchase of arms and ammunition by which they might further their cause.

The Berets also began to stockpile weapons including pistols and shotguns which were to be used when the time was ripe for 'revolution' (3) 24 obsolete Bermuda Regiment drill rifles, due to be disarmed at the Bermuda Technical Institute, were stolen. Police believed Black Beret members, who had infiltrated the Bermuda Regiment, were responsible. Furthermore, a Bren gun, part of another consignment of surplus rifles used by the Regiment which had been due to be taken out to sea and dumped was also stolen. Police later discovered the weapon wrapped in sacking and partially hidden in a hedge where it had been due to be collected by a Beret member, believed to be Dionne Bassett. Bassett, who had an intense hatred for Police Commissioner George Duckett, and who fled the island shortly after Duckett's murder, was subsequently charged with possession of the stolen firearms. However, he jumped bail and never returned to Bermuda. The arrest warrant was not dropped until 1994. Bassett had planned on visiting Bermuda in 1996 but died before he had the opportunity. Bassett had spent the remainder of his life as a fugitive and died in Syracuse, New York, aged 49.(4)

These facts are in direct contradiction to those presented by Bermudian writer and Black Beret apologist Quito Swan in his 2010 book '*Black Power in Bermuda*'. Swan alleges Bassett was 'forced into exile' by a racist colonial government.

*

Filled with rage at a community that had relegated them to the bottom of the heap Burrows and Tacklyn adopted the belief they could commit crimes in the name of 'racial justice'. It was the kind of thinking prevalent at the time amongst young black criminals in the United States who took their cue from American black radicals. Left wing 'revolutionary' groups urged African Americans to seek retribution for "300 years of slavery" and claimed that criminal acts in the name of "justice" were not immoral. It was the kind of thinking that led many black criminals to justify their illegal enterprises as an anti-dote to the historical sufferings of black people. It was a form of 'revolutionary self-help'.

Following Burrows' release from Casemates, Police Chief Duckett felt sympathetic to his circumstances. He immediately re-hired him as the headquarters janitor and handyman. It was then that Duckett had purportedly learned that Burrows had been subjected to an 'interrogation by night stick'. (5) According to a former police officer, "Duckett didn't believe 'Buck' (Burrows) was guilty of the break-ins but the Berets played on the fact that Buck's so-called 'friend' (the police chief) hadn't been able to prevent what had happened, hadn't been able to stop him being beaten up and going to jail. They planted the seeds of doubt in his head, they confused him, they made him feel that Duckett – as Commissioner of Police – was ultimately responsible for what had happened to him, that he was in fact the living embodiment of the oppression and unhappiness (he) had endured all of his life. They tried to dehumanise Duckett in Burrows' head – to turn him into a symbol of Colonial oppression…."(6)

The Royal Gazette opined, "Burrows, it is believed, never recovered from the psychological trauma the Berets knew would occur when they primed him to kill the man who had become the most important mentor and role model in his lonely, fatherless, life…….Spraying the kitchen of Bleak House with .22 shots in an attempt to also kill Duckett's wife Jane, and 17 year old daughter Marcia, it seems likely Burrows' mental equilibrium never properly recovered from this attack on what amounted to his extended family."(7)

The evidence in the murder investigation files clearly reveals that Burrows and Tacklyn were aided in the conspiracy to assassinate the Governor and this fact was confirmed by Burrows in his confessions. The trial prosecutor, John Marriage, reasoned that as one or two people ran onto North Shore Road by Audrey Armstrong's house and two men had been seen by Barbara Francis and Ray Bascombe running across Marsh Folly to the railway line, it was extremely likely there were four people involved in the shooting at Government House because it seemed most unlikely that the two who ran past Mrs. Armstrong's house would be the same people who ran across Marsh Folly.

Accordingly, there can be no doubt Tacklyn and Burrows were assisted by one or more conspirators when they entered the grounds of Government House to assassinate the Governor. As the *Royal Gazette* stated, "At least two members of the Black Berets were on hand to watch the Governor and (Captain Sayers) being shot down in cold blood by one of the pair of petty criminals they had indoctrinated with their Black Power militancy and counter-culture rhetoric, brainwashed into believing they were the vanguard for a Bermudian revolution that would never come."(8)

Beret participation in the assassination of the Governor is further corroborated by Burrows' written confession and the statement he made to Neville Darrell - "Buck, all this shooting and killing shit man, I know you were not alone, who else was with you?" Burrows replied, "Neville, you'll be surprised, man, who was involved. Yes sir, man, you'll be surprised."(9)

The political/criminal 'unholy alliance' was the operative term to describe the Governor's assassins and the people who assisted them. This description of the conspiracy was used by the murder investigators and the Acting Governor I.A.C. Kinnear. Kinnear wrote, "This combination of revolutionary and criminal elements provides both the motive for assassination and the means to achieve it without outside assistance."(10)

The conspiracy to assassinate the Governor was likely hatched at Greene's Grill. Burrows and Tacklyn were regulars at the restaurant along with other well-known members of the criminal fraternity. Tacklyn not only did menial jobs there but also took part in Greene's drugs and robbery enterprises. The group of criminals were frequently joined by Beret members. Greene befriended and used the young 'revolutionaries' and armed them with weapons to protect his 'drug turf'. The half-dozen or so remaining Beret ringleaders was all that remained in 1973 of a movement that at its peak boasted more than 200 full-time members who had by now fled after coming under close police scrutiny.

Scotland Yard detectives and the Bermuda Police believed that their major suspects in the murders were all "…either members or supporters of the Black Beret Cadre and it must be accepted that other members of this organization may well have conspired, incited or even aided in the commission of the murders of Sir Richard Sharples, Captain Sayers and Mr Duckett. The suspects all frequented the Court Street area of Hamilton and their headquarters was 'Greene's Grill' which is run by Bobby Greene, 42, the self-styled 'Godfather' of the criminal fraternity."(11)

Scotland Yard detectives and Bermuda police officers concluded, as a result of their enquiries and reliance on informants, that it was likely Buck Burrows had been recruited when he was in Casemates Prison in 1971. Burrows had been serving time for breaking into police officers' homes (according to some sources these were 'trumped-up' charges) and a number of Berets were serving prison sentences at that time.

This group of violent prone Berets knew that Burrows had every reason to feel intense anger against a society that had relegated him to the bottom of the heap. His outward appearance was that of a shy and retiring young man who was always smiling. Beneath the façade, however, lay an embittered and violent personality which had been severely damaged by the circumstances of his upbringing. Burrows has been characterized by those who knew him as a 'child-like soul', 'very naive' and 'very trusting'. And the gullible Burrows must have been flattered to have been given the role of a 'secret agent'. In effect, Burrows was a 'Trojan Horse' who could not only feed information about Police Headquarters to the Berets – collecting names, car licence numbers and the addresses of police officers – but also do it without arousing any suspicion.

Following his release from prison Burrows met regularly with the militant faction of the Berets and they encouraged the malleable young ex-convict to attend the Beret's meetings at their new Bassett Street Building headquarters on Court Street. They now had within their grasp a committed, violent criminal who had access to police headquarters and the inner sanctum of the Berets' main enemy – the Bermuda Police Force. As the *Mid Ocean News* stated, the Berets' "propaganda" was spoon-fed to, "a largely uncomprehending Burrows by his Black Beret Cadre handlers." (12)

The indoctrination and recruitment to the cause of Buck Burrows and Larry Tacklyn had been in the hands of one Black Beret in particular, the 'third man'. He held an almost psychic hold over them.

Police intelligence revealed that both killers had been indoctrinated in Marxist anti-colonial ideology which was essentially built upon racial resentments, hatred and, indeed, some suffering. Burrows and Tacklyn had been 'taught' by leading members of the Black Berets in the rhetoric of revolutionary violence. Following his conviction for the murders, Burrows had shouted "Viva Fidel!" and other pro-Castro slogans when led from the Supreme Court. At some point during his indoctrination he had told friends he was '*The Cuba Kid*' or '*Cuba*'.

Burrows and Tacklyn had both been heavily influenced by the black 'revolution' as expressed by many an American black militant. Burrows echoed the sentiments of these radical groups in his writings when he parroted phrases straight out of left-wing radical literature and black racist sloganeering. He frequently made reference to the violent overthrow of the 'white colonialist society'. It is no coincidence that by the time Burrows came to trial he was describing himself as the '*Commander of All Anti-Colonialist Forces*'. It was a form of language that clearly emulated 'Field Marshall' Donald Defreeze, or 'Cinque', the leader of the Symbionese Liberation Army, the criminal revolutionary gang that kidnapped Patty Hearst in 1974. The military title had also been suggested to Burrows by the Black Berets who hero-worshipped Black Panther leader David Hilliard, a man who adopted the title 'Field Marshall'.

According to former police officer Territt Cabral, "Having known these petty criminals personally, they would have never done these things without some type of reward offered or some thought of a gift or something down the road. The killers are the killers but the reasons they were picked is because those behind the conspiracy, the Black Beret Cadre, used them to change the Government…. They succeeded to some extent and have kept that within the walls of the BIU and PLP."(13)

The small group of Black Beret fanatics began to do more than indoctrinate and manipulate Burrows. They trained him in the use of firearms and took him to the abandoned quarries and the moats around Fort Hamilton to practice target shooting. The 'third man' persuaded them they were active revolutionaries who could change Bermudian society at a stroke and help usher in a revolutionary-type government. Additionally, Tacklyn and Burrows were told to rob banks and other places of business owned by whites to secure funds for the 'revolution'.

A high Bermudian official who was familiar with the murder investigations had no doubt as to who was responsible for Burrows' criminal acts. "I remember when he confessed to robbing the Bank of Bermuda and the Piggly Wiggly in 1974," the former official said, "and he was led out of the courtroom shouting… leftist slogans. Christ, 'Buck' Burrows didn't know Fidel Castro from castor oil but he was the ultimate empty vessel, one the militants in the Black Berets filled with their poison, with their revolutionary propaganda, and he was so lonely, so desperate for acceptance, that he swallowed all this stuff without objection. They styled him as '*Commander in Chief of All Anti-Colonial Forces in Bermuda*' and the poor guy never realised he was in charge of an army of one; himself. The Berets were setting him up to do the dirty work they in fact themselves were too cowardly to carry out. You have to recognise that the handful of militants in the Black Beret the real hardcore types were criminals masquerading as revolutionaries, manipulative and cowardly thugs. They exploited the naiveté of the Black Beret mainstream who were, by and large, a bunch of teenagers and college students caught up in the revolutionary spirit of the times this was the late 1960s, early 1970s, remember, when young people really believed they were going to change the world and when every other kid had a poster of Che Guevara on their wall and Chairman Mao-Tse Tung's on their bedside table." (14)

Beret members also told Burrows that they had to "…get Duckett first." Scotland Yard detectives also believed Dionne Bassett had assisted Burrows in the murder of the police chief. Bassett was known to, "… have had a deep hatred for Mr Duckett. (He) left the island on the 30th September 1972 and to this date has not returned. He is believed to be in the United States or Canada."(15)

Although Burrows said the assassination of the Governor was on his 'direct orders' and 'inspired efforts' the murder was in fact planned and directed by this coterie of Berets with Burrows and Tacklyn playing the secondary role of hit men using weapons supplied to them by the Berets. Most of the weapons used by Burrows and Tacklyn were stolen during a break-in at a store in Antigonish, Nova Scotia and then smuggled into Bermuda.

The strongest testimony suggesting the existence of a conspiracy involving the Black Berets came from Sylvan Musson. (A confidential police source has revealed that Musson was a 'police plant' in the Berets .His 'reward' had been acceptance into the police force following his undercover role.) Musson gave a convincing and compelling statement to police that a group of militant Black Beret members had planned the assassinations.(16)

In the last of Sir Richard Sharples's monthly memos to the Foreign Office regarding internal security, dated 6th March 1973, the Governor displayed a remarkable insight into the political implications of George Duckett's murder. Sharples wrote, "…the members of the remaining (Beret) small hardcore (following Dionne's fleeing the island after the Police Chief's murder) held a number of meetings during (February) three of those being held at a private house….(the third man) has become increasingly vocal and is understood to be planning to acquire a new headquarters for the group. He is reported to have said that the Black Beret Cadre is to be re-organized and to have urged other members to gather weapons 'in preparation for the struggle'. (He) is also reported to have said that once the Black Beret Cadre was reformed a member would be sent to Cuba or Tanzania for guerrilla training. Although (his) previous attempt to revive the Cadre have met with little success, the present frequent contacts between certain members suggests that he could be more successful this time and a close watch is being kept on developments… (The reorganization) of the hard core of the Black Beret Cadre and the possibility of further arms being in the hands of (members) is a disquieting development." (17) Four days later the Governor was assassinated.

Scotland Yard detectives, who believed there were four men involved in the Governor's assassination, admitted there was 'little evidence' to charge anyone else with the conspiracy to murder the Governor and Police chief but they were satisfied that one suspect, the 'third man', had undoubtedly participated in all of the murders. Most especially, they knew that Tacklyn and Burrows had been known to express the greatest admiration, even hero worship, for him. "(The third man) is a very cunning individual who refused to answer any questions when interviewed and is sufficiently intelligent to have carefully planned all of these assassinations", their report stated, "The only evidence against him to date is the shotgun cartridge found in his possession which is identical to those used in all the shotgun incidents. Whilst his alibi for the time of the Government House murders is weak he succeeded in visiting numerous premises that evening to cause confusion in the minds of people later interviewed to corroborate him....their appears little doubt that many Bermudians and close criminal associates fear him and consequently avoid involvement."(18)

However, information I received in a letter from former police officer Darrel Geddings, (pseudonym) states the report failed to include details of a search of the third man's girlfriend's house where police found a gun and lists of politicians' car numbers and addresses. They were taken to Police Headquarters and handed over to Special Branch officers.

Scotland Yard detectives also learned that the pistol Wayne Michael Jackson had found at his home following the Governor's assassination was the same weapon he observed handed to Larry Tacklyn and the 'third man' by Bobby Greene.

The home of the 'third man' was searched. As he was interviewed the Beret leader hit a police officer and escaped. According to the police report, "… whilst being arrested for possession of ammunition assaulted police and (he) made good his escape."(19)

Former police officer Nick Bolton remembered the time the 'third man' was arrested. Bolton said, "…Detective Inspector Laurie Jackson… and a couple of detectives went to arrest him… (He) attacked Jackson and knocked him down a flight of stairs and then took off. This led to an arrest warrant for assault on police and possession of ammunition, we were then looking for him for some time (I remember it as months) before he made it off the island…..it was amazing that with the huge manhunt he just slipped away, he was supposed to have left via the airport dressed as a woman/girl on a regular flight."(20)

The third man fled the island after the Governor's assassination disguised as a Black Muslim woman and using a borrowed passport (*His biological daughter who lives in the United States confirmed the story in an email to the author*). According to the Scotland Yard files, after he fled to Canada he became addicted to heroin. As the third man had assaulted a police officer before he made his escape these charges alone were sufficient to ask Canadian police to implement his extradition. There has been no official explanation why Bermuda's police did not ask the Canadian authorities to return the third man to the island. He did not return to Bermuda until many years later. He remained there for a short period until the early 1980s before leaving, never to return.

The 'third man' is also mentioned in another report by Scotland Yard detectives on the occasion Commander Morrison, Chief Inspector Donald and Detective Inspector Swan visited Bobby Greene in Casemates Prison on the 21st July 1973. The police report of the interview stated, "Although (the third man) was close to Green and in fact occasionally worked in his restaurant Greene made no mention of his involvement in the murders. It is thought to be that he is afraid of (the third man) or his father….." Greene told detectives he was fearful of receiving a prison sentence for the (unrelated) charges against him and that if he did receive one he would, "….. supply (more) information in respect of the murders. The report stated, "He will readily do so for his release, excepting perhaps the Shopping Centre murders in which he may be involved."(21)

Following the Governor's assassination, Acting Governor Kinnear wrote to the Foreign Office and informed them, "The evidence available suggests that… (the third man)…knew what was going to happen…His behaviour on the night in question was most uncharacteristic as he went out of his way to be conspicuous and to be seen by people not connected with the Cadre and with whom he would never mix normally….Unlike the occasion of the murder of the previous Commissioner of Police, there is no wall of silence. There is a good deal of information coming in and everyone interviewed in the house-to-house enquiries being conducted has been most cooperative...In the absence of any firm evidence, I must proceed on certain basic assumptions. I think these must be that Sir Richard's murder and the murder of the Commissioner of Police were connected: that the motive must be political (although there may be a criminal element involved); that if the two murders are connected they establish a pattern of assassination of the principal symbols of colonialism and law enforcement and we can, therefore, expect a further attempt or attempts."(22)

Bringing the real leaders of the conspiracy to justice was a problem for the authorities as the evidence against them was meagre. Police believed one of the conspirators who influenced Burrows and Tacklyn, (the third man), might only be sentenced to a short prison term if he returned to Bermuda. With this in mind a senior British official stationed in Bermuda said the Beret's return to the island would, "do more harm than good to the whole situation. Therefore it seems to me infinitely preferable that he should stay up in Canada and the more we can harry him the better. The more we can drop stories into the Press the better - our only means of communication with him - that might make him say, 'God, they know that do they! I wonder how much more they know!' The more we can make his friends, still here in Bermuda, against whom we have no case at all, feel nervous and jittery, the better. If it is true, as we have been told, that (he) has started taking heroin, then it is good news: far better that he should drug himself to death in Canada than come back to Bermuda, do a few months in jail and thereafter be a bigger menace to the community than ever before. We must employ skilful propaganda to help worry him to further foolish acts, anything but return to Bermuda, to causing his own death by drugs if possible." (23)

According to Scotland Yard files, a warrant for the third man's arrest was issued but was never acted upon. Additionally, Baroness Sharples was told by "Scotland Yard detectives" that he was "a *suspect* and had fled the island and went to the United States but returned to Bermuda." When the suspect returned a few years later Baroness Sharples was told by Bermuda police they "were keeping an eye on him" and "if he puts a foot out of place they would arrest him." (24) A Government House document also states that US police had been contacted and asked to 'keep an eye' on him but they never asked for him to be extradited. When he returned to the island a few years later the arrest warrant had mysteriously disappeared. The circumstances remain a mystery.

However, a clue may be found in a comment Baroness Sharples made. In September 2004 Sir Richard's widow told this author she knew about the suspect and was aware he had powerful connections on the island.(25)

Former police officer Nick Bolton said, "…. it was amazing that with the huge manhunt (the third man) just slipped away." Bolton said a Special Branch detective responsible for surveillance of the airport, "was suddenly transferred back to uniform shortly afterwards." (26) He added, "When (the suspect) voluntarily returned all the paperwork was missing, therefore no charges, no proceedings, nothing." (27) The motive for stealing or destroying the arrest warrant was a fear that riots would ensue, Bolton said.

In 1975 Baroness Sharples had blamed her husband's successor, Sir Edwin Leather, for not pursuing more thoroughly who was behind the murders. She told a Foreign Office official in a private 1975 interview that, "It was clear he would have preferred to put a decision off indefinitely … he had cold feet." An internal Foreign Office memo confirmed Lady Sharples' assessment that with suspected murderers Burrows and Tacklyn behind bars on armed robbery charges, the Governor would have been content to allow the murder cases to remain unsolved. A 1975 Foreign Office memo reported that, "Acting on the advice of the Attorney General, the Commissioner of Police and Ministers, but against his own inclinations, the Governor agreed in May of this year to lift the inhibition on the inquest into Mr. Duckett's death……He had been apprehensive that such an action would be against the public interest, opening a 'Pandora's box' at a time when the security situation in Bermuda has returned to one of calm. In any case the Police were convinced that those responsible for all five deaths were already in prison on other charges."(28)

To summarize, there was sufficient evidence against the 'third man' to charge him in a court of law with conspiring to assassinate the island's Governor -

• The 'third man' had expressed hatred for the Governor on more than one occasion.

• The 'third man' was the most vehemently vocal of the Berets who advocated the elimination of the island's political leaders and the institution of a revolutionary Marxist government.

- A witness testified he had 'reconnoitred' the Governor's mansion with the 'third man' on at least four occasions. The 'third man' had also drawn up sketch plans of Government House and Police headquarters.
- A live shotgun shell was found in the apartment of the 'third man'. It was linked to the weapons used in the shootings.
- A search of the third man's girlfriend's house revealed a gun, lists of politicians' car numbers and addresses. They were taken to Police Headquarters and handed over to Bermuda's Special Branch officers.
- On the 14th March 1971 the 'third man' had threatened to kill a senior police officer, Detective Inspector John Joseph Sheehy.
- The 'third man' was observed handling a pistol. The gun had been handed to the 'third man' by Bobby Greene outside Greene's restaurant.
- The 'third man' had showed a consciousness of guilt by fleeing the island under disguise when police eventually connected him to the assassination.
- At one time the 'third man' had shared an apartment with convicted assassin Larry Tacklyn.
- On the night of the assassination the 'third man' went out of his way to be conspicuous, seeking to be seen with non-Berets with whom he normally did not associate with.
- Police compiled evidence that the quick-tempered and violently anti-white 'third man' had a controlling influence over convicted assassins Tacklyn and Burrows.

However, as we have seen, the authorities decided it was not in the interests of Bermuda to bring the 'third man' to justice. As Former police officer Territt Cabral said, "My impressions of the whole thing were to get bodies, which they did and moved on. We don't need another insurrection. The local police did a good job in my view.......the UBP did not want to upset the whole political field. Get some bodies, put them in court, get convictions for something and let it die. They did not want anymore turmoil. Let the tourists come, let's get on with offshore banking. The economy is going downhill, I need to make money....we will deal with (the third man) later." (29)

ELEVEN

EXECUTIONS AND RIOTS

"I guess if you had polled people at the time, a good majority of blacks in Bermuda would have said 'no' to the executions, and a good number of whites would have said 'yes'. As an ex-policeman, I thought … (Burrows and Tacklyn) were rightly convicted of a group of heinous crimes."
Former Police Sergeant Roger Sherratt

HARRY SOUSA WAS the last man to go to the gallows in Bermuda for the 1941 murder of Margaret Stapleton. He was executed in 1943. The last woman to be hanged was Martha Annette Outerbridge in June 1934. She murdered her boyfriend Herbert Leslie by striking him 119 times with a hatchet. Outerbridge sang hymns as she walked to the gallows. Earlier she had insisted on pleading guilty and said, "He is dead. I am satisfied to pay the penalty."(1)

On 18ᵗʰ July 1976 Larry Tacklyn was found guilty of the murders of Victor Rego and Mark Doe and sentenced to death. On the 20ᵗʰ July 1976 he was found not guilty of the murder of the Governor and his ADC, despite the overwhelming evidence against him. He was not charged with the murder of the Police Commissioner. Buck Burrows had been found guilty of the murders of the Governor, Captain Sayers, the Commissioner of Police George Duckett and the Hamilton shopkeepers Victor Rego and Mark Doe. He was sentenced to death on 6ᵗʰ July 1977.

Larry Tacklyn did not want to die. He always thought he would get a last minute reprieve. Following his written confession, Burrows said little to enhance any understanding of what really occurred on the night of the

Governor's assassination. Both murderers stewed in prison from the time
of their capture in 1973 until their executions in December 1977. Tacklyn
passed his time playing table tennis and exercising. Burrows took a vow of
silence, communicating his thoughts on scraps of paper then handing them
to prison officers and fellow inmates.

According to 'Food Officer' Edward Robinson, "The food officer had to
deliver (Tacklyn and Burrows) meals personally.....We built up somewhat
of a rapport. Tacklyn was very eager to learn, he was always exercising....
Burrows never verbally communicated with many officers, myself included.
But he was always smiling. If he wanted to say anything, he would write
it down. In one instance he didn't want yeast in his bread, he wanted
unleavened bread. He wrote a note asking me to make bread without yeast,
which we did. We tried to accommodate him."(2)

Prison Officer Roy Carden said that Burrows became resigned to his fate
and wanted to go down in history as the 'Commander-in-Chief' of all anti-
colonialist forces in Bermuda. He wanted to be a 'hero of the revolution'
who had resisted any attempts to get him to show remorse for his actions
or to give up the names of his fellow conspirators. Carden said Tacklyn was
at first a 'model prisoner' but as time passed he resorted to his old ways,
frequently issuing threats and voicing his racist sentiments to expatriate
officers.(3)

Following the rejection of Larry Tacklyn's last appeal, which was heard
on 1st December 1977, it became possible for Bermuda's new Governor,
Sir Peter Ramsbotham, a former distinguished diplomat who had served
as Ambassador to the United States, to commute Tacklyn's and Burrows'
sentences to life imprisonment. However, the Governor declined. He
believed he could not go against a decision made in 1975 by Bermuda's
House of Assembly (which consisted of 22 black and 18 white members) to
retain the death penalty.

Although the death penalty had been abolished in Britain in 1965 the
British Foreign Secretary, David Owen, explained why he had advised
the Queen not to commute the death sentences of the Governor's killers.
The Times of London summarised Owen's dilemma: "The decision not to
reprieve the two black murderers of Governor Sharples and of three other

persons was made by the government of the ruling United Bermuda Party, who constitute the only body able to assess the wisdom or otherwise, quite apart from the justice, of such action. It is a multi-racial government, of five black and six white ministers. The House itself has 22 black and 18 white members, and in 1975 (after the murders) voted 25 to 9 to retain capital punishment. It is quite clear, therefore, that the decisions were all properly made in Bermuda. Under the so-called Creech-Jones rule of 1947, as Dr Owen told the House (of Commons) yesterday, the British Government did not intervene. That rule lays down that the Secretary of State does not advise the Queen to use the prerogative when the local governor has decided not to intervene, except in blatant miscarriages of justice."(4)

The Queen's response to the plea for clemency was not well met. When a privy councillor handed her the document setting out Burrows' appeal for mercy she signed it "with a flourish", adding "He's got a cheek, asking me for clemency. Do you know he even shot the dog?"(5)

On 25th November 1977 the Bermudian Government announced the death sentences would be carried out on December 2nd. Premier Sir David Gibbons stood up in the House of Assembly and announced the executions would be carried out. His comments were met with astonishment by a large section of his audience who believed that it, "aggravated a large section of the community who saw it as a racial thing. Both of them had been black and at that time the majority of the justice system had been white."(6)

Following the Governor's announcement protests and demonstrations were organized. According to the Governor, the island became, "increasingly full of unease and foreboding…suspicions and tensions mounted. Black youngsters appeared more sullen and more hostile. There were isolated acts of violence".(7)

A petition of 6,000 signatures was signed and sent to the Governor. Organisers claimed they had collected a further 2,200 signatures at the 'People's Parliament' and 4,800 by the National Committee Against Capital Punishment. Protesters therefore claimed 13,000 Bermudians had protested against the death sentences. In fact, the PLP were taking a rather disingenuous approach. On the one hand they knew that capital punishment was popular and did not wish to take a stand against it. On the other hand they could fuel discontent and take advantage of the riots that many guessed would likely follow.

The Bermudian Police were prepared for trouble when the Government's announcement was made. It had a police unit of 26 men on standby outside the House of Assembly. Concern was also voiced by Government officials about the tourist industry. 2,000 to 3,000 mostly American tourists were in Bermuda at the time (unlike the 12,000 per week during the high season of mid-winter).

The first incident of violence protesting the death sentences occurred on November 29th. A white youth was pulled from his car on Victoria Street, Hamilton, and assaulted. Police discovered that young blacks had been asking white Bermudians for their opinions on the death sentences. If whites answered in the positive they were attacked.

On 30th November police officers were put on 12 hour shifts. Later that evening two petrol bombs were thrown at houses in Cavendish Heights, Devonshire. Fearful that demonstrators would march to Casemates Prison where Burrows and Tacklyn were being held, 52 police officers were stationed in the area around the prison. No incidents, however, were reported.

According to former Police Sergeant Roger Sherratt, "It was a very volatile time in Bermuda's history. In the lead up to the executions, it was a very difficult time for the police...on the night of the executions I was one of the police officers up by HMS Malabar (near Casemates Prison) on guard duty. We had police officers outside (the prison) just in case there was any kind of disturbance. We were aware of the rioting in town and the fire at the Southampton Princess where a number of people were killed.... It was a nerve-wracking time – it sent shock waves around the world. Visitors were killed as a result of the rioting that took place."(8)

On the night of the executions, 1st December, a crowd gathered in the Till's Hill/Court Street district of Hamilton and some members of the crowd exhorted others to march on Casemates Prison, the Supreme Court and Government House in Hamilton. Although prison officers at Casemates reported no disturbance the crowd did proceed to Parliament Street in the capital. They were prevented from continuing to the Court of Appeal by barriers that had been placed by police at the junction of Church and Reid Streets.

At 10.10pm Julian Hall, Tacklyn's junior counsel, emerged from the Supreme Court and gave the thumbs down sign. The streets erupted in an orgy of violence. Hall said, "I remember I came out of the court that night and was surprised to see this enormous crowd. There were people as far as the eye could see. Someone shouted out 'what is the verdict?' and I just gave the thumbs down signal to tell them we had lost, without even thinking. I never intended, with an innocuous hand sign, to start the riots, but they were based on long simmering anger not just that day's events".

Hall was taken to a police car for his own safety. As he was driven to a safe house he saw Molotov cocktails being hurled and people began screaming. "It was like a dark cloud descended; you could smell the anger and feel it" he said. Hall described the feeling amongst the crowd as one of anger at a white establishment that had, "...decided to kill these black young men, come what may".

Twenty-four-year-old Dale Butler, who was later to become an MP, was one of the junior founding members of the National Committee against Capital Punishment and witnessed the riot in Hamilton that night. "I was scared", he said. "There were all these people running around and the lights were out, they had all been smashed. There was always the possibility that there could be a fire in your home, many buildings were ablaze. Molotov cocktails were flying and, even inside my house, you could feel the sting of the pepper spray (from riot Police). There was a glow from all the buildings and people running around in masks. I went out and screamed, 'Stay calm, go home' but people just ignored me. There was this immense frustration and they were taking out anything that represented white privilege, some buildings just went up in smoke".(9)

The crowd, which by now had grown into an unruly mob, tore down the barriers the police had erected at Church and Reid streets. Some demonstrators scaled the boundary wall of the Supreme Court building and began to smash windows but rioters were prevented from gaining entry. The crowd then moved to the junction of Reid Street and Front Street but turned around and marched to Parliament Street. They were confronted by a police riot unit, backed up by four Land Rover personnel carriers, which had been called out. The police officers formed a line across Parliament Street, south of the Supreme Court and proceeded to rebuild the barrier that had been torn down.(10) During the melee crowds tipped an unmarked CID car on its side.

Aware their route had been blocked by police the crowd proceeded to march to Victoria Street. En route two police vehicles and a number of parked motorcycles were attacked causing considerable damage. Private homes and business premises were then set upon and windows were smashed. The riot police stationed on Parliament Street then came under attack as a wave of bottles and petrol bombs were thrown. The police responded by firing tear gas into the crowd which had the effect of dispersing rioters, some of whom moved to the Court Street area and firebombed business premises. The disturbances spread throughout Bermuda and police reported numerous incidents of fire bomb damage to mostly white-owned businesses, including Gosling Brothers' liquor store in Hamilton and a supermarket in Shelley Bay.

Firemen who attempted to put out the fires came under attack from gangs. It became necessary to give police protection each time the Fire Brigade was called out. According to the Governor Sir Peter Ramsbotham, "The news that they were setting fire to commercial property in Hamilton soon prompted groups of black youngsters in other parts of the island to follow their example. So the arson was widespread: within 36 hours several million dollars worth of damage had been done, and three people had lost their lives in a fire which burnt out the top floor of the largest hotel here."(11)

Ramsbotham believed the rioters were 'PLP allies', 'gangs of criminals from Court Street'. They, "…attacked property belonging to black members of the UBP as well as that of whites. No black UBP members of Parliament ventured into Court Street, where the gangs congregated…until the PLP becomes more responsible, Bermuda will continue to be at risk."(12)

The Governor's memo made reference to an incident that occurred at the Southampton Princess Hotel, approximately five miles from Hamilton, on the night before the executions. One Bermudian hotel worker and two American tourists had been killed in what police determined was a deliberate arson attack. It had been rumoured that the two hangman appointed by the Government to carry out the executions had been staying at the hotel. A hotel worker had made enquiries as to which room they were staying in and had apparently relayed this message to the arsonists. Instead of killing the hangmen they murdered two innocent tourists and an innocent hotel worker. Later a suspect in the Southampton Princess Hotel murders was arrested and housed in the same Casemates Prison unit as Burrows and Tacklyn. According to former prison officer Roy Carden, "I was in the Special Section which is part of the old section 3….. We… had the chap who was charged with three murders during the riots last year when he set fire to the Southampton Princess."(13)

The anonymous executioner was British, in his early forties and lived in Canada and his assistant was from Trinidad. Their names were kept secret for their own safety. They had both carried out numerous executions in the Caribbean and were selected from a register of executioners that was kept by the Prisons Department. The hangman had arrived in Bermuda on the evening of the executions and left early the next morning on a flight to New York. It was rumoured he wore a tuxedo to carry out the hangings.(14)

Tacklyn was hanged at 4am, December 2nd 1977, and pronounced dead at 4.20am. Burrows was hanged at 4.40am and pronounced dead at 4.55am. Tacklyn was 25 years of age, Burrows 33. There were no reported 'last words' but government reports reveal that as the two condemned men walked from their cell to a holding cell beside the newly constructed gallows, Casemates prison erupted in an orgy of shouting and screaming. Both men were buried in the grounds of the Prison.

At 9am on December 2nd, some five hours after the executions, the Governor announced a State Of Emergency and a dusk to dawn curfew. The announcement initially had some calming effect but rioting soon ignited.(15)

At 1pm on the following day, 3rd December, a large crowd of approximately 500 gathered in the Court Street area and rioted until 6pm when a heavy downpour helped disburse them. The entire police force was called out to deal with the rioters and the officers were forced to use riot gas grenades to break up the crowds.

However, aware that the police could not deal effectively with such a large crowd, the Governor requested troop reinforcements be sent from Britain. On Saturday, 3rd December, the Governor called for British troops to reinforce the local security forces, who were by then nearing the point of exhaustion. According to Governor Ramsbotham, "…the public soon became alarmed by the Government's apparent inability to restore order. There was a danger that groups of vigilantes might be formed, and that US tourists might be officially advised against coming here, unless prompt action was taken to restore confidence". On Sunday 4th December 80 British troops arrived from Belize, followed by 120 from the UK. The Belize troops, led by Major John Varley, arrived by an RAF troop transport VC 10 and landed at the US Naval Air Station. The troops were then transported to Hamilton by a convoy of buses.

By the time the troops arrived there was, "an uneasy calm". The troops were "deployed unobtrusively to avoid any risk that their appearance might be provocative."(16) The Bermuda Regiment was not used for crowd control as it was believed that some black soldiers would side with the rioters.(17)

During the period 4th – 8th December there were a number of incidents including firebombing, but generally the violence had subsided. *The State of Emergency* was lifted on the 9th December. A total of 14 factories and stores had been firebombed across the island.

The riots shocked Bermudian society and led to a wave of finger-pointing. Black militants felt that the UBP government should have done more to prevent the executions. White Bermudians were horrified that the island's black community had sympathy for two murderers who had no regrets in killing their victims. Although many black Bermudians felt 'colonialism' had been responsible for the Governor's assassination, they had been hard pressed in adopting that excuse for the vicious murders of Mark Doe and Victor Rego. Additionally, PLP leader Lois Browne Evans' remarks, with reference to the executions, that it was "…time for us to stop treating wrong doers as if they were animals" was also met with incredulity by the majority of the white population.(18)

In response to the rioting the Bermuda Sun editorialized, "There is no man, woman or child in the island who does not share in the ignominy of this horrid day. We are paying a very dear price for a decision over which we were repeatedly told, we had no control. Emotions ran high, too high, and so they burst into a hideous wave of violence, despite the last minute pleas from all sides." (19) Governor Ramsbotham said the destruction was, "…on a scale unprecedented in Bermuda. The mood of some participants was menacing, and their evident race hatred came as a shock to most Bermudians."(20)

A young woman who was present during the riots said she was "… convinced that they weren't going to let those two men hang and so were a lot of other people who were on Court Street Thursday night. The violence was an expression of disappointment and rage and the complete feeling of disaster to individual human beings that produced these burnings."(21)

Dale Butler, a member of a group called 'Bermuda For Bermudians' said young blacks, "…were only responding to the frustrations that adults have created…It was adults who failed to remove capital punishment from the statute books. It was adults who brought the racial element into this issue. It was adults who introduced drugs into the community…Adults created a fringe society…It is that fringe that is reacting today to untold other pressures."(22)

*

A Riot Commission, headed by Lord Pitt of Hampstead, was instituted to look into the reasons for the riots. A witness who appeared before the Commission said that a great number of black Bermudians "cheered" the rioters. A 'young black man' told the Commissioners, "I am inclined to agree with the lady who said there were quite a few Bermudians cheering from the sides during the riots, and I include myself in that category and for one reason only, and that is because the only thing the businessmen know is dollars and cents. The riots…hurt them financially and so for that reason I sat back and cheered…What happened …was people's natural reaction… (The people) had spoken in some instances until they were blue in the face and were not heard, and so…the only avenue for them to take was to loot and burn and riot….(23)

These sentiments were not adopted by the majority of white Bermudians who were incredulous that the same type of sympathy given to Burrows and Tacklyn had not been extended to the victims. Former Police Sergeant Roger Sherratt said, "I guess if you had polled people at the time, a good majority of blacks in Bermuda would have said 'no' to the executions, and a good number of whites would have said 'yes'. As an ex-policeman, I thought … (Burrows and Tacklyn) were rightly convicted of …heinous crimes."(24)

The Commission, which called many witnesses, stated that one of the reasons for the disturbances was that the hangings were seen by many, "as a vindictive action to which the government adhered in the face of mounting evidence that it was contrary to the wishes of a very substantial part of the population ….."(25)

The Commission also reached a number of other conclusions about the long-term contributory causes. The Commission, under a chapter entitled '*The Causes of the Disorders*' listed the following factors:

* Bermuda's history was that of a colonial society, small and isolated and until recent years, racially segregated. And, because of its size islanders felt 'claustrophobic and had the need to travel periodically in order to preserve a sense of equilibrium'. In a society where everyone knew everyone else it was easy for grievances to spread and take hold.

*The Commission recognised that white Bermudians rarely understood how 'deep the wounds of discrimination (could) strike into an individual's personality'. The Commissioners noted how many black Bermudians still remembered racial slights decades after the incidents occurred.

* The Commission noted that the white population was more readily able to take advantage of the new economic opportunities following the First World War, especially tourism.

* The Commission noted how most working class jobs in the tourist industry were held by black Bermudians. The black man's self-esteem was thus damaged by 'continually waiting upon white males who project…an image of wealth, success and power.'

*The Commission recognised that the wealth and power of Bermuda could not have been so rapid had the Bermudian Government not recruited expatriates from overseas who brought the skills that Bermudians could not command. However, Bermudians resented the privileged position the expatriates occupied. Some Bermudians told the Commission that they felt like second-class citizens and said Bermuda should be for Bermudians.

*Although racial segregation should be condemned, the Commission maintained, it did help build a sense of black solidarity which made it easy for black Bermudians to sympathize with lawbreakers. The Commission quoted one white Bermudian as saying, "I ran as a white candidate for the PLP and I can remember talking to an old black man in Paget. When he was asked if he would put his name to the form proposing me as a candidate, he told me: "I am heart and soul PLP but it is as much as my life is worth to put my name on that paper; they have got me right here and I am too old to lose everything and start again". I thought he was being over-dramatic. I found later he was speaking the truth."(26)

*The Commission recognized that the 1960s social revolution in the Western nations contributed to a sense of injustice. Black Bermudians came to identify with black Americans rather than the black community in Britain. The extreme rhetoric of Black Power groups in America contributed to a 'new tone' adopted by blacks.

*The Commission said that 'race' was at the center of the riots. As the UBP leaders testified, "If our current practice of racially separated social lives is so pernicious to our collective long-term interests, how can we generate effective peer-group pressure which will nudge us along the path of genuine, effective and broadly-based integration?"(27)

*The Commission did not hold the Bermuda Police responsible for igniting the riots or handling them in a way that would further incite trouble. The Report stated, "The police anticipated the course of disorders in Hamilton with precision, their discipline was well maintained and they performed their duties very creditably. Yet, paradoxically, our hearings became a setting for the voicing of many complaints about them. Perhaps this is characteristic of the position of the police in contemporary society: whatever they do someone is dissatisfied." (28) The Commission did however recommend that the Bermuda Police force appoint more black Bermudians.

* The Commission also recognized the influence America had played in forging a new identity for black Bermudians. The report stated, "(In the

past) it would have been a society oriented towards the United Kingdom and during his youth (the black Bermudian's) national identity would have been that of a subject of King George V. A young black man today grows up in an international society oriented towards North America; his political conceptions are influenced by racial identifications with blacks in the United States.....so that he cannot easily fashion an identity based upon loyalty to the British Crown. The advance of Rastafarianism movement with its conception of a black God and a black homeland can be understood as an attempt to furnish a new kind of identity........ (A witness said) Many of our parents send children to North America. Others send them to England. We are still tied to Great Britain in terms of historical and cultural heritage. Somewhere in there, in Bermuda, lie a very confused people. They don't really know which way to go....somewhere along the line they lose their personal identity...every country should be able to produce something of their own that kids and other people can identify with. We haven't produced that yet.......This leads us, inexorably, to the discussion of independence, and to the question of whether those who are presently alienated from the social order would identify themselves more effectively with an independent Bermuda."(29)

One Commission witness, BIU president Ottiwell Simmons Sr, said the establishment in Bermuda looked upon the island as its own big company with the rest of the community treated as servants. He said the "dichotomy within the community set whites against blacks, employers against workers and rich against poor. It also breeds attitudes which make conflict and civil disturbances inevitable." Simmons believed the decision to carry out the hangings was taken by the Premier and his Cabinet, regardless of the feelings of the people. "And who knows if they have even hanged the right persons. It is the opinion of our union that much of the fire damage and the consequential bad publicity etc, etc, could have been avoided because all the anti-hanging protests were reasonable and justified warnings to the government. Therefore the responsibility for all the damage Bermuda has suffered must rest at the feet of the Premier and his Cabinet...To effect (change) either the present establishment must change; or it must be removed."(30)

Commission witness Police Inspector Barrie Meade partly agreed with Simmons but placed the blame for the riots not on the Premier and his Cabinet but on the opposition PLP and others who had made irresponsible remarks in the lead up to the hangings. Meade said that the campaign to abolish the death penalty and to save Burrows and Tacklyn from the gallows was so timed and conducted in such a manner that it was "certain to produce tension". He added that the effect of many of the speeches delivered during the campaign to commute the death sentences was "to increase the tension".

On the night preceding the hangings, Meade said, legal steps were taken to attempt to prevent the hangings and public meetings and a march was held resulting in the "climate of tension" reaching a "boiling point". He said the police believed that the tension was deliberately caused for "political purposes and rioting was the natural and foreseeable result....What alarms our members (of the police force) is that there are people who have the power and the will to disrupt the entire community, and yet these people are responsible to no one. A single percentage point in the population can effectively ruin the economy and way of life of the remaining 99%."(31)

The Governor, Sir Peter Ramsbotham was in agreement. He believed the situation had been exacerbated by the PLP, "...who (treated) anyone with a grudge against the establishment as an ally. So the back of town youth gangs are encouraged to identify with it – and to look upon themselves as its hatchet men."(32)

In a secret memo to the Foreign Office Ramsbottom also pointed out that the judge who sentenced Burrows and Tacklyn to death was not only black and Bermudian but part of a family whose career achievements were acclaimed by the PLP. Ramsbotham said the PLP chose not to become actively involved in the pleas for clemency because of the "apparent lack of popular support for abolition of capital punishment". The PLP also believed, "reprieves would be granted anyway, just as they had always been for more than 30 years". The PLP had done nothing, he said, "to raise the issue of capital punishment in the House of Assembly, although it could quite easily and quite properly have been raised early last summer (1977)". This indifference "led to occasional squabbles with PLP militants".(33)

Ramsbottom also noted that following the announcement on Friday, 25th November, that both men would, in consequence, be executed a week later, "… the PLP remained silent: although the House of Assembly met on the day of the announcement, the subject was never mentioned during its meeting. But the group of PLP militants (*Author's note: some of whom were formerly members of the Black Beret Cadre*) took swift and energetic action. Over the weekend, they pressured the party's leaders and some members of the Ministerial Association of Churches here into sponsoring a protest campaign; they arranged to feed slanted information to left-wing members of Parliament in the UK and to the press there; they lobbied international bodies opposed to capital punishment and they formed a local body to oppose it. They thus set the stage for a week of inflammatory activity, throughout which they were themselves never averse to inciting racial hatred – and, I suspect, always hopeful of provoking the riots which eventually erupted."(34)

The Governor believed the militants who started the campaign against capital punishment may have had "ulterior" motives. (35) He regarded the PLP leaders as "dangerous" and that, as the party drew its support from the majority black community, "…they have a moral right to power; and that they must have been unfairly deprived of it by a trick. They are unwilling to believe that the electorate might have rejected them for their own deficiencies of excesses. So they denounce the present electoral arrangement in exaggerated and misleading terms. They also, much more dangerously, tend to regard any black who joins the governing UBP as a traitor to his race…."(36)

Ramsbotham believed the campaign against capital punishment had been characterized as a black struggle to save "two underprivileged blacks who were at times represented as the victims of injustice." He also believed that many of the rioters were not sincere in their protests because, "…none of the 90 odd people arrested for serious emergency offences even mentioned Burrows or Tacklyn when asked by police why they had taken part in the riots. They were plainly not protesting against the executions: those were no more than the occasion for their rebellion." Two thirds of the rioters arrested had previous criminal records and the average age was just over 23.

Ramsbotham said the rioters who were arrested were, "…a problem group of youngsters who resent authority and always react quickly and viciously to any incident involving the Police. That group is made up of hard cases, who probably provided the hard core of the rioters."(37)

The PLP leader and defence attorney for Larry Tacklyn, Lois Browne Evans, came under particular criticism from Sir Peter and he accused her of abusing the legal system by trying to, "force a stay of execution" and that the appeal hearing provided a focal point for an unruly mob of demonstrators who gathered in the streets outside the Supreme Court building. "We must endeavour to convince Mrs Browne Evans and her colleagues", he said, "that their future success will depend upon their making discernible attempts to appeal to a wider section of the community", (i.e. white Bermudians as well as black "and upon more evident respectability."(38)

TWELVE

TWIN LEGACIES - COLONIALISM AND BLACK POWER

"Fanaticism often begins with a sudden, dramatic shift in world view, often due to an overwhelming disturbing experience….sometimes this involves betrayals and deep disappointments….The second step…is exposure to a fanatic ideology. The third step usually involves a persona; connection to a charismatic leader who appears to embody the 'purity' promised by the ideology…."
Steve K. Dubrow-Eichel, Wilmington Delaware News, 23.9.2001

LARRY TACKLYN AND Buck Burrows came from deprived backgrounds - by Bermudian standards. They displayed an anger that was the result of an impoverished childhood and a 'brutalization' experience growing up. Consequently, a lot of what they did was based on a bitter resentment of many of their fellow citizens, particularly the minority white population which for centuries held a privileged position on the island. And the white community did not have the disadvantage of unemployment and poor health which arose from deprivation of the kind suffered by Burrows and Tacklyn. As psychologically malleable young men they were also influenced and coached by leaders of the Black Beret Cadre who raised their self-esteem and taught them that what they were doing was in conformity with 'revolutionary principles'. They would be recognised as 'heroes' in the fight to eliminate 'colonialism and racism' from the islands.

*

Independence had been one of the PLP's central principles since the party's inception in 1963 and continued to inspire black politicians throughout the 1960s and 1970s. In 1968 the PLP election platform stated that, "No government can be either responsible or democratic while under the rule of another country. Colonialism is a cancer which must be removed from the tissue of human affairs....Therefore we shall return to London to examine with the British Government what arrangements can be made for our independence."(1)

From the beginning Deputy Governor Kinnear knew that the murders of the Police Chief and Governor were the work of black militants bent on eliminating colonial control over Bermuda. In a memo to the Foreign Office he described the legacy of racism in Bermuda. "You have in Bermuda a country which contains the inevitable frictions of any multi-racial society," he wrote "but which, by standards elsewhere, works pretty well with the races living alongside each other harmoniously enough". Kinnear said the wealth was evenly distributed amongst the population and was not "fertile ground for revolutionary philosophies". However, he cautioned, "the two-thirds black majority, quite contrary to the normal pattern elsewhere, is not reflected in a wholly black government".

Another weak position, Kinnear observed, was the reluctance of the ruling white dominated ruling party to even consider independence. Additionally, the Progressive Labour Party was ineffective and produced a sense of frustration among the young black people which was directed primarily at the symbols of colonialism and the police which was another symbol of the colonial heritage. Kinnear said the resentment existed because the colonial symbols were "foreign" and there was abroad a mistaken belief that Britain was holding Bermuda back from independence. Certainly there is a known small number of bitter young men", Kinnear wrote, "… I am quite convinced that the frustrations that do exist among black youth (and others)…are going to grow rather than diminish; and that for every person who considers the Governorship an expensive anachronism now, there will be two in two to three years' time."(2)

Underlying this anti-colonial attitude was a belief that anything the British people accomplished in their desire for an Empire was wrong or malevolent or a simple desire to dominate 'lesser peoples'. Most of the radicals in Bermuda took their cue from left wing ideologues in the United

States. The radical left in Bermuda, like their American counterparts, promoted romantic visions of black Africa, blaming every atrocity from slavery to civil wars on the 'colonial heritage' - essentially ignoring the fact that black Africans had participated in that trade and animosities between tribes had existed long before any white man set foot on the continent.

The issue of seeking freedom from colonial control wasn't new and it was not confined to the shores of Bermuda. Anti-colonialism was one of the dominant political currents of the 20th century, as dozens of European colonies in Asia and Africa became free. And apologists for terrorism, including former Black Beret members, argued that terrorist acts were an understandable attempt on the part of subjugated non-Western peoples to lash out against their long-time Western 'oppressors'. These views still remain with many left-wing and radical commentators who call on the West to pay reparations to the ancestors of slaves and the victims of colonialism.

It can be argued, however, that this attitude towards 'colonialism' as expressed by Bermuda's left wing elite, including some members of the PLP, was always seriously flawed. Contrary to the opinions expressed by left-wing historians it can be argued that the British Empire was, in general, not always a good thing, but it was a vital component in the formation of the modern world. Revisionist historians are now realising that anachronistic thinking has been responsible for many of the negative judgements made about the Empire.

These historians have come to understand how people have been trying to impose the values of the 20th century on things that were done long ago in a wholly different world. For example, we rightly condemn the British atrocities committed in the wake of the Indian Mutiny but in recent years many Indian historians have acknowledged the debt Indians have to Britain for opening India to science, justice and European civilization. As Indian writer Nirpal Dhaliwal wrote, "(The English)…introduced (Indians) to the English language, parliamentary democracy, the rule of law and the protection of individual rights. (It is) an admission of the crucial role (England) played in their history….For all they extracted from India, the British left behind a practical network of transportation, governance and values without which India would not be the dynamic democracy it is today.

It is a mark of India's quiet appreciation as well as its great self-confidence that it asks for no apology for the past. Out of respect no Briton should be condescending enough to offer one."(3)

In his book '*Empire*' British historian Niall Ferguson points out the dark side of colonialism - outright piracy and theft, the slavery, the racism, the exploitation, the refusal to recognise that the introduction of British principles led inevitably to independence and the erosion of the Empire. However, Ferguson also argues that the British Empire was one of the world's greatest modernizing forces.

Ferguson argues that the world we know today is in large measure the product of Britain's *Age of Empire*. The reason the West became so affluent and dominant in the modern era, he maintains, is that it invented three institutions: science, democracy, and capitalism. All those institutions are based on universal impulses and aspirations, but those aspirations were given a unique expression in Western civilization. The spread of capitalism, the communications revolution, the notion of humanitarianism, and the institutions of parliamentary democracy-all these can be traced back to the extraordinary expansion of Britain's economy, population, and culture from the seventeenth century until the mid-twentieth.

Ferguson's narrative traces the history of the empire from its beginnings in the 16th century. As Ferguson argues, by the 18th century British consumers had developed a strong taste for sugar, tobacco, coffee, tea and other imports. The empire's role was to supply these commodities and to offer cheap land to British settlers. Not until the late 18th century did Britain add a 'civilizing mission' to its commercial motives. Liberals in Britain, often inspired by religious feelings, abolished the slave trade and then set out to Christianize indigenous peoples. He admits that the British sometimes responded to native opposition with brutality and racism. Yet he also argues that other empires, especially those of Germany and Japan, were far more brutal and "much worse". Ferguson reminds critics of how much the United Kingdom did for free trade and he also contends that Britain nobly sacrificed its empire in order to defeat these imperial rivals in WWII.

Although it is obvious to us now that slavery is wicked it was completely accepted by all human beings until the 18th century. St Paul and Aristotle, two great moralists of the ancient world, insisted on the kindness to slaves but did not object to slavery. Far more slaves were sold in Africa to other Africans than were shipped abroad to England and the United States. The anti-slavery movement grew up in the 18th century and it was almost entirely a British initiative. As A.N Wilson has observed, "Note that (the anti-slavery movement) was not started in Gambia or Senegal....nor by the other men on the other side of Africa, in the Sudan, who went on doing a lively trade in slaves until the 20th century."(4)

Author Lawrence James agrees with Ferguson and believes that, "....on balance the British Empire was a force for good and should be a source of national pride. It provided an interlude of stability in which countries divided by race and religion could develop and, in the case of India, discover a national identity......Alongside railways, schools, universities and sanitation projects, the empire introduced political and social ideas dear to the British. These included extending civil rights to women, a free press and, most important of all, a culture of popular consent and reasoned debate. English spread as the language of learning and commerce...... (and) millions of (the empire's) former subjects have chosen to settle in Britain."(5)

The assault against colonialism and imperialism is predicated on a number of premises – Colonialism is a distinctively Western evil that was inflicted on the non-Western world. And, as a consequence of colonialism, the West became rich and the colonies became impoverished – therefore, as the left argues, the descendants of colonialism are worse off than they would be had colonialism never occurred. Such attitudes, often expressed in the Bermudian media by purported experts from the United States and home-grown arbiters of popular culture, contribute no sense of history or have forgotten about the Egyptian empire, the Persian Empire, the Macedonian empire, the Islamic empire, the Mongol empire, the Chinese empire, and the Aztec and Inca empires in the Americas. In response to the left's position it may be argued that the Arabs should be paying reparations for their destruction of the Byzantine and Persian empires. Furthermore do they argue that Muslims should reimburse the Spaniards for their 700-year rule?

Moreover, the Western nations could not have reached its current stage of wealth and influence by simply stealing from other countries. Before

British rule, there were no rubber trees in Malaya, no cocoa trees in West Africa and no tea in India. This is not to deny that the colonialists exploited native resources. However, colonialism was the central force that brought to Asia, Africa, and South America the positive values of Western civilization. Although many African nations continue to experience serious problems of tyranny, tribal and religious conflict, poverty, and underdevelopment, it is not due to the 'evils' of Western colonialism. Instead, it is because those countries are insufficiently westernized. Colonialism in Africa lasted a mere half-century therefore the ills those countries experience now cannot be used to blame 'colonialism'. Instead, the problems they suffer are due to too short a time for Western institutions to effectively change their societies. Accordingly, after their independence, most African nations have retreated into a kind of tribal barbarism that can be remedied only with more Western intervention and influence, not less. Africa needs more Western capital, more technology, more rule of law, and more individual freedom.

If stronger leadership within the black community in Bermuda had adopted these enlightened views and renounced their beliefs that colonialism and the British presence were altogether 'evil', it is unlikely that radical and criminal elements, embracing a perfidious political agenda, could have prospered. If the PLP had not embraced the ideology of the US Black Power movement with all its talk of the corrupt white man and the 'white devils', Bermuda's past may have looked much different and a different history may have emerged – a history based upon true equality and a common sense of purpose between the white and black communities.

*

Bermuda differed from the Caribbean nations in several important ways. About 40% of the population were white. Unemployment was not a major problem; indeed manpower had to be imported specifically from the United States and the UK. The staple economy was not bananas or sugar, but tourism. An annual inflow of 400,000 visitors, mostly Americans and Canadians, sustained a higher standard of living than that of a single crop Caribbean island economy.

Black resentment of white privilege of the old traditional kind appeared to have been reduced by the changes of 1968 and later. Internal self-government had been extended; constituency boundaries, which had been grossly discriminatory, had been revised; the UBP accepted a black leader in the person of Sir Edward Richards; even the predominantly white police force boasted some senior black officers. As the British newspaper, *The Guardian*, described it at the time of the murders Bermuda was a country in which, "… (Although) the wealth seems not to be badly distributed, bearing in mind it is still very much a colony. The blacks, who make up two-thirds of the Bermudian community, don't live all that badly. Unemployment is almost non-existent, poverty is rare. Many people seem to own their own homes …and consumer goods are easily available and not too pricey. Tax is low, the sunshine is constant…."(6)

That these efforts towards racial change and complete equality occurred at the time the United States and Britain were experiencing revolutionary changes in race relations was no coincidence. By the mid-century racial equality had become the major concern for Bermudian citizens and it echoed the changes that were occurring in the United States and Britain. The catalyst for change was the civil rights movement whose moral passion destroyed the legitimacy of societies that were structured on segregation and legalized discrimination. From the beginning American Civil Rights leaders called for a partnership with white liberals to end an inhumane system. They were committed to a 'brotherhood of ideals'.

During the late 1950s Bermudians looked to the Rev Martin Luther King for inspiration in their own efforts to abolish the system of segregation on the island. American black leaders like King showed the way for Bermudians in calling for a society where all Bermudians would enjoy the fruits of a successful and rich community without the destructive apartheid which dehumanized blacks. Black activists in Bermuda echoed King's call for a world in which people would be judged not by the 'color of their skin but by the content of their character'.

The movement to secure equal rights for black Bermudians began at the time the American civil rights movement was just beginning. During the 1950s US Civil Rights leaders called for non-violent demonstrations and marches designed to provoke the consciences of their fellow citizens. However, as a new decade began the adoption of different attitudes towards protest that occurred in the United States soon spread to Bermuda. As the Pitt Report recognised, "The 1960s were a decade in which black opinion in (America) was mobilised as never before and the revolution in self-conceptions was dramatised in the adoption of the designation 'black' in place of 'coloured'. Black Bermudians came to identify more with black Americans and to believe that they might learn from the tactics employed by them. Black racial consciousness in Bermuda took on a new tone. The rhetoric of Black Power, the Afro hairstyles and the affirmation that 'Black is Beautiful' came to Bermuda."(7)

Union dockworkers struck in 1959 and inspired a new militancy in union workers. It also affected the racial issue as the BIU worked hand-in-hand with the newly formed PLP. Following full adult suffrage in 1968 it appeared that three centuries of aristocratic white rule would come to an end. This did not happen. The PLP gained only one third of the popular vote and a quarter of the Parliamentary seats in the 1968 election. Four years later the paradoxical situation of continued white rule was repeated. As the left-wing of the PLP moved towards more radical solutions it disturbed a core of working class black Bermudians who feared radical socialist policies would derail their continued battle for equal rights. The PLP's left-wing policies, they believed, were untenable at the polls. The growing militancy of the PLP also upset many religious black Bermudians by criticising the Christian faith in Marxist terms as 'the opiate of the people' and an obstacle to political mobilization.

There were further reasons why the PLP failed to achieve power. The UBP pre-empted many PLP policies including desegregation, free secondary school education and full equal adult suffrage, government financed social services and they made a commitment to the Bermudianization of the work force. The UBP also appointed Sir Edward Richards, an Afro-Caribbean lawyer as the new Premier and nominated Sir John Swan, Bermuda's most successful black businessman, as a candidate for the exclusive white enclave of Paget East.

However, even as the Civil Rights movement was reaching its apex there were militants at work trying to undermine everything Martin Luther King and other non-violent blacks fought for. During the early 1970s the PLP appealed to black militants and angry youths. It referred to blacks who worked for the UBP as 'Uncle Toms'. The UBP, on the other hand was committed to desegregation and a 'partnership between white and black'. It nominated racially mixed 'tickets' in approximately three fifths of Bermuda's constituencies and recruited influential blacks to take leading positions in the party and government. The Wooding Report also recognized that in 1968 and 1977 the riots in Bermuda were associated with activities sponsored by the PLP. In 1968 the violence was preceded by a PLP use of provocative rhetoric at a rally and in 1977 the PLP's efforts to prevent the hangings of Tacklyn and Burrows provoked youthful street gangs to riot. The PLP, the report concluded, needed to take some responsibility for inciting racial animosity.(8)

There were, of course, elements within Bermudian society that did not wish to see any change at all for the black majority. The attitude of some whites towards black Bermudians would never change no matter which government was in power. Similar attitudes towards Bermudian black men were experienced by many Afro-Caribbean youth in Britain especially in the 1970s and 1980s. David Matthews, who grew up in London's East End recalled his memories of his youth when he saw, "…how my hard working parents were treated with disdain and resolved never to lead the life they had….Racism had eaten into me….I was resentful towards a society that carved up the pie to suit a privileged minority. …so I rebelled…… (However) we have become complacent because slavery, colonialism and racism have always been ideal fuel for our anger, bitterness and cynicism towards the white man. But the tide is changing and the time for excuses is running out."(9)

The white racists in Bermuda in the 1960s were gradually marginalized by a society that was determined to throw away the old and embrace the new. Because most black Bermudians felt quite content to seek progress by constitutional means a small minority of blacks, (although having a large support network of young black Bermudians) decided that assassination was the best means of destroying the island's tranquillity and creating the sort of climate that suited its 'revolutionary' ends. They adopted the mantle of the 'outlaw' rebel' in 'primitive revolt' against social oppression by the defenders of that injustice – the 'racist police'.

Out of this climate of political protest there developed a new call for change 'by any means necessary' as young blacks took to the streets to demand change in Bermudian society. The call for 'equal rights' was no longer led by Church groups and mature, moderate black Bermudians. Young men now identified with militant blacks in the United States and were willing to commit violent acts to further their agenda. This new militancy appealed to young black men like Burrows and Tacklyn who did not have the moral grounding to reject indiscriminate violence and unlawful acts.

Bitter resentment also existed because of a lack of understanding between white police officers and black Bermudian youth. This can be no better expressed than by a comment made by a former white expatriate police officer who related his experiences when he lived on the island 30 years ago. "What was condemned as racism was actually 'rational discrimination.'", he opined, "Unjust as it may have been, when you entered certain parts of Hamilton you acted differently, not because you were racist but because most young black men in that area were usually drug pushers or criminals."(10)

*

The 1972/73 spate of murders in Bermuda was inexcusable but not inexplicable. There are killers in every society. It isn't true that young black Bermudians were intrinsically more violent or valued human life less than white Bermudians. But in the late 1960s and early 1970s there was something especially corrosive within Bermudian society that conditioned young blacks to accept murder as a justifiable act against what they perceived as an alleged racist regime and it is arguable that the Black Power agenda, imported from the US, was the catalyst.

By June 1968 violence and protest in the United States had reached a crescendo and it was having its affects on Bermudian youth. Radicals, both white and black, were justifying violence as a legitimate tactic in seeking political ends and they had been enunciating the use of violent methods of 'liberation'. The Black Berets had given their approval to some of these groups, specifically the Black Panthers and the Black Muslims. Such rhetoric from these American anti-establishment groups had frequently been a prequel for physical assaults against police and other establishment figures.

The Black Power movement in America was led by young men who embraced communist and socialist theories (now discredited) as the answer to the call for equal rights for black people. Young men who had close links to the United States and who made frequent visits there returned home with a new perspective about how black people could go about challenging the system. When they returned to the island they began to talk of how most jobs on the island were sophisticated forms of labour exploitation. Some began to believe in the idea that black men could rob homes, steal from local shops, engage in scams, and assure themselves that all of it was okay because they were 'attacking' a system that needed to be dismantled. Followers of the Black Berets were taught that, "All black males are victims. All black prisoners were political prisoners". A radical double standard existed whereby anything the Berets did was justified by the historical sufferings of black people.

American Black Panther literature, which inspired the Black Beret Cadre, played an important role in promoting a hostile attitude to the Bermudian Police force. The Panthers believed that the chief impediment to organizations in the black community came from the activities of the police department. The police, they alleged, functioned like an occupying army in the black community intimidating black people. The Panthers aim was to remove them from their communities. They told their followers that it was a form of 'community imperialism' to have a police force occupying their neighbourhoods which they believed were controlled by the white power structure. To further their aims, the Panthers alleged police officers carried out murders of black citizens.(11)

A flood of literature glorifying and romanticising the use of crime to make amends for past injustices towards black people were endemic in Bermuda in the late 1960s and early 1970s. These manifestos included George Breitman's '*Malcolm X Speaks*', Eldridge Cleaver's '*Soul on Ice*', and George Jackson's '*Blood In My Eye*'. The Marxist Black Panthers' newspaper was used as a model for the Black Berets own publication. Many Panther articles were simply re-written for a Bermudian audience. In one issue it compared the plight of the criminal to the exploitation of the working class. Invoking the name of a notorious criminal the paper said, "He's going to trial on or about four or five different alleged crimes, and the crimes are *seeking justice*. The society views any person who's striving after justice and freedom and to end exploitation as a 'criminal'. We know that if we are criminals, the criminals have received their ultimate revenge when Karl Marx indicted the bourgeoisie of grand theft. We realize that it's they who are criminals and it's they who will have to be brought to justice. We will have to go on fighting in spite of the losses and in spite of the hardships that we're bound to suffer, until the final downfall of the reactionary power structure."(12)

It was also Black Panther influence that persuaded many Black Berets that the use of firearms was legitimate in their pursuit of alleged brutalities committed against them. According to the Black Panther manifesto, published in the Beret newspaper, "We believe the Second Amendment to the Constitution of the United States gives a right to bear arms. We therefore believe that all black people should arm themselves for self-defense....We want freedom for all black men held in federal, state, county and city prisons and jails. We believe that all black people should be released from the many jails and prisons because they have not received a fair and impartial trial."(13)

Following the Governor's assassination, there were a number of black radical groups around the world, many supportive of Marxist terror groups, who praised Burrows' and Tacklyn's murderous acts. Effectively, these groups 'sanctioned' the killing as a 'legitimate' act against a capitalist, unjust and racist society. As former American left-wing political activist Jonathan Lerner stated, describing his own journey towards radicalism, "Like many children of affluence, I was horrified by racism and poverty, and filled with idealism...I started out wanting to humanize the world, but ended up perverting my own best instincts...any damage would satisfy...With a group of ...SDS comrades, I watched the film "The Battle of Algiers" about the successful urban guerrilla war against the French; unannounced bombs in coffee bars, weapons hidden beneath chadors....we felt ourselves to be more heroic and inventive, closer to people like Che Guevara....It has taken me until now... to realise how foolish and wrong we were...."(14)

Many black Bermudians did not understand the innate underpinnings of what the American Black Panthers stood for. Some young men thought the Panthers were heroic martyrs targeted by a fascist American government. Black Beret leaders indoctrinated their members with the notion that the British Government and its colonial representatives were no less fascist. Other new Beret recruits simply 'played' at being 'revolutionaries' and were unaware of how dangerous the organization was becoming.

Although some young Black Beret recruits had romanticised views of the US Black Panthers, others came to see the Panthers for what they really were – a criminal and violent organisation and a few sane Beret members voiced their objections to indiscriminate violence against the 'white Bermudian power structure'.

Black Panther leaders had held the notion that the American government were engaged in 'genocide' against them, a view that was echoed by Black Beret members with reference to the Bermudian government and the Bermuda Police Force. The 'genocide' argument is one of many myths constantly resurrected by left wing historians to excuse the Panthers. In 1971 writer Edward J. Epstein investigated these allegations and found them completely erroneous. According to Epstein there was a difference between 'harassment' and 'genocide'. When the Panthers were stockpiling weapons and engaging in drug dealing and robberies the FBI was 'making prank phone calls' and sending out notes and letters designed to put Panther and Black Power gangs at each others throats. An omniscient and malevolent FBI trying to take down the Panthers was a ludicrous idea, Epstein discovered. (14)

Over the past 30 years the truths about the Panthers have finally been exposed by a number of authors including David Horowitz and Edward J Epstein as well as former Panther members who have stated that the radical organisation was rightly targeted by the FBI. The Black Panthers constituted a definite threat to domestic security, these authors discovered. It was a 'militia' that used extra-legal methods to promote its cause. And, as former

Panther David Hilliard came to realize, "(The Black Panthers) ...talked about arriving at its destiny with arms, through revolutionary methods, and was in coalition with revolutionary peoples all over the world. *(It) certainly made us a threat to the United States of America"* (15) Some former left-wing advocates now recognise that it would have been criminally negligent if the FBI had ignored, in the name of Civil Rights, a violent organization like the Black Panthers. If the Bermudian Government had taken a similar stand the murderous events of 1972/1973 would likely have taken a different course.

It is not surprising, therefore, that many black Bermudian criminals, including Tacklyn and Burrows, displayed no shame or remorse for their crimes which were committed in the name of 'Black Power'. Many of the prisoners at Casemates believed that their criminal activities were in accordance with the fight for civil rights. Some even spoke of getting even with white society for the injustices made against them in their 330 year struggle against slavery. They believed they were fighting the 'white power establishment'. Additionally, the Berets promoted the idea that Casemates prison held innocent victims therefore all its inmates were 'innocent'.

QUO FATA FERUNT - WHITHER THE FATES CARRY (US)

"(Often the attitude is) 'I'm black. I am therefore a victim of racism and am not responsible for my actions. What's more, being black, I am incapable of racism, so you cannot use this excuse against me.' This means we have one law for the black, and one for everyone else. This cannot be a good basis on which to run a society, and, sure enough, our community is disintegrating as a direct consequence."

Letter from Bermuda: *'Seeing Racism Everywhere, Except In The Mirror',*
KYC News, Inc., November 4, 2005

"No sane person can either rationalize or minimise the increasing ubiquity of violence in Bermuda. Mini-riots in Hamilton on weekends are so commonplace they rarely make the news now let alone trigger the states of emergency once employed to combat occasional outbreaks of widespread violence in the 1970s."

Royal Gazette, *'The Human Zoo',* 23 April 2004

THE STRUGGLE FOR equal rights was the high point in Bermuda's history; the assassination of the police chief, the Governor and his aide and the murders of the Hamilton shopkeepers, its lowest.

The Black Beret Cadre believed they had a God-given right to inflict their pathologies on the rest of Bermudian society and in so doing caused great harm to the history of the islands and its people. The role they played has been whitewashed by consecutive Bermudian Governments and began with

Sir Richard Sharples' successor, Ted Leather, who was afraid that further investigations into the Governor's murder would open up a 'can of worms'. Over time history becomes myth and what people believe happened enters into the culture and memories of generations to come. The truth lays buried. However, those who forget the past are condemned to repeat it.

It is also clear that the events of the early seventies were viewed by many politicians as a stain upon the character of the islanders. The response by successive Bermudian governments was to sweep this affair under the carpet. In effect, the politicians turned a blind eye to a blot on the landscape of a beautiful island and they became increasingly aware that the main economic engine of their community – tourism – must not be damaged.

Looking back to 1970 -1973 it is evident that tourist expectations of Bermuda were strongly influenced by industry-produced images designed to sell a place and people to the travel consumer, as it is today. In brochures, travel features, and advertisements, islanders were beautiful, sun-loving people, lounging on the warm, white sands of the island's beaches. At first glance the travel brochures added historical and cultural depth to the constructed image of a happy, peaceful people inviting you to share their paradise. But, on arrival, the passive scenes of a happy and friendly people were juxtaposed with the reality of Court Street, which became synonymous with drug dealing and anti-social activity, race riots and black militants demonstrating and chanting their slogans calling for the end to colonialism and the destruction of an 'evil racist regime'.

In the early 1980s, following the period of turmoil Bermudians had experienced in the 1970s, *Barry, Wood, and Preusch* presented the authentic side of the Bermudian tourism experience. The authors noted that, although some call Bermuda, "…the little Switzerland of the Atlantic, the facade of peace hides deep racial resentment…."(1)

The history of Bermuda in the 1970s could have been different were it not for the leadership of the Progressive Labour Party. The reality is that the PLP could have won power in Bermuda decades before their accession to government in 1998 except for the fact that the militant socialism of Lois Browne Evans - egged on by black militants - frightened most mature black Bermudians as well as the white population. If the PLP had embraced the democratic socialism of

Britain's Labour Party or Canada's New Democrats, it is likely they would have been triumphant much sooner. Despite the rhetoric of extreme left politicians there was a defined constituency of like-minded black and white voters who would have tilted the balance of power had it not been for the extremist talk of leading PLP politicians and their links to fanatical groups like the Black Berets. Instead, the PLP repeatedly missed the chance to create a multi-cultural voting base by opting for the racially exclusive, militant Third World socialism of the type preached by the far left in Britain.

Following the racial turmoil of the 1970s Bermuda's social, political, and economic institutions remained relatively stable but the increasing prosperity of Bermudians did not prevent Bermuda from suffering the same fate as most western nations – fatherless children, degrading educational standards, high prices for even the basics of existence, burgeoning and increasingly violent crime and a growing sense of fear for the future.

Since that time the island has been awash in cocaine and heroin and during the late 1990s the new PLP government did nothing to effectively stem its tide or the tide of corruption and crime. As the *Mid-Ocean News* observed, "The widely publicised looting of the Bermuda Housing Corporation coffers, the multi-million-dollar Berkeley Institute boondoggle, the grace-and-favour terms of the Coco Reef lease and the widening pension fund scandals leave little room for doubt there's more corruption in Bermuda's Government than you'd find in the average graveyard." (2) And, as *Mid-Ocean News* reporter Christian Dunleavy wrote, "The PLP political model is simple: stoke the fires of racial hatred; keep those fires burning and the public will turn a blind eye to neglect over housing, education, crime, healthcare and seniors."(3)

In recent years the crime rate in Bermuda has been high (especially for burglary) compared to industrialized countries. An article by Reuters in August 2006 highlighted acts of violence on the island. It was listed as one of *Yahoo News'* most popular stories. The story, headlined "Bermuda grapples with gangland-style shootings" described, "a drive-by shooting, a gunman spraying bullets into a bar and a teenager gunned down in his car in a gangland-style hit" as proof of escalating violence on the island. The article reported the island's gang problem "… (was) heading the way of urban American or other island getaways in the nearby Caribbean". At the core of the problem was Bermuda's "burgeoning drug trade". The article also described how the U.S. Consulate had issued travel advisories warning visitors about an increasing gang problem and the tendency for assaults in the back streets of Hamilton after dark.(4)

In a related article, the *Bermuda Sun* reported the views of a former senior police officer who was dismayed at how, "Lawlessness could spiral out of control unless the gang culture is smashed and with it the 'code of silence' that effectively renders killers and thugs immune to prosecution." The newspaper went on to describe how many crimes in Bermuda were unsolved because, "Would-be witnesses need stronger support and protection under the law because as the gang culture expands, the pressure to remain silent intensifies. Meanwhile, gangsters roam free to create the kind of deadly mayhem that has shocked Bermuda in recent weeks." The former police officer told the Bermuda Sun that he had seen too many investigations collapse because people were too afraid to testify.(5)

The shocking crime statistics of recent years were highlighted when a Canadian girl, Rebecca Middleton, was brutally murdered on a visit to the islands. Rebecca had been waiting for a cab on Mullet Bay Road, St George's, when she and her friend Jasmine Meens were approached by three youths on two motorcycles. St. George's had been busy that night, with a cruise ship berthed in the town, and the two girls had been socializing at a friend's house on Mullet Bay Road before going outside. Jasmine and Rebecca were driven away on separate bikes. Jasmine was taken back to her father's home in Smith's Parish, where the two girls were staying, but Rebecca did not make it. She was found naked and stabbed near bushes on quiet Ferry Road. Over a period of many years, the judiciary of Bermuda and its governor have declined to review the case and to charge those responsible (who are well known) with aggravated sexual assault and other serious charges, notwithstanding overwhelming evidence which supports those charges. This farce was the result of police 'prosecution incompetence'. As Dr Carol Shuman has documented in her excellent book *Kill Me Once...Kill Me Twice: Murder on the Queen's Playground* , Colin Coxall, who was Police Commissioner of Bermuda at the time that Becky was murdered, tried to make amends at the injustice of the case. Unfortunately, a year after Becky's murder, Bermuda terminated his contract. Coxall is on record as referring to Becky's murder as "the most disgraceful miscarriage of justice" of his career.(6)

Despite fears that an independent Bermuda would lead to closer ties with 'socialist' regimes in the Caribbean both political parties have discussed the possibility of complete independence from Britain. However, critics of the present day PLP government maintain Bermuda's relationship with the United States should not be put in jeopardy by embracing countries like Cuba.

Moderate Bermudians both black and white were therefore pleased that a 1995 independence referendum was resoundingly defeated. Just over 58% of the electorate voted. Of those voting, over 73% voted against independence, while only 25% voted in favour. Vote results may have been distorted by the Progressive Labour Party's call to boycott the referendum. The boycott was also supported by the BIU. In 2006 a poll revealed that seven out of ten Bermudians opposed breaking ties with England.(7)

However, six years after the PLP's election victory Premier (and PLP party leader) Alex Scott announced his decision to commence an open and objective debate on the subject of independence from the U.K. Since that time, there has been only minimal discussion, with the focus more on the pros and cons of autonomy than on the mechanics of delivering independence. There was great concern, however, that former Black Beret leader Phil Perinchief, a vocal advocate of independence, was appointed by the government to lead the enquiry into the prospects for an independent Bermuda. Ewart Brown, who was sworn in as prime minister in October 2006 after ousting three-year incumbent Alex Scott, also supported an independent Bermuda. As a college student in America Brown supported the Black Panthers and the Black Berets.

The issue of independence for Bermuda would appear to be more of a concern for the United States than Britain. Critics in Bermuda allege that present day government policy puts the Bermudian economy at great risk and say that Bermuda's move towards closer ties with undemocratic regimes causes more alarm in Washington DC than in London.

In recent years many Bermudians have been dismayed at their government's attempts to facilitate closer links with Castro's Cuba - a country which allegedly contributed assistance to the Black Beret Cadre in the early 1970s. The connection arose because of the influence black American leaders and black writers had on the Black Beret Cadre, some of whom are now well established in lucrative government appointed positions.

Bermuda's connections with Cuba stemmed from links to American ideas about slavery, the dream of going back to Africa, the work of Marcus Garvey in Cuba, and various cultural interactions. In the 1960s when the critical fracture occurred in the American Civil Rights movement creating a new group of black nationalists, the burgeoning militant wing of the movement believed it had found a natural ally in Fidel Castro's Cuban revolutionary regime and a close relationship was forged with militant black leaders. Revolutionary Cuba offered solidarity and support to civil rights leaders and urban militants alike. The Cubans certainly believed there could be a U.S. revolution, and the Panthers believed they were the vanguard action group that would lead by setting examples. It was Castro's way of influencing American domestic policies. There were also the manipulations that took place by the Soviet Union. Eldridge Cleaver, Former Minister of Information for the Black Panther Party said, "The Black Panther Party was very present in the early years of U.S. black relations with the Castro regime … The Cubans never argued with us about our vanguard role. There was no time for arguments."

Whilst the British take the position that they would not mind in the least if Bermuda became independent Washington cares a great deal. In fact, many British politicians over the years found the continued possession of colonies particularly irksome – ergo, The Falklands, Hong Kong, and Gibraltar – the proximity of the island is still important to the United States.

American interests in Bermuda have, on occasion caused Bermudians to protest. In 1984 Ottiwell Simmons Sr. told the Sunday Times, "For many years we Bermudians have lain back and let the British rule and do as they wish. But we are getting tired. We want a say in our own destiny. We want some say in what is being done here on our island. But we do not control foreign treaties and defence and so everyone can do as they wish. We don't even get any rent for the (military) base. Nothing at all, just the suspicion that the Americans are using us a great aircraft carrier, making us a target for attack, without our say so at all."(8)

America left her bases in Bermuda in 1995.The bases had occupied more than 10 percent of the land which were formally returned in 2002. With the Soviet Union gone and NATO restructured, Bermuda's importance as a military base ended. For years the Bermuda Government got more than US $60 million a year from the bases, even though their real estate had been rent free. Now Bermuda's taxpayers and visitors pay the shortfall.

*

Bermuda had its share of the anger about the historic mistreatment of its black citizens However, despite the successes of the PLP, many white Bermudians cannot understand the continuing 'black rage' that exists in the face of enormous social, cultural and economic gains made by the majority of black Bermudians. And the racial tensions in Bermuda continue to distort the efforts of many Bermudians of both races to build a multi-racial society. Ergo, some Bermudian politicians, taking their cue from PLP politicians like Renee Webb, still claim Bermuda's politics is about race and always will be.

In 1995, more than twenty years after the 1977 riots, the fires of racial discord were still being stoked when a Bermuda radical magazine, believed to be published by Bermuda college students under the name Nationalist Youth Alliance, commemorated the 17th anniversary of Erskine Durrant `Buck' Burrows' hanging in 1977. On the magazine's cover is a photocopied picture of Burrows with his birth dates and a banner headline depicting the words: "Murdered!'" The authors described as a martyr and "truly revolutionary individual...a brother who was willing to sacrifice his life in an effort to end a three-century legacy of oppression of the Afrikaans Bermudian population by the Island's white minority". Additionally, the magazine declared the group, "(understood) the motivation behind the murder and offer no condemnation whatsoever against our fallen comrade". Two earlier editions urged blacks in Bermuda to mount a violent freedom fight against whites and condemned the government for allegedly neglecting blacks. The magazine described the Queen as "a syphilitic whore".(9)

Ten years later black Bermudian youth and the politicians who led them were still calculating their lives along the sum of their grievances rather than the sum of their blessings. As Larry Burchall of the *Bermuda Sun* wrote, "Last time I looked, every sitting member of the ruling party was black. The CEO of the Bank of Bermuda/HSBC and the chairman of the Board of Directors of Butterfield Bank were black. There are plenty of black doctors, dentists, nurses, lawyers, accountants, civil servants... Why then are there still cries that blacks are being disadvantaged because of their race? Racial prejudice is the least of the young black man's obstacles."(10)

Other critics allege that the PLP government routinely meets any criticism of its actions with accusations of racism. Anyone who opposes independence for Bermuda, for example, is often branded a racist. "The (PLP) was elected mainly by repeatedly blaming its predecessor in government of being racists or Uncle Toms, depending on their skin colour", KYC News editorialized, "Meanwhile, a black businessman who was unhappy with the way a local bank had treated him has been suing the bank for racist behaviour. His logic was that his skin colour was the only factor in some of the bank's dealings with him. The notion that his business model was not a good one in the first place never crossed his mind. He alleged that in 1996 a bank officer leaked word of cash flow difficulties to a party he was negotiating to partner with in a cable television business. He alleged that the bank's CEO and 16 past and present bank directors did not properly investigate the alleged breach because he is black."(11)

The present racial climate is not helped by the continuous flow of radical guest speakers who arrive in Bermuda to give their ideologically-biased versions of black history and culture. Since the election of the PLP a succession of Black Power advocates have been invited to Bermuda. Amongst these are the hatemongers Louis Farrakhan (who called Jews 'the bloodsuckers of the black community') and Al Sharpton, a promoter of the concept of 'police racism' within the New York Police Department. These arbiters of political correctness have replaced icons like Martin Luther King in the pantheon of black heroes.

From the white Bermudian perspective, liars like Sharpton's client, Tawana Brawley, have replaced true victims like Emmet Till. As Peter Collier and David Horowitz observed with respect to American black history, "The people holding this attitude truly believe that the worst blight on human history is what white America did to blacks. Most of them haven't read a single book of history that would indicate, for instance, that Jews and a variety of white ethnic groups have also suffered atrocities at the hands of others, atrocities every bit as horrible as, and in some cases worse than, what black Americans have suffered. These narrow-minded arbiters of black history promote romantic visions of black Africa, ignoring the history of interethnic rivalries that caused most of the slaves taken from the continent to be captured and sold to Europeans by other black Africans. They blame what's happening in Rwanda in the 1990s on colonial history, as though the Hutus are so mindless that they cannot themselves be held accountable for brazenly pulling the trigger on and applying machetes to Tutsis. 'The legacy left by the French made them do it' state black romantics who insist on turning all of black history into fairy tales of glorious kings and queens who lived blissful lives until the white man arrived in their territory."(12)

Some black politicians in Bermuda also make positive references to American black leaders like Jesse Jackson (who endorsed the idea that the CIA had conspired to flood African-American communities with crack cocaine in order to suppress the African-American population), convicted drug user and Washington DC Mayor, Marion Barry, ex-convict and convicted drug addict, Rodney King, and characterize them as 'heroes of the struggle'. Black Bermudian youth have no conscious memory of real black heroes like Medgar Evers. Instead they look to 'gangsta rappers' and celebrity criminals for their inspiration and fall victim to exploitative left-wing black intellectuals who glorify the murderous Black Panthers.

It is a bone of contention amongst white Bermudians that associating with such radical and racist 'celebrities' can only widen the racial divide. Black Bermudians, they contend, should also recognise that the United Kingdom views incitement to racial hatred as an arrestable offence and racial incitement to hatred is protected in the United States under the Constitution.

It would appear that the racial problems that have that have scarred the island's political and social life are destined to remain. Although the white community have, for decades, accepted black Bermudians as full partners in the economic, social and political life of the island, the race issue is still, even today, at the centre of public discourse.

*

The Black Berets continue to form an important part of Bermuda's history, at least from the perspective of left wing elements in Bermudian society. This was the Black Beret Cadre of which former Bermudian Premier Jennifer Smith had this to say, "The late 60s and early 70s saw the emergence of Bermuda's Black Beret Cadre and like many of her peers Jennifer Smith gravitated to their message of liberation. The freedom preached by the politics of the movement had its corresponding impact on cultural and artistic freedom of expression and Jennifer's creative soul found a natural home. She founded a dance troupe called the 'Liberation Dancers', where she combined African, modern and interpretive dance to express and tell stories'."(13)

The left wing intellectual elite within the PLP have repeatedly characterized the Berets as 'freedom fighters' and honourable men and women who were fighting for equal rights and the 'empowerment' of black Bermudians. As we have seen, nothing could be farther from the truth and it would appear former members of the Black Beret Cadre, some of whom now hold high office, are in complete denial.

In recent years former Berets have continued to court controversy. Former Black Beret member Mel Saltus, who Scotland Yard detectives did not implicate in the 1972/1973 spate of murders, became the leader of the Black Hebrews in Bermuda. Saltus is representative of former Berets who have not abandoned their racist views. Ben Aaharon, as Saltus later became known, spoke at a memorial for Dionne Bassett who died at the age of 49 in 1998. Saltus, who was acting as spokesman for former Black Beret members said he expected at least 50 people to be at the memorial. Still glorifying the Berets, Saltus said people who viewed Black Berets as 'rebels without a cause' would get to see what they had achieved in the years since the group disbanded.(14)

Phil Perinchief, who was also never implicated in the string of murders and assassinations, was recently a member of the Bermudian Government's Independence Commission. Decades after the Berets came to prominence the former chief ideologue of the organization had not abandoned his extremist political rhetoric as evidenced by a statement he made on the death of Dominican President 'Rosie' Roosevelt Douglas in 2000 in which he reiterated his respect for 'Marxist revolutionaries' Malcolm X, Che Guevara and Stokely Carmichael. In 2000 he also stated that, "Any black person who is not prepared to play the rules the way the white supremacists want them played will suffer….(We should) continue the struggle for independence from Colonial Britain and the establishment of true democracy…free yourselves from your total immersion into selfish capitalistic opulence."(15)

Another former Beret supporter, Randy Horton, who did not figure in any of the murder investigations, was appointed to a position in the Bermuda Government which, incredibly, placed him in charge of Bermuda's law enforcement agencies. He too became a controversial figure when he appeared on a Bermuda television programme. Horton claimed a the steward aboard a flight he took returning to Bermuda was, 'in (my) face, and (I) shouted at him twice to get out of (my) face during a heated confrontation". The steward insisted that Horton said, "How come the white man next to me can use the washroom? Do you treat blacks differently?"(16)

*

It may be argued that racial segregation still exists in Bermuda – a situation that is made by choice rather than laws. Black Bermudians still associate as a race in social settings and white Bermudians act similarly. It is reflected in Sunday morning church attendance and the cultural factors which keep the races apart, including choice of music, dress, entertainment and historical outlook.

No society can exist without a common history. The Bible says that, "the sins of the fathers will be visited on the sons up to the seventh generation". In the Bermuda context it may well be seven generations for the great sins of segregation and racism to be put aside by those who have been wronged. It may also take another few generations for whites and blacks to agree on a common and unbiased history which can set the stage for a society where both communities can truly work as one. A solution might begin with the PLP's version of Bermudian history which has little or no mention of the

English, Portuguese, American and Canadian teachers, police, nurses, doctors, ministers, who built the island up so that all Bermudians could have the highest standard of living in the world.

This could be difficult to achieve because it would appear nothing the white Bermudian can do will alleviate the racial problem. Black Bermudians still accuse whites as being totally insensitive, and that whites subconsciously continue to look down on blacks in covert ways. Very few politicians have found a solution in which both races can traverse a middle ground. Such a solution would perhaps require white Bermudians to create greater opportunity for young black Bermudians to integrate into the economic life of the island and for black Bermudians to acknowledge that the black militants of the 1960s and 1970s exacerbated the island's racial problems.

Bermuda's leading newspaper, *The Royal Gazette* and the *Mid Ocean News*, which published a series of exposes over the past 10 years, did much to rectify the false official accounting of an important era in Bermuda's history. However, they did not tell the full story as readers who are familiar with the series will now be aware.

In light of the new information which has been discovered in the Scotland Yard files, it would behove PLP leaders to cease characterizing the Black Beret Cadre as 'freedom fighters'. Additionally, if Bermuda is to continue to build an equal society it may also require politicians to call for the justice that was denied some 40 years ago. Such a move would inevitably require the Bermudian Government to emulate the American, Israeli and German governments, who have brought ex-Nazis to justice for their crimes more than 50 years after the end of the Second World War, and to re-open the 1972/73 murder cases and bring those who were co-conspirators of Burrows and Tacklyn to justice. The government could begin with a commission of enquiry to look into the evidence which indicates a small group of Black Berets, in particular the 'Third Man', plotted the murders and assassinations – a group that were the inspiration for, and the co-conspirators of, Tacklyn and Burrows. Until that time the ghosts of George Duckett, Sir Richard Sharples, Captain Hugh Sayers, Victor Rego and Mark Doe will continue to haunt all Bermudians – a testament about the times and a reproach to those leaders who don't want to hear the bad news lest it interfere with their 'perfect paradise'.

BIBLIOGRAPHY

GOVERNMENT REPORTS AND PUBLICATIONS

Inquests Report prepared by Bermuda Police – Mr George Duckett, Sir Richard Sharples, Capt. Hugh Sayers, Mr Victor Rego, Mr Mark Doe - December 5th 1974.

The Scotland Yard Files – Statements of Witnesses compiled by the Bermuda Police Force and Scotland Yard Detectives and '*The Final Report*' written by Detective Chief Inspector Basil Haddrell to Commissioner of Police – Division: Murder Squad, 9th December 1976 (CR 201/65/73) Supplied to the author by David Capus, Assistant Departmental Records Officer, Metropolitan Police, Records management Branch, Wellington House, 67 – 73 Buckingham Gate, London SW1E 6BE (2003).

Metropolitan Police: Registered Files, Crime (CR Series) MEPO 26/223/1 Part 1 of 3. Part 1 of 3 Sir Richard SHARPLES (Governor of Bermuda) and Capt H SAYERS: murdered by E D BURROWS and L W TACKLYN at Government House, Bermuda on 10 March 1973 Date range: 1973 - 1978. FORMER REFERENCE CR 201/73/65 http://www.nationalarchives.gov.uk/catalogue/displaycataloguedetails.asp?CATLN=6&CATID=8540755

Metropolitan Police: Registered Files, Crime (CR Series) MEPO 26/223/2 Part 2 of 3 . Part 2 of 3 Sir Richard SHARPLES (Governor of Bermuda) and Capt H SAYERS: murdered by E D BURROWS and L W TACKLYN at Government House, Bermuda on 10 March 1973 Date range: 1973 - 1978. FORMER REFERENCE CR 201/73/65 http://www.nationalarchives.gov.

uk/catalogue/displaycataloguedetails.asp?CATLN=6&CATID=8540755

Metropolitan Police: Registered Files, Crime (CR Series) MEPO 26/223/3 Part 3 of 3 . Part 3 of 3 Sir Richard SHARPLES (Governor of Bermuda) and Capt H SAYERS: murdered by E D BURROWS and L W TACKLYN at Government House, Bermuda on 10 March 1973 Date range: 1973 - 1978. FORMER REFERENCE CR 201/73/65 http://www.nationalarchives.gov.uk/catalogue/displaycataloguedetails. asp?CATLN=6&CATID=8540755

Wooding, Hugh, *Bermuda Civil Disorders 1968 (The Wooding Report), Report of the Commission and Statement by the Government of Bermuda.* Hamilton, Bermuda: Government Publication, 1969

Report of the Royal Commission into the 1977 Disturbances (Pitt Report),
The Rt. Hon. Lord Pitt of Hampstead, MB, ChB, DCH, JP, Chairman;
Professor Michael P. Banton, PhD, DSc, JP
Reginald C. Cooper, Esq.
John I. Pearman, Esq.
Walter N. H. Robinson, Esq.
William A. Scott, Esq.
To His Excellency the Governor of Bermuda, 14th July 1978
Printed In Bermuda by The Bermuda Press Ltd, 1978

Foreign and Commonwealth Office Files (FCO Files) – The National Archives – *Bermuda FCO Records 1971- 1973:*
   FCO 44/541   *Bermuda intelligence reports, including activities of Black Beret Cadre* - January 1971 to September 1971
   FCO 44/542   *Bermuda intelligence reports, including activities of Black Beret Cadre* September 1971 to December 1971
   FCO 63/946   *Bermuda intelligence reports, including activities of Black Beret Cadre* 1 January 1972 – 31 December 1972

FCO 86/50   *Appointment of Sir Richard Sharples as Governor of Bermuda* 1 January 1972 – 31 December 1972

FCO 63/1101 1 January 1973 – 31 December 1973 - *Murder of Sir Richard Sharples, Governor of Bermuda 10 March 1973*

FCO 63/1102   1 January 1973-31 December 1973 *Murder of Sir Richard Sharples, Governor of Bermuda 10 March 1973*

FCO 63/1103   1 January 1973-31 December 1973 *Murder of Sir Richard Sharples, Governor of Bermuda 10 March 1973*

FCO 86/206   1 January 1973 – 31 December 1973

Staffing problems in Bermuda arising from assassination of Sir Richard Sharples, Governor of Bermuda.

PREM 15/1313 11 March 1973 – 21 November 1973. *Prime Minister's Office: Correspondence and Papers, 1970-1974. Situation in Bermuda: Assassination of Governor Sir Richard Sharples and Captain Hugh Sayers, Aide De Camp to governor.*

BOOKS

Barry, Tom, (et al). *The Other Side of Paradise: Foreign Control in the Caribbean.* New York: Grove Press, 1984.

Cashill, Jack. *Sucker Punch.* Nashville, Tennessee: Nelson Current, 2006.

Cleaver, Eldridge. *Soul on Ice.* New York: Dell Publishing, 1968.

Crotty, William J., ed. *Assassinations And The Political Order.* New York: Harper and Row, 1971.

Darrell, Neville T. *Acel D'ama – The Untold Story of the Murder of the Governor of Bermuda, Sir Richard Sharples.* (Self-published), Printed by Coastline Mountain

Press (1983) Ltd, Surrey, B.C. Canada, 2003

DeGroot, Gerard. *The Sixties Unplugged*. London: Macmillan, 2008

Dennis, Norman, and George Edos. *Families without Fatherhood*. London: IEA Health And Welfare Unit, 1993

_____*Rising Crime And The Dismembered Family*. London: Institute of Economic Affairs 1993

Douglas, John and Mark Olshaker, *The Cases That Haunt Us*. New York: Pocket Books, 2000.

_____*The Anatomy Of Motive*. New York: Pocket Books, 1999.

_____*Mindhunter: Inside The FBI Elite Serial Crime Unit, London:* Arrow Books, 1997.

Dubowitz, Howard. *Neglected Children – Research, Practice and Policy*. London: Sage Publications, 1999

Elliott, Paul. *Assassin! The Bloody History Of Political Murder*. Poole: Dorset: GB Blandford, 1999.

Ferguson, Niall. *Empire: How Britain Made the Modern World*. London: Penguin Books Ltd, 2004

Gurian, Michael. *A Fine Young Man*. New York: Jeremy P. Tarcher, 1999

Hannau, Hans. *The Bermuda Isles*. Bermuda: Argos Inc, 1973

Hare, Robert D. *Without Conscience: The Disturbing World Of The Psychopaths Among Us*. New York: The Guilford Press, 1993

Hazelwood, Roy and. Michaud, Stephen G. *Dark Dreams: A Legendary FBI Profiler Examines Homicide And The Criminal Mind*. New York: St Martins Paperbacks, 2001

Hireson, Gordon (Ed). *Sir Richard Christopher Sharples*, Bermuda: Kiwanis International, 1973

Horowitz, David. *Hating Whitey – And Other Progressive Causes*. Dallas: Spence Publishing Company 1999

_____ (Ed with Peter Collier), *The Race Card – White Guilt, Black Resentment, And The Assault On Truth And Justice*. Rocklin, CA: Forum, 1997

Hunter, Barbara Harries. *The People Of Bermuda – Beyond The Crossroads*. Bermuda: Self-Published, Printed In Canada by Gagne-Best, Toronto, 1993

Hurwood, Bernhardt J. *Society and the Assassin: A Background Book on Political Murder. New York:* Parents Magazine Press, 1970.

Hyams, Edward. *Killing No Murder: A Study of Assassination As A Political Means*. London: GB Nelson, 1969

Jones, Liz Ziral. James *Insider's Guide, History of Bermuda, 2nd edition*. Bermuda: Insider's Guide NC, 1999

Kirkham, James (with Levy, S. and Crotty, W) *Assassination and Political Violence – A Report to the National Commission on the Causes and Prevention of Violence*. New York: Bantam Books, 1970

Kittrie, Nicholas. *Rebels With A Cause – The Minds And Morality Of Political Offenders*. Oxford: Westview Press, 2000

Manning, Frank E. *Bermuda Politics In Transition- Race Voting And Public Opinion*. Bermuda: Island Press 1978

McKnight, Gerald. *The Inside Story Of The Murder Squad Of Scotland Yard*. London: WH Allen, 1967

Pearson, Hugh. *The Shadow Of The Panther. Cambridge, MA:* Da Capo Press, 1996

Rhodes, Richard. *Why They Kill*. New York: Vintage Books, 2000

Schafer, Stephen. *The Political Criminal: The Problem Of Morality And Crime*. New York: The Free Press, 1974

Shuman, Carol *Kill Me Once...Kill Me Twice: Murder on the Queen's Playground* by Authorhouse, (2010)

Steele, Shelby. White *Guilt – How Blacks And Whites Together Destroyed The Promise Of The Civil Rights Era*. New York: HarperCollins Publishers, 2006

Tucker, Terry. *Bermuda: Today And Yesterday*. Bermuda: Robert Hale Ltd, 1983

Uviller, Richard H. *Virtual Justice: The Flawed Prosecution Of Crime In America*. New Haven: Yale University Press, 1996

Zimbardo, Philip. *A Situationist Perspective On The Psychology Of Evil.* Palo Alto, Ca: Stanford University 2003

PREFACE

1. See: History News Network, http://hnn.us/articles/29986.html, 9/10/2006, *The Black Panthers: Their Dangerous Bermudian Legacy* by Mel Ayton

INTRODUCTION

1. Sunday Times, *Racial Tension Is No Stranger In Bermuda Paradise*, 18 March 1973, 8

2. Tim Hodgson, Royal Gazette. Email to the author, 8 October, 2004

3. Baroness Sharples. Letter to the author, 8 September 2004

4. Philip Swift. Letter to the author, 7 April 2005

5. Letter from Bermudian Senior Police Officer involved in the assassination investigations and who wishes to remain anonymous, 28 March 2005

CHAPTER 1
FLAWED PARADISE

Hart, Keith *Bermuda's Name*, World History Archives – The Contemporary Political History of Bermuda, 8 October 1995, http://www.hartford-hwp.com/archives/43/041.html

This historical fact has come under scrutiny of late, however. Keith Hart, a history teacher in Bermuda has argued that the name derives from one of the three kings of the Galacia and Leon regions of Northern Iberia. The Bermudos reign was from 760 to 1034, the last Bermudo dying in the battle of Tamara in 1034. Hart believes that Juan had named the island in honour of one of these kings. In any event, they became known as the 'Somers Islands' after Sir George Somers who first settled them in the early 17th century.

2. Jones, Liz Ziral. James *Insider's Guide, History of Bermuda, 2nd edition.* Bermuda: Insider's Guide NC, 1999, 14

3. Burchall, Larry. Bermuda Sun, *We Should Celebrate What Makes Us Bermudian* 7 May 2003, 4

4. Hunter, Barbara Harries. *The People Of Bermuda – Beyond The Crossroads.* Bermuda: Self-Published, Printed In Canada by Gagne-Best, Toronto, 1993, 20

5. Hunter, *The People Of Bermuda – Beyond The Crossroads,* 27

6. Hunter, *The People Of Bermuda – Beyond The Crossroads,* 157

7. Hunter, *The People Of Bermuda – Beyond The Crossroads,* 161

8. Hunter, *The People Of Bermuda – Beyond The Crossroads,* 163

9. Hunter, *The People Of Bermuda – Beyond The Crossroads,* 164

10. Philip Swift. Email to the author, 12 August 2004

11. Hunter, *The People Of Bermuda – Beyond The Crossroads,* 167

12. *Report of the Royal Commission into the 1977 Disturbances (Pitt Report),* The Rt. Hon. Lord Pitt of Hampstead, MB, ChB, DCH, Chairman, HM Government, Printed In Bermuda by The Bermuda Press Ltd, 1978, (Pitt Report), 2

13. Hunter, *The People Of Bermuda – Beyond The Crossroads,* 208

14. Pitt Report, 2

15. Pitt Report, 3

16. The Royal Gazette, *Ex-Governor Ramsbotham's Riot Report Declassified.* 15 April 2005, 5

17. Hunter, *The People Of Bermuda – Beyond The Crossroads, 166-167*

18. Hunter, *The People Of Bermuda – Beyond The Crossroads,* 208

19. Hunter, *The People Of Bermuda – Beyond The Crossroads,* 211

20. Hunter, *The People Of Bermuda – Beyond The Crossroads,* 212

21. Hunter, *The People Of Bermuda – Beyond The Crossroads,* 214

22. The Royal Gazette, *Foreign Secretary Feared For Prince's Safety On*

Island, 28 March 2003

23. Ibid

24. Ibid

25. Ibid

26. Territt Cabral. Email to the author, 11 January 2005

27. Peter Clemmet. Email to the author, 17 October 2005

28. The Royal Gazette, *Foreign Secretary Feared For Prince's Safety On Island,* 28 March 2003

29. Ibid

30. FCO Files. *Cable - Lord Martonmere to Foreign Office,* 11 October 1970

31. The Royal Gazette, *Foreign Secretary Feared For Prince's Safety On Island,* 28 March 2003

32. The Royal Gazette, Magazine section untitled, September 2005

33. The Royal Gazette, *Foreign Secretary Feared For Prince's Safety On Island,* 28 March 2003

34. Ibid

35. Ibid

CHAPTER 2
POLITICAL TARGETS

1. The Bermuda Police Magazine, *George Duckett*, October 1972, 28

PAUL BELVIN – AUTHOR'S NOTE - For a few months he was held in solitary confinement in the 'dark cells' of Casemates Prison, a fortress-like structure on Ireland Island. The maximum security prison was situated near the entrance to the dockyards. HMS Malabar, the stationary base for the Royal Navy, was nearby. Belvin was guarded around the clock by Prison Officers, including the intake of UK expatriate officers who had arrived on the island in October 1971 and who were known locally as the 'Dirty Dozen'. According to a number of expatriate officers Belvin was "definitely mentally unstable" and this fact probably accounted for a commutation of his death sentence to life imprisonment in 1972. Roy Carden. Letter to the author, 6 June 1977

2. Ibid

3. Ibid

4. The Royal Gazette, *A New Dimension*, 11 September 1972, 4

5. The Royal Gazette, *Editorial*, 8 March 1972, 4

6. Territt Cabral. Email to author, 11 January 2005

7. Nick Bolton. Email to the author, 7 February 2005

8. Alan Armstrong (pseudonym). Email to the author, 26 November 2004

9. The Royal Gazette, *A New Dimension*, 11 September 1972, 4

10. Baroness Sharples. Letter to the author, 8 September 2004

11. Daily Telegraph, *Obituary: Sir Richard Sharples, Governor of Bermuda.* 12 March 1973, 15

12. Baroness Sharples. Letter to the author, 8 September 2004

13. Ibid

14. Hireson, Gordon (Ed). *Sir Richard Christopher Sharples*, Bermuda: Kiwanis International, 1973, 20

15. Ibid

16. Daily Telegraph, *Obituary: Sir Richard Sharples, Governor of Bermuda*, 12 March 1973, 15

17. Baroness Sharples. Letter to the author, 8 September 2004

18. Daily Telegraph, *Obituary: Sir Richard Sharples, Governor of Bermuda*, 12 March 1973, 15

19. Bermuda Sun, *The Man Who Did Not Want To Interfere*, 17 March 1973, 10

20. Ibid

21. Hireson, *Sir Richard Christopher Sharples*, 20

22. Bermuda Sun, *The Man Who Did Not Want To Interfere*, 17 March 1973, 10

23. Hireson, *Sir Richard Christopher Sharples*, 21

24. Bermuda Sun, *The Man Who Did Not Want To Interfere*, 17 March 1973, 10

25. Bermuda Sun, *The Man Who Did Not Want To Interfere*, 17 March 1973, 11

26. Bermuda Sun, *The Man Who Did Not Want To Interfere*, 17 March 1973, 10

27. TIME, 'Clouds Across The Sun' 26 March 1973, 52

28. FCO Files. Memo from Acting Governor Kinnear to the UK Foreign and Commonwealth Office, 1 May 1973

29. Mid Ocean News, *MPs lobbied London to appoint Lady Sharples as Governor*
http://www.midoceannews.bm/ siftology.midoceannews/Article/ article.jsp?sectionId=49&articleId=7 d423123008002a
6 February 2004

30. Ibid

31. Mid Ocean News, *When Horsa's Birthday Party Gave FCO Paws For Thought,* 20 February 2004 http:// www.midoceannews.bm/siftology. midoceannews/Article/article.jsp?se ctionId=49&articleId=7d42a12300 80023

32 Ibid

33. Daily Mail, *Yard Team Links Holiday Isle Murders* by Dermot Purgavie, 13 March 1973, 2

34. Sunday Times, *Racial Tension Is No Stranger In Bermuda Paradise*, 18 March 1973, 8

35. Ibid

36. Bermuda Sun, *The Man Who Did Not Want To Interfere* 17 March 1973, 10

March 1973, 4

37. Baroness Sharples. Letter to the author, 8 September 2004

38. TIME, 'Clouds Across The Sun' 26 March 1973, 52

39. Bermuda Sun, *The Shock That Began On Saturday, March 10, 1973*, 17 March 1973, 5

40. Ibid

41. Bermuda Sun, *Don't Quote Me, Said The Pressman*, 17 March 1973, 9

42. Bermuda Sun, Tourism *Rides The Blow*, 17 March 1973, 9

43. Royal Gazette, *Editorial*, 12 March 1973, 1

44. Mid Ocean News, *Buck Burrows' desperate plan to kidnap Premier is exposed*, 30 January 2004 http://www.midoceannews.bm/ siftology.midoceannews/Search/ results.jsp?dateOrdered=false&articl eIndex=9

45. Daily Express, *Guns – For Black Power leaders, This Tiny Colony Sticks out like a Sore Thumb by Ivor Key*, 12

46. Daily Express, Untitled, 19 March 1973, 7

47. Daily Express, *Guns – For Black Power leaders, This Tiny Colony Sticks out like a Sore Thumb by Ivor Key*, 12 March 1973, 4

48. Birmingham Post (UK), *Troubled Waters Of The Caribbean*, 13 March 1973, 5

49. Daily Telegraph, *Murder in Bermuda*, 12 March 1973, 2

50. Daily Mail, *Yard Team Links Holiday Isle Murders'* by Dermot Purgavie, 13 March 1973, 2

51. The Guardian, *Tourist Trap*, 12 March 1973, 4

52. The Guardian, *Rumblings Of Discontent Under Bermuda Calm* by Simon Winchester, 13 March 1973, 3

53. The Sun, *Hired Gunmen Clue To Island Killings* by Steve Dunleavy, 13 March 1973

CHAPTER 3
THE BLACK BERETS 1969-1970

1. The Guardian, *Rumblings Of Discontent Under Bermuda Calm* by Simon Winchester, 13 March 1973, 3

2. Ibid

3. Ibid

4. Reed Irvine and Cliff Kincaid, *Black Panthers Still Growling*, Media Monitor, www.aim.org, 3 March 2002

5. Michael Kaufman, *Stokely Carmichael, Rights Leader Who Coined 'Black Power' Dies at 57*. The New York Times, 16 November 1998. http://www.nytimes.com/1998/11/16/us/stokely-carmichael-rights-leader-who-coined-black-power-dies-at-57.html?scp=1&sq=stokely+carmichael+died&st=nyt

6. DeGroot, Gerard. *The Sixties Unplugged*. London: Macmillan, 2008, 270

7. Libcom.org. *The Black Panther Party For Self Defense.* http://libcom.org/library/the-black-panther-party-for-self-defense, September 2006

8. Kirkham, James (with Levy, S. and Crotty, W) *Assassination and Political Violence – A Report to the National Commission on the Causes and Prevention of Violence*. New York: Bantam Books, 1970, 348

9. DeGroot, Gerard. *The Sixties Unplugged*. London: Macmillan, 2008, 271

10. The Black Panther, *Editorial*. April 6, 1969, 14. http://www.itsabouttimebpp.com/BPP_Newspapers/bpp_newspapers_index.html

11. The Black Panther, May 1967, *A Pig* http://www.itsabouttimebpp.com/BPP_Newspapers/bpp_newspapers_index.html

12. Horowitz, David. *Hating Whitey – And Other Progressive Causes*. Dallas: Spence Publishing Company 1999, 212.

13. Sol Stern. *Ah, those Black Panthers! How Beautiful!* City Journal, 27 May 2003. http://www.city-journal.org/

html/eon_5_27_03ss.html

14. Pearson, Hugh. *The Shadow Of The Panther. Cambridge, MA:* Da Capo Press, 1996, 221

15. Brian Carnell. *City Journal vs New York Times on the Black Panthers.* 4 June 2003 http://www.leftwatch. com/articles/2003/city-journal-vs-new-york-times-on-the-black-panthers/

16. Jamie Glazov, *Bobby Seale's Confession: David Horowitz was Right On.* History News Network. 6. May 2002 http://hnn.us/articles/695.html

17. Kate Coleman. *The Panthers For Real*, 23 June 2003, FrontPage magazine. http://www. frontpagemag.com/readArticle. aspx?ARTID=17579

18. Horowitz, David (Ed with Peter Collier), *The Race Card – White Guilt, Black Resentment, And The Assault On Truth And Justice.* Rocklin, CA: Forum, 1997, 166

19. Cleaver, Eldridge. *Soul on Ice.* New York: Dell Publishing, 1968, 26

20. Horowitz, David. *Hating Whitey – And Other Progressive Causes.* Dallas: Spence Publishing Company 1999, 213

21. Ibid

22. Sol Stern. *Ah, those Black Panthers! How Beautiful!* City Journal, 27 May 2003. http://www.city-journal.org/ html/eon_5_27_03ss.html

23. Horowitz, David. *Hating Whitey – And Other Progressive Causes.* Dallas: Spence Publishing Company 1999, 121

24. Horowitz, David. *Hating Whitey – And Other Progressive Causes.* Dallas: Spence Publishing Company 1999, 120, 214

25. Ibid

26. Ibid

27. Kate Coleman. *The Panthers For Real*, 23 June 2003, FrontPage magazine. http://www. frontpagemag.com/readArticle. aspx?ARTID=17579

28. Alvin Williams. *Blacks Have Turned On Blacks In Tribalism That Has Brought Grief To Many Bermudian Families*. Mid Ocean News, 9 June 2004, http://www.midoceannews.bm/siftology.midoceannews/Article/article.jsp?sectionId=49&articleId=7d3548e3008000f

29. FCO Files. Bermuda Intelligence Committee Report 5 January 1971 – 2 February 1971, FCO 44/541

30. Ivor Key, *10 Black Power Men Quizzed.* Daily Express, 13 March 1973, 7

31. Alvin Williams. *The Times In Which We Really Came Of Age.* Mid Ocean News 13 June 2003 http://www.midoceannews.bm/siftology.midoceannews/Article/article.jsp?sectionId=49&articleId=7d3668e3008000e

32. *The Cuba Kid Who Didn't Know Castro From Castor Oil*, Mid Ocean News, 12 May 2006. http://www.midoceannews.bm/siftology.midoceannews/Article/article.jsp?ar ticleId=7d6560e30080020&sectionId=60

33. Territt Cabral. Email to the author, 8 December 2005

34. FCO Files. Bermuda Police Intelligence Report for Foreign Office, February 1971

35. Ibid

36. Mid Ocean News. *Inside The Black Beret Cadre,* 6 June 2003 http://www.midoceannews.bm/siftology.midoceannews/Article/article.jsp?sectionId=49&articleId=7d3630e30080007

37. Mid Ocean News. *The Cuba Kid Who Didn't Know Castro From Castor Oil*. 12 May 2006. http://www.midoceannews.bm/siftology.midoceannews/Article/article.jsp?ar ticleId=7d6560e30080020&sectionId=60

38. Alvin Williams. *The Times In Which We Really Came Of Age.* Mid Ocean News 13 June 2003 http://www.midoceannews.bm/siftology.midoceannews/Article/article.jsp?se

ctionId=49&articleId=7d3668e300
8000e

39. FCO Files. Lord Martonmere -
Memo to the Foreign Office, March
25 1970.

40. Ibid

41. *Deeper Inside The Black Beret
Cadre…* Mid Ocean News, 13 June
2003 http://www.midoceannews.
bm/siftology.midoceannews/Article/
article.jsp?sectionId=49&articleId=7
d3668e3008000d

42. FCO Files. Bermuda Police
Report, 7 October 1970

43. Alvin Williams. *The Times In
Which We Really Came Of Age.* Mid
Ocean News 13 June 2003 http://
www.midoceannews.bm/siftology.
midoceannews/Article/article.jsp?se
ctionId=49&articleId=7d3668e300
8000e

44. FCO Files. Government House
memo, 9 October 1970

45. FCO Files. Bermuda Police
Report, 11 October 1970

46. FCO Files. Bermuda Police
Intelligence Report November 1970

47. FCO Files. Memo, Chief
Secretary to West Indian Dept of the
FCO, November 1970

48. FCO Files. Bermuda Intelligence
Committee Report 5.1.71 – 2.2.71,
FCO 44/541

49. FCO Files. Bermuda
Government House Intelligence
Report, 15 February 1971

CHAPTER 4
THE BLACK BERETS 1971-1972

1. FCO Files. Bermuda Intelligence
Committee Report, 5 January 1971 –
2 February 1971, No 1 of 1971, FCO
44/541

2. Ibid

3. Ibid

4. FCO Files. Internal memo from
A.R. Powell, 24 February 1971, FCO
44/541

5. Ibid (*Author's Note: The files do not indicate the reason for Perinchief's conviction and the Bermuda Police Force responded negatively when a request was made for his police records. Additionally, Mr Perinchief refused a request for interview.*)

6. Ibid

7. Ibid

8. Ibid

9. Ibid

10. Ibid

11. FCO Files. Bermuda Intelligence Committee Report 5 January 1971 – 2 February 1971, FCO 44/541

12. FCO Files. Government House, Despatch to the Foreign Office, 15 February 1971, FCO44/541

13. Ibid

14. Ibid

15. Ibid

16. FCO Files. Bermuda Intelligence Committee Report 5 January 1971 – 2 February 1971, FCO 44/541

17. FCO Files. Government House memo, 5 March 1971

18. FCO Files. Bermuda Intelligence Committee Report 5 January 1971 – 2 February 1971, FCO 44/541

19. Ibid

20. Metropolitan Police Report entitled "Criminal Investigation Department, New Scotland Yard, 8.5.74, (name redacted by author) Criminal Records Office, No 4990. Also - Bermuda Intelligence Committee Report, 7.7.71 – 3.8.71, FCO 44/541

21. Bermuda Intelligence Committee Report 3.2.71 –2.3.71, FCO 44/541

22. Ibid

23. Ibid

24. Government House, Despatch to the FO, 15th February 1971, FCO44/541

25. Bermuda Intelligence Committee Report, July 1971

26. Bermuda Intelligence Committee Report, 3 Feb-2 March 1971 FCO 44/541

27. *Royal Gazette* 6 June 2003

28. Foreign Office memo to Lord Martonmere, May 1971

29. *Royal Gazette* 6 June 2003

30. Bermuda Intelligence Committee Report July 1971

31. Ibid
32. Ibid

33. Bermuda Intelligence Committee Report, 7.7.71 – 3.8.71, FCO 44/541

34. Ibid

35. Ibid

36. Ibid

37. Ibid

38. Ibid

39. Ibid

40. Ibid

41. Bermuda Intelligence Committee Intelligence Report 29.10.71 – 30.11.71, FCO 44/542

42. Bermuda Intelligence Committee Report 3.2.71 – 2.3.71, FCO 44/541

43. Government House, Despatch to the Foreign Office, 15th February 1971, FCO44/541

44. Bermuda Intelligence Committee Report December 1971

45. Government House Report by Lord Martonmere to Foreign Office, December 1971

46. Ibid

47. Bermuda Intelligence Committee Report 1.7.71 – 3.8.71, FCO 44/541

48. Bermuda Intelligence Committee Report 29.10.71 – 30.11.71, FCO 44/542

49. Government House Intelligence Report, 5.9.72

50. *Royal Gazette* 20 June 2003, Jonathan Kent

51. Bermuda Intelligence Committee Report 5 September 1972

52. Minutes of Intelligence Committee Meeting, Foreign Office papers, 5.9.1972

53. FCO memo, 23 November 1972

54. Bermuda Intelligence Committee Report, 8.11.72 – 5.12.72, FCO 63/946
55. Bermuda Intelligence Committee Report December 1972

56. FCO memo, 23 November 1972

57. Government House memo to Foreign Office December 1972
58. Government House memo to Foreign Office 6.3.1973

59. Government House memo to Foreign Office, 1.5.1973

* Former Black Beret Cadre supporters:

Mel Saltus - the Black Berets 'Minister of Information' and who later changed his name to Eliyahtsoor Ben Aaharon.
Ottiwell Simmons Jr – who left the island in 1973 and eventually joined a black Hebrew sect in Israel.
Randolph Horton - former Black Beret supporter and a former PLP Minister of Labour, Home Affairs and Public Safety.
Ewart Brown - a former Black Beret apologist and present Premier of the PLP government.
Jerome Perinchief – former Black Beret 'Minister of Defense', brother of Bermuda Member of Parliament Wayne Perinchief and Senator Phil Perinchief, former Attorney General of Bermuda.
Malcolm Marsden Dears - Beret supporter and known violent criminal.
Calvin 'Shebaz' Weeks - former Black Berets 'Treasurer'.
Dennis Alan Bean - former

convict who robbed the Masters store and received money from the Shopping Centre robbery. He is currently a cab driver and appears frequently on Bermuda 'Talk Shows'. He was a parliamentary candidate in the 2003 election. Scotland Yard Files. Statement of Witness, Dennis Bernard Bean, 29 June 1976.

Beverley Lottimore - became the Communications Director for Premier Alex Scott.

Glen Fubler - an associate of Black Beret Cadre members and joined in protest marches on Front Street, Hamilton.

'Baby Face' Evans, convicted criminal notorious amongst Bermudian Police for possessing firearms.

Donald Scott, former financial secretary for the PLP government.

Keith Adderley, convicted of arson (Devonshire Church) and sentenced to 7 years imprisonment

CHAPTER 5
THE MURDER OF BERMUDA'S POLICE CHIEF

1. Time. *Terror on Pleasure Island*, 19 October 1959

2. Scotland Yard Files, Metropolitan Police Criminal Investigation Department, New Scotland Yard, 11th February, 1973 - To Commissioner of Police, Bermuda, 11 February 1973

3. The Scotland Yard Files – Statements of Witnesses compiled by the Bermuda Police Force and Scotland Yard Detectives and '*The Final Report*' written by Detective Chief Inspector Basil Haddrell to Commissioner of Police – Division: Murder Squad, 9th December 1976 (CR 201/65/73) Supplied to the author by David Capus, Assistant Departmental Records Officer, Metropolitan Police, Records Management Branch, Wellington House, 67 – 73 Buckingham Gate, London SW1E 6BE (2003). Statement of Witness, Sheena Duckett.

4. Ibid

5. Ibid

6. *Inquests Report prepared by Bermuda Police* (Inquests Report) – Mr George

Duckett, Sir Richard Sharples, Capt. Hugh Sayers, Mr Victor Rego, Mr Mark Doe - December 5th 1974 Para 206

7. Inquests Report paras 20-21

8. Inquests Report para 24

9. Inquests Report para 107

10. Inquests Report para 35

11. Philip Swift. Email to the author from, 12 August 2004

12. Royal Gazette. *Editorial - A New Dimension*, 11 September 1972, 4

13. Royal Gazette. *New Dimension To The Crime, Says Acting Governor*, 11 September 1972.

14. Mid Ocean News, *The Execution of Commissioner Duckett*, 27 June 2003 http://www.midoceannews. bm/siftology.midoceannews/Article/ article.jsp?articleId=7d6680e3008004 7&sectionId=60

15. Government House memo to FCO, 1 May 1973

16. Ibid

17. Mid Ocean News. *Trial Of Buck Burrows – Now You Have The Confessions…* 28 July 2006 http:// www.midoceannews.bm/siftology. midoceannews/Article/article.jsp?ar ticleId=7d67e0e30080036&section Id=60

18. Scotland Yard Files, Metropolitan Police Criminal Investigation Department, New Scotland Yard, 11th February, 1973 - To Commissioner of Police, Bermuda, 11 February 1973

19. Bermuda Police Statement of Witness Basil Haddrell, 31 May 1975

20. Nigel Regan., *The Buck Burrows Few People Knew*. Bermuda Sun 13 December 2002 http://bermudasun. org/main.asp?Search=1&ArticleID= 14756&SectionID=82&SubSectionI D=231&S=1

21. Ibid

22. Matthew Taylor. *Darrell Plans More Revealing Sequel*, Royal

Gazette, 21 January 2004 http://www.royalgazette.com/siftology.royalgazette/Article/article.jsp?sectionId=60&articleId=7d41a9230030013

23. Darrell, Neville T. *Acel D'ama – The Untold Story of the Murder of the Governor of Bermuda, Sir Richard Sharples.* (Self-published), Printed by Coastline Mountain Press (1983) Ltd, Surrey, B.C. Canada, 2003, 6

24. Government House Report to FCO 23 October 1973

25. Nick Bolton. Email to the author, 3 February 2005

26. Territt Cabral. Email to the author, 11 January 2005

27. Ibid

28. Scotland Yard Files. Psychiatric Report by Dr PG Eames – *Interview with Erskine Burrows, St Brendan's Hospital*, 26 May 1976

29. Peter Clemmet. Email to the author, 17 October 2005

30. Inquests Report, para 68

31. Mid Ocean News. *The Cuba Kid Who Didn't Know Castro From Castor Oil.* 12 May 2006. http://www.midoceannews.bm/siftology.midoceannews/Article/article.jsp?articleId=7d6560e30080020&sectionId=60

32. Inquests Report para 198

33. Inquests Report para 212

34. Nick Bolton. Emails to the author, 7.2.2005, 3.2.2005

35. Royal Gazette, *Leaders Deplore The Murder*, 11 September 1972, 2

36. Ibid

37. Bermuda Police Magazine. *Police Commissioner George Duckett*, October 1972, 9

CHAPTER 6
THE ASSASSINATION OF THE ISLAND'S GOVERNOR

1. Scotland Yard Files. Statement of Sylvan Musson Jr, 23 May 1976

2. Nick Bolton. Letter to the author, 7 February 2005

3. Scotland Yard Files. Statement of Sylvan Musson Jr, 23 May 1976

4. Ibid

5. Scotland Yard Files, Statement of Wayne Michael Jackson, 18 November 1975

6. Scotland Yard Files. Statement of Wayne Michael Jackson, 16 July 1975

7. Ibid

8. Ibid

9. Ibid

10. Scotland Yard Files. *The Final Report*, 4

11. Scotland Yard Files. Statement of Witness, Wayne Michael Jackson, 18 November 1975

12. Scotland Yard Files. *Report: Government House and Shopping Center Murders*, Bermuda CR 201/73/65

13. John Smith. The People, *I warned Sir Richard – you could be murdered next*, 18 March 1973, 2

14. Ibid

15. FCO Files. Government House memo to FCO, December 1972

16. Mid Ocean News. *MPs lobbied London to appoint Lady Sharples as Governor*, 6 February 2004 http://www.midoceannews.bm/siftology.midoceannews/Article/article.jsp?sectionId=49&articleId=7d423123008002a

17. Dorothy-Grace Elder. Glasgow Herald, *Where the style of the raj lives on,* 13 March 1973, 3

18. The Daily Telegraph, *Murder in Bermuda*, 12 March 1973, 2

19. Bermuda Sun, *Government House – An Easy Target In The Dark*, 17 March 1973, 11

20. Mid Ocean News. *Foreign Secretary Feared For Prince's Safety on Island Tri, 28 March 2003* http://www.midoceannews.bm/siftology.midoceannews/Article/article.jsp?sectionId=49&articleId=7d33e1230080001

21. Inquests Report, para 132

22. Scotland Yard Files. *Report: Government House and Shopping Center Murders*, Bermuda CR 201/73/65 - Burrows' confession

23. Inquests Report para 133

24. Inquests Report para 138

25. Inquests Report para 142

26. Inquests Report para133

27. Inquests Report para 149

28. *The Final Report*. 35

29. Inquests Report para 151

30. Scotland Yard Files. Statement of Witness, James McMaster, 24 May 1976

31. Inquests Report para 168

32. Inquests Report para 169

33. Inquests Report paras 170-189
34. *The Final Report*, 73-74

35. Scotland Yard Files. Statement of Witness, Barbara Blane, nee Francis, 10 November 1975

36. Inquests Report para 189

37. Scotland Yard Files. Statement of Witness, Barbara Blane, nee Francis, 10 November 1975

38. Inquests Report para 190

39. Patrick Burgess. Email to the author from, 25 September 2004

40 Letter to the author from Alan Armstrong (pseudonym), 26 November 2004

41. Mid Ocean News. *UK faith in island's long-term prospects was a victim of Sharples' assassination,* 12 March 2004 http://www.midoceannews.bm/siftology.midoceannews/Article/article.jsp?se

ctionId=49&articleId=7d43612300
8002b

42. FCO Files *Statement by the Secretary of State for Foreign and Commonwealth Affairs*, 12 March 1973

43. Ian Ball, Daily Telegraph, *FBI Join Bermuda Manhunt*, 22 March 1973, 6

44. Sir Duncan Watson Deputy Under Secretary, FCO. Letter to IAC Kinnear, 22 May 1973

45. FCO Files ANE 14/5. E.N Larmour to H.E. Mr K.R. Creek, EXT/REL/GOV, 22 March 1973

46. Scotland Yard Files. Statement of Witness, Wayne Michael Jackson, 18 November 1975

47. *The Final Report*. 7

48. Ibid

49. *The Final Report. 9*

50. *Ibid*

51. *The Final Report*. 14

52. *The Final Report*. 15

53. Inquests Report, para 205

54. Inquests Report, paras 206 - Para 211

55. Inquests Report para 214

56. Inquests Report paras 244-251

57. FCO Files. Cable From President Richard M. Nixon to HM The Queen via American Embassy, London - FCO AHE/14/5. FM FCO 1612352, 16 March 1973

58. Sidney Young. Daily Mirror, *His Duty – By Widow of Governor*, 14 March 1973, 3

59. Mid Ocean News. *MPs lobbied London to appoint Lady Sharples as Governor*, 6 February 2004 http://www.midoceannews.bm/ siftology.midoceannews/Article/ article.jsp?sectionId=49&articleId=7 d423123008002a

CHAPTER 7
THE UNHOLY ALLIANCE

1. FCO Files. Government House memo to the Foreign Office, May 1973

2. Mid Ocean News. *A Conspiracy to Murder*, 26 June 2006 http://www.midoceannews.bm/siftology.midoceannews/Article/article.jsp?sectionId=49&articleId=7d66b8e30080032

3. Scotland Yard Files, Metropolitan Police General Registry MEPO 26/223 CR 201 /65/73 *Murder of the Governor of Bermuda*

4. Nick Bolton, Email to the author, 7 February 2005

5. FCO Files. Government House Memo to Sir Duncan Watson, FCO, 23 May 1973

6. Email to the author from anonymous source, 'Jadejezz', Bermuda Free Speech Forum, 19 April 2005
7. Nick Bolton. Email to the author, 7 February 2005

8. Ibid

9. Ibid

10. Mid Ocean News. *A Conspiracy To Murder*, 23 June 2006 http://www.midoceannews.bm/siftology.midoceannews/Article/article.jsp?sectionId=49&articleId=7d66b8e30080032

11. Scotland Yard Files. Statement of Wayne Michael Jackson, 18 November 1975

12. Scotland Yard Files, Statement of Witness, Anthony Brown Mello, 26 February 1973

13 Ibid

14. Ibid

15. Scotland Yard Files. Statement of Albert Rodriguez Cabral, 27 February 1973

16. Ibid
17. Ibid

18. Inquests Report para 341

19. Territt Cabral. Email to the author, 23 September 2005

20. Ibid

21. *The Final Report* 25

22. Inquests Report paras 315-319

23. Inquests Report para 268

24. Inquests Report para 269

25. Inquests Report para 257

26. *The Final Report* 24

27. Inquests Report para 259

28. Inquests Report para 344

29. Inquests Report para 345

30. Inquests Report para 347

31. Inquests Report para 349
32. *The Final Report* 30

33. Nick Bolton. Emails to the author, 3 February 2005, 7 February 2005

34. Scotland Yard Files. Metropolitan Police General Registry MEPO 26/223 CR 201 73 65, *Murder of The*

Governor of Bermuda

35. Ibid

**CHAPTER 8
ARREST AND
IMPRISONMENT**

1. Inquests Report para 305

2. Inquests Report para 192

3. *The Final Report* 42

4 Inquests Report paras 46-50

5. *The Final Report* 10

6. *Royal Gazette*, Buck: I have made My Peace With The Lord, 25 May 2006
7. *The Final Report* 10

8. *The Final Report* 23

9. Inquests Report para 61

10. Inquests Report para 59

11. *The Final Report* 38

12. Tim Ewart, *The Shootings - Police*

Warn: Gunman Could Kill. Bermuda Sun, 29 September 1973, 1

13. Ibid

14. Mid Ocean News.
Buck Burrows' desperate plan to kidnap Premier is exposed
http://www.midoceannews.bm/siftology.midoceannews/Article/article.jsp?sectionId=49&articleId=7d41f123008003630 January 2004

Former PLP candidate Neville T. Darrell was a young police officer at the time of the murders and shootings. He joined the Bermuda Police Force in 1960 and remained there until he was fired from his job in 1978. Darrell had been promoted to the rank of Detective Sergeant but was later demoted. He blamed a 'racist police administration' for his dismissal. (Royal Gazette 27 January 2005, *Why Neville Took To The Pen Instead Of The Gun* by Heather Wood) Arthur D.O. Hodgson, who wrote the Foreword to Darrell's short memoir, described Buck Burrows as a man who had "…decisiveness in political action" who "(displayed) strength of character, which is lacking in most politicians." (*Acel D'Ama*, page 6)

In his book published in 2003, Darrell related how he once considered killing one of his superior officers. He told Royal Gazette reporter Heather Wood, "No, I did not commit murder, although I had thought about it and had planned to murder one of my police administrators. One of the differences between Buck (Burrows) and me was the fact that Buck, because of frustration, took to the gun and committed murder, while I took to the pen and wrote this book." Wood wisely asked Darrell, if the administration was racist, why was he promoted in the first place? Darrell's reply was that he "was too advanced for the Bermuda Police Force"(RG 27.1.2005, *Why Neville Took To The Pen Instead Of The Gun* by Heather Wood) It was a statement contradicted by the true facts of his dismissal and the testimony of some of his former colleagues in the police force. According former police officers, Territt Cabral and Nick Bolton, both of whom worked with Darrell, some officers distrusted him because he associated with criminals on Court Street and also involved in high stakes card games. The officers said that Darrell was considered to be a "hard man" amongst the criminal fraternity. He also carried a revolver on and off duty. According to the two former officers, Darrell's failures were certainly not the result of any racism. According to both the former police officers Darrell was demoted from Police Sergeant to constable and then eventually fired because he forged or falsified a sick note. (Royal Gazette 27 January 2005, *Why Neville Took To The Pen Instead Of The Gun* by Heather Wood)

Darrell's claims he, "… masterminded the capture of Buck Burrows". However, the police files indicate Darrell exaggerated his role which was, essentially, providing intelligence of Burrows' whereabouts.

15. Nigel Regan. *Special Report: How We Collared Burrows*, Bermuda Sun, 4 December 2004 http://bermudasun. org/main.asp?Search=1&ArticleID= 14585&SectionID=82&SubSectionI D=231&S=1

16. Ibid

17. Ibid

18. Ibid

19. Nigel Regan. *Bermuda's Thwarted Revolutionary*. Bermuda Sun, 31 January 2003 http://bermudasun.org/ main.asp?Search=1&ArticleID=153 69&SectionID=82&SubSectionID= 231&S=1

20. Nigel Regan, *The Buck Burrows Few People Knew*. Bermuda Sun, 13 December 2003 http://bermudasun. org/main.asp?Search=1&ArticleID= 15369&SectionID=82&SubSectionI D=231&S=1

21. Mid Ocean News. *The Dream/ Nightmare World of Buck Burrows*. 12 May 2006 http://www.midoceannews.bm/ siftology.midoceannews/Search/ results.jsp?dateOrdered=false&articl eIndex=9

22. *The Final Report* 29

23. *Author's Note*: I was a former

resident of the island between September 1971 and December 1973 and I was, in fact, employed by the Bermudian Prison Department and knew the two conspirators who were tried for the murders and eventually executed. I also worked closely with some of the people mentioned in this book. However, the book was never meant to be a 'memoir' therefore I have, as far as possible, removed myself from the events described and instead have relied, for the most part, on the recollections of my former colleagues.

I had previously worked in a maximum security psychiatric prison in England, a prison that specialized in the treatment of psychopaths. I was therefore used to looking after violent and disturbed individuals. It came as a surprise, therefore, to discover that Bermuda's criminals were far more violent from any I had previously known.

I had occasion to be responsible for Larry Tacklyn for a short period of time when I was placed in charge of 'A' wing. I had the exacting task of unlocking Tacklyn each morning and as I entered his cell doorway he would invariably be standing in the corner staring aggressively at me. Of all the prisoners I came into contact during the two years I spent working in Casemates Tacklyn stood out as the most malevolent. He did not threaten me in any overt way but he did make it absolutely clear that he hated me because I was white and English.

I also recall the time I was in charge of Section 2. A Dirty Dozen colleague, Terry Jamieson, was instructed by Divisional Officer Dean to allow Dennis Bean out for exercise and to put him in the yard next to Tacklyn. I told Jamieson that the security instructions regarding Burrows, Tacklyn and Bean would be negated if this was allowed to continue. Officer Jamieson complained to the Chief Officer but no disciplinary action was taken.

There were a number of incidents in the prison I remembered well. On Thursday 23 June 1972, for example, I was supervising exercise in the basketball court. There were over 30 inmates. The remainder of the prisoners, who refused exercise, were locked away in the block. A senior officer informed me that extra officers would soon join me in supervisory duties. None appeared the whole time the exercise was taking place. During the Basketball game a fight between two inmates erupted and I was forced to separate the inmates alone. Had the rest of the prisoners turned on me I would have been unable to call for assistance.

I also recall the time I was placed on a death list by a particularly violent and unstable prisoner by the name of Matthews, a Black Beret supporter and alleged member of the organization. Matthews had been imprisoned after he was caught without a tax certificate for his 50cc bike. In court Matthews jumped out of the dock and stabbed the reporting police officer in the neck. He was given three years for grievous bodily harm. Matthews, who stood over six foot tall and sported an Afro hairstyle, was one of the most belligerent and aggressive of prisoners. He frequently erupted in rage when challenged for even the most minor infringement of the rules.

On one occasion I placed him on report for 'violent behaviour towards prison staff'. When he was called by the prison governor to answer the charges he attacked two Bermudian officers who unlocked his cell. I came to the aid of the officers and we took Matthews to the segregation unit. Matthews threatened reprisals and purportedly put my name on a 'death list'.

24. Scotland Yard Files. Statement of Witness, E.L Dyer, Scotland Yard File, C.O. 20172209

25. Scotland Yard Files. Psychiatric Report by Dr PG Eames – *Interview with Burrows at St Brendan's Hospital*, 26 May 1976

26. Roy Carden. Letter to the author, 22 September 1976

27. Roy Carden. Letter to the author, 10 January 1975

28. Roy Carden. Letter to the author, 2 June 1974

29. Roy Carden. Letter to the author, 30 June 1975

30. Nigel Regan. *Retired Prison Officer Unlocks The Memories.* Bermuda Sun, 5 April 2001. http://www.midoceannews.bm/siftology.midoceannews/Search/search.jsp

31. Ibid

32. Ken Wright Letter to the author, 5 March 1974

33. Roy Carden. Letter to the author, 10 January 1975

34. Roy Carden. Letter to the author, 11 September 1979

CHAPTER 9
CONSPIRATORS ON TRIAL
1.Territt Cabral, Email to the author, 27.9.2005

2.Final Report pages10 - 22

3. Hunter, *The People Of Bermuda – Beyond The Crossroads* 249

4. Scotland Yard Files. Statement of Eric McLean Davis, 17 June 1976
5. Scotland Yard Files. Photocopies of Burrows' letters of confession.

6. Ibid

7. Darrell, Neville T. *Acel D'ama – The Untold Story of the Murder of the Governor of Bermuda, Sir Richard Sharples.* (Self-published), Printed by Coastline Mountain Press (1983) Ltd, Surrey, B.C. Canada, 2003 96

8. Scotland Yard Files. Statement of Witness, Dennis Bernard Bean, 29 June 1976.

9. *The Final Report* 50

10. *The Final Report* 15

11. Hunter, *The People Of Bermuda – Beyond The Crossroads* 256

12. Ibid

13. Ibid

14 Ibid

15. Hunter *The People Of Bermuda – Beyond The Crossroads* 257

16. Ibid

17. *The Final Report* 39

18. Inquests Report para 332

19. *The Final Report* 27

20. *The Final Report* 52

21. Hunter *The People Of Bermuda – Beyond The Crossroads* 259

22. *The Final Report* 40

23. *The Final Report* 40, 51

24. *The Final Report* 44 (Criminal Registry File Number 950/76C)

25. *The Final Report* 45

26. Ibid

27. *The Final Report* 46

28. *The Final Report* 49

29. *The Final Report* 40

30. *Ibid*

31. *The Final Report* 41

32. *The Final Report* 42

CHAPTER 10
WHAT REALLY HAPPENED?

1. Uviller, Richard H. *Virtual Justice: The Flawed Prosecution Of Crime In America.* New Haven: Yale University Press, 1996 242

2. FCO Files. Bermuda Intelligence Committee Report, 8 November 1972 – 5 December 1972 - FCO 63/946

3. FCO Files. Foreign Office memo, 23 November 1972

4. Meredith Ebbin, *Memorial Service For Black Beret Founder.* Bermuda Sun, 22 March 1996, 9

5. Mid Ocean News. *Buck Burrows' desperate plan to kidnap Premier is exposed,* 30 January 2004 http://www.midoceannews.bm/ siftology.midoceannews/Article/ article.jsp?sectionId=49&articleId=7 d41f1230080036

6. Nick Bolton. Letter to the author, 7 February 2005

7. Mid Ocean News. *Trial of Buck Burrows: 'Now you have the confessions . . .', 28 July 2006 http://www.midoceannews.bm/siftology.midoceannews/Article/article.jsp?articleId=7d67e0e30080036&sectionId=60

8. Royal Gazette, "The Trial Of Buck Burrows", http://www.royalgazette.com/article/20060714/NEWS/307149917) July 14 2006

9. Darrell, Neville T. *Acel D'ama – The Untold Story of the Murder of the Governor of Bermuda, Sir Richard Sharples.* 8

10. Government House Report to Foreign Office, May 1973

11. Scotland Yard files, Metropolitan Police General Registry MEPO 26/223 CR 201 73 65

12. Mid Ocean News. *Trial of Buck Burrows: 'Now you have the confessions . . .', 28 July 2006

13. Territt Cabral. Letter to the author, 11 January 2005

14.. Mid Ocean News. The 'Cuba Kid' who 'didn't know Castro from castor oil', 12 May 2006 http://www.midoceannews.bm/siftology.midoceannews/Article/article.jsp?articleId=7d6560e30080020&sectionId=60

15. Scotland Yard Files. Memo to Commissioner Bermuda Police from Metropolitan Police Criminal Investigation Department, New Scotland Yard, 11 February 1973

16. *The Final Report* 43

17. FCO Files. Government House memo to Foreign Office, 6 March 1973

18. Scotland Yard Files. *(Name redacted by author) CRO No 4990.* Metropolitan Police General Registry MEPO 26/223 CR 201 73 65, 8 May 1974. *Author's Note:* However, the report failed to include details of a search of the third man's girlfriend's house where police found a gun and

lists of politicians' car numbers and addresses. They were taken to Police Headquarters and handed over to Special Branch officers.

19. Ibid

20. Nick Bolton. Letter to the author, 7 February 2005

21. Scotland Yard files, Metropolitan Police General Registry MEPO 26/223 CR 201 73 65, "Murder of The Governor of Bermuda"

22. Mid Ocean News, *Although there is little evidence against Beret Yellow, he has undoubtedly participated in all of the murders'* 11 April 2008 http://www.midoceannews.bm/siftology.midoceannews/Article/article.jsp?sectionId=60&articleId=7d845d330080035

23. Royal Gazette, 'Although there is little evidence against Beret Yellow, he has undoubtedly participated in all of the murders', http://www.royalgazette.com/article/20080411/NEWS/304119979

24. Baroness Sharples. Telephone interview with the author, 8 September 2004

25. Baroness Sharples. Letter to the author, 8 September 2004

26. Nick Bolton. Email to the author, 7 February 2005

27. Nick Bolton. Email to the author, 7 December 2004

28. Royal Gazette, Fearful Leather was reluctant to open Pandora's box . . .http://www.royalgazette.com/article/20060519/NEWS/305199922, 19 May 2006

29. Territt Cabral. Email to the author, 11 January 2005

CHAPTER 11
EXECUTIONS AND RIOTS

1. Nigel Regan. *Brit Ruling Raises Spectre of Bermuda's Darkest Hour*. Bermuda Sun, 25 October 2002 http://www.bermudasun.bm/archives/2002-10-25/01News05

2. Nigel Regan. *Retired Prison Officer Unlocks The Memories - After 30 plus*

years, Edward Robinson escapes rigours of a life in prison work, 25 April 2001 http://www.bermudasun.bm/archives/2001-04-25/01News08

3. Roy Carden. Letter to the author, 22 September 1976

4. The Times, *Editorial*, 5 December 1977, 10

5. Daily Mail, *Review Section*, 14 August 2011, "*He's got a cheek, asking me for clemency....*" By Chris Mullen, page 2

6. Jeanine Klein. *Signing Off* Bermuda Sun by 3 October 2003 http://www.bermudasun.org/main.asp?Search=1&ArticleID=18390&SectionID=82&SubSectionID=231&S=1

7. Royal Gazette, *The Still Vex'd Bermoothes*, 15 April 2005

8. Nigel Regan. *Brush With Anarchy* Bermuda Sun by, 4 December 2002 http://bermudasun.org/main.asp?Search=1&ArticleID=14584&SectionID=82&SubSectionID=231&S=1

9. Ruth O'Kelly-Lynch. *When*

Hamilton Burned. Royal Gazette, 3 December 2007 http://www.royalgazette.com/siftology.royalgazette/Article/article.jsp?sectionId=48&articleId=7d7c1b730030014

10. Pitt Report 5

11. Royal Gazette. *Ex-Governor Ramsbotham's Riot Report Declassified*, 15 April 2005 http://www.theroyalgazette.com/apps/pbcs.dll/article?Date=20050415&category=MI

12. Royal Gazette, *The Still Vex'd Bermoothes*, 15 April 2005

13. Roy Carden. Letter to the author, 28 September 1978

14. Nigel Regan. *A Tale Of The Gallows.* Bermuda Sun 26 January 2005 http://bermudasun.org/main.asp?Search=1&ArticleID=24147&SectionID=82&SubSectionID=231&S=1

15. Pitt Report, 5

16. Royal Gazette, *The Still Vex'd Bermoothes*, 15 April 2005

17. Hunter, *The People Of Bermuda – Beyond The Crossroads* 267

18. Nigel Regan. *Brit Ruling Raises Spectre of Bermuda's Darkest Hour.* Bermuda Sun, 25 October 2002 http://www.bermudasun.bm/ archives/2002-10-25/01News05

19. Nigel Regan. *How the Sun Reported* It. Bermuda Sun, 4 December 2002 http://bermudasun. org/main.asp?Search=1&ArticleID= 14586&SectionID=82&SubSectionI D=231&S=1

20. Royal Gazette, *The Still Vex'd Bermoothes*, 15 April 2005

21. Nigel Regan. *How the Sun Reported* It. Bermuda Sun, 4 December 2002 http://bermudasun. org/main.asp?Search=1&ArticleID= 14586&SectionID=82&SubSectionI D=231&S=1

22. Ibid

23. Pitt Report 10

24. Nigel Regan. *Brush With Anarchy* Bermuda Sun by, 4 December 2002

http://bermudasun.org/main.asp?Se arch=1&ArticleID=14584&SectionI D=82&SubSectionID=231&S=1

25. Pitt Report 9

26. Pitt 27

27. Pitt 8

28. Pitt 30

29. Pitt 35

30. Hunter *The People Of Bermuda – Beyond The Crossroads* 277

31. Hunter *The People Of Bermuda – Beyond The Crossroads* 267

32. Royal Gazette, *The Still Vex'd Bermoothes*, 15 April 2005

33. Ibid

34. Ibid

35. Nigel Regan. *A Tale Of The Gallows.* Bermuda Sun 26 January 2005 http://bermudasun.org/main.asp?Se arch=1&ArticleID=24147&SectionI

D=82&SubSectionID=231&S=1

36. Royal Gazette, *The Still Vex'd Bermoothes*, 15 April 2005

37. Ibid

38. Ibid

CHAPTER 12
TWIN LEGACIES –
COLONIALISM AND BLACK
POWER

1. Manning, Frank E. *Bermuda Politics In Transition- Race Voting And Public Opinion*. Bermuda: Island Press 1978, 129

2. FCO Files. Memo from Acting Governor Kinnear to the Foreign Office 14 March 1973

3. Nirpal Dhaliwal, "Britain Has No Need To Apologise To India…" Daily Mail July 29th 2010.

4. A N Wilson. Get Off Your Knees. Daily Mail, 23 June 2006, 6

5. Lawrence James. *Nailing The Lie of the Evil Empire*. Sunday Times, News Review 18 June 2006 2

6. Simon Winchester. *Rumblings of Discontent Under Bermuda Calm*. The Guardian, 13 March 1973 9

7. Pitt Report 8

8. Wooding, Hugh, *Bermuda Civil Disorders 1968 (The Wooding Report), Report of the Commission and Statement by the Government of Bermuda*. Hamilton, Bermuda: Government Publication, 1969 11/12

9. David Matthews. *The Trouble With Black Men*. Sunday Times News Review, July 31 2004 16

10. Ken Wright. Letter to the author, 5 March 1974

11. The Black Panther, *Pigs Ambush Panthers*, May 4 1968, 4 http://www.itsabouttimebpp.com/BPP_Newspapers/pdf/Vol_II_No5_1968_1.pdf

12. The Black Panther May 4th, 1969. *Message from Huey - Taped in Prison*". 2 http://www.itsabouttimebpp.com/BPP_Newspapers/bpp_newspapers_

index.html

13 The Black Panther, September 28, 1968. 6, 14 http://www.itsabouttimebpp.com/BPP_Newspapers/bpp_newspapers_index.html

14. Jonathan Lerner. *I Was A Terrorist.* The Washington Post Magazine, 24 February 2002 http://www.washingtonpost.com/ac2/wp-dyn/A41899-2002Feb20?language=printer

15. Horowitz, David (Ed with Peter Collier), *The Race Card – White Guilt, Black Resentment, And The Assault On Truth And Justice.* Rocklin, CA: Forum, 1997 25

16. Horowitz, David (Ed with Peter Collier), *The Race Card – White Guilt, Black Resentment, And The Assault On Truth And Justice.* Rocklin, CA: Forum, 1997 23

AFTERWORD

1. Barry, Tom, (et al). *The Other Side of Paradise: Foreign Control in the Caribbean.* New York: Grove Press, 1984 217

2. Royal Gazette. *Where The Fates Takes Us…* 24 June 2005 http://www.royalgazette.com/siftology.royalgazette/Search/search.jsp

3. Christian Dunleavy. *PLP Dinosaurs Cling To The Past.* Royal Gazette, 15 February 2006 http://www.royalgazette.com/siftology.royalgazette/Article/article.jsp?sectionId=75&articleId=7d6279230030034

4. Terri Mello. *Gang Story Goes Global.* Bermuda Sun, 14 August 2006 http://www.bermudasun.bm/searchform_advanced.asp

5. Coggie Gibbons. *Code Of Silence A Threat To Our Safety.* Bermuda Sun, 14 August 2006 http://www.bermudasun.bm/main.asp?SectionID=24&SubSectionID=270&ArticleID=30379

6. Rebecca Middleton .org – Standing Up For Becky. *Getting Away With Murder.* http://rebeccamiddleton.org/index.html

Shuman, Carol *Kill Me Once…Kill Me Twice: Murder on the Queen's Playground* by Authorhouse, (2010)

7. Ruth O'Kelly-Lynch. *Support For Split From UK Falls To New Low.* Royal Gazette, 31 July 2006 http://www.royalgazette.com/siftology.royalgazette/Article/article.jsp?sectionId=60&articleId=7d67f8e30030018

8. Simon Winchester. *Whose Colony?* Sunday Times, 23 March 1984 14

9. Royal Gazette, Buck Burrows called a 'martyr' by magazine by John Burchall. 27/1/1995 http://www.royalgazette.com/siftology.royalgazette/Article/article.jsp?sectionId=60&articleId=7cb1d933003003a

Royal Gazette, Opinion Column, 17 June 2003 http://www.royalgazette.com/siftology.royalgazette/Article/article.jsp?sectionId=75&articleId=7d3688e3003001a

10. Larry Burchall, *Opinion*, Bermuda Sun, 8 June 2005 http://www.limeyinbermuda.com/latest_news/2005/06/education_not_r.html

11. *Letter from Bermuda*, KYC News, Inc., November 4, 2005 http://www.kycnews.com/story_library.asp

12. Quoted in - Horowitz, David (Ed with Peter Collier), *The Race Card – White Guilt, Black Resentment, And The Assault On Truth And Justice.* Rocklin, CA: Forum, 1997, 69

13. Jennifer Smith website. *Biography of Jennifer Smith*. www.jennifersmith.com

14. Meredith Ebbin, *Memorial Service For Black Beret Founder*. Bermuda Sun, 22 March 1996, 9

15. Politics.bm. *Comrade Google*. 15 December 2004, http://www.politics.bm/archives/2004/12/15_000476.html

16. Sam Stevens. *Minister Involved In Angry Air Spat With Steward.* Royal Gazette, 26 April 2005 http://www.ttalpa.org/news/news_item.asp?NewsID=26

17. Patrick Burgess. Letter to the author, 25 September 2004

18. Jerusalem Post 'FBI, US probing Black Hebrews For Fraud', by Yaakov Katz, 8.12.2005 http://www.jpost.com/servlet/Satellite?cid=1132475704455&pagename=JPost%2FJPArticle

%2FShowFull

19. Ibid

CURRENT AND FORTHCOMING TITLES FROM
STRATEGIC MEDIA BOOKS

QUEENPINS
Notorious Women Gangsters of
the Modern Era

SCAPEGOAT
The Chino Hills Murders and
The Framing of Kevin Cooper

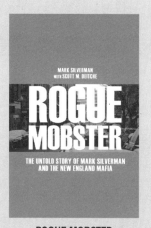

ROGUE MOBSTER
The Untold Story of Mark
Silverman and The New
England Mafia

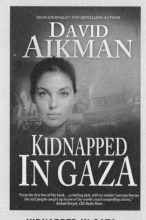

KIDNAPPED IN GAZA

AVAILABLE FROM STRATEGICMEDIABOOKS.COM, AMAZON, AND MAJOR BOOKSTORES NEAR YOU.